Casebook on Company La

Casebook on Company Law

Josephine R. Bisacre

Pitman Publishing

Pitman Publishing
128 Long Acre, London WC2E 9AN

A Division of Longman Group UK Limited

First published in 1992

© Longman Group UK Limited 1992

British Library Cataloguing-in-Publication Data

A catalogue record for this book is available from the British Library

ISBN 0 273 03425 1

Printed and bound in Great Britain by
Dotesios Ltd, Trowbridge, Wiltshire.

Contents

Preface

This casebook is a sister volume to *Casebook on Contract Law* by W T Major. Each chapter of the casebook contains a summary of the law to enable the reader to view the cases in their context. The case reports appear in the order in which they are given in the summary. The name and year only are quoted in the summary for those cases which are further reported upon. Occasionally a case is mentioned in the summary but is not further reported upon, and for such cases a full citation is given. Since much of company law is now statutory, the summaries do not purport to be complete statements of the law, and accordingly the book should be used in addition to, and not instead of, a textbook.

The casebook includes some Scottish material which is clearly marked as such by an asterisk preceding the title of the case.

The book is intended for students taking a first course in company law as part of a BTEC or SCOTVEC HND Accounting, a degree in Accounting or Business Studies, or the various professional examinations. For law students also, the book will serve as a useful and accessible summary of case law, although it cannot substitute for systematic consultation of the law reports themselves.

Josephine R Bisacre

Acknowledgments

The publisher and compiler are grateful to the Incorporated Council of Law Reporting for England and Wales, Butterworths, The Scottish Council of Law Reporting and The Law Society of Scotland, who kindly gave permission to include extracts from the Law Reports, the Weekly Law Reports, the All England Law Reports, Butterworths Company Cases, LEXIS case transcripts, Session Cases and Scottish Civil Law Reports.

Extracts from *British Company Cases* (BCC) are reproduced with the kind permission of CCH Editions Limited, Telford Road, Bicester, Oxfordshire OX6 OXD.

Nine of the Scottish cases are reproduced from *Scots Law Times* by permission of W Green – the Scottish Law Publisher.

Quotations from the First Council Directive of March 1968 are reproduced by permission of the Commission to the European Communities.

Latin words and phrases

ad hoc for a particular or special purpose
ad interim in the meantime
alter ego other self
bona fide(s) in good faith, good faith
cadit quaestio the matter admits of no further argument
cestui que trust a person for whom another is a trustee
damnum injuria datum loss caused by a legal wrong
de facto in fact
dicta statements
ejusdem generis of the same kind
ex debito justitiae a remedy applicable as of right
ex facie apparently
ex hypothesi according to the argument
ex proprio motu of its own motion
inter alia among other things
inter se among themselves
inter socios among partners
intra vires within the powers of
mala fide(s) in bad faith, bad faith
mandamus an order from a Divisional Court of the Queen's Bench
 Division to some person or body to compel the performance of a
 public duty
mens rea guilty mind or intention
non est factum it is not his deed (a plea denying that a deed
 mentioned in the plaintiff's pleading was truly that of the
 defendant)
per by means of, through
per contra on the contrary
per curiam by the court
per pro. on behalf of
persona personality
prima facie at first sight
pro tanto to a certain extent
qua as

quantum meruit according to his deserts

res inter alios acta things transacted between strangers do not injure those who are not parties to them

respondeat superior let the superior person answer (e.g. where an employer is responsible for the acts of an employee committed in the course of employment)

scire facias lit. 'that you cause him to know'. A writ based on a judgment directing the sheriff to warn the person against whom it was brought to show cause why the person bringing it should not have the benefit of judgment (abolished in 1947)

ultra vires beyond the powers of

vires powers

Glossary of legal terms

B list of contributories A list of persons who were members of a company within a year before the commencement of a winding up, and who may be liable in the liquidation.

Constructive trust A trust which arises by operation of law where a person acquires property which he is not entitled to retain.

Estoppel An admission which cannot be denied by the party whom it affects (**personal bar*).

Hiving down agreement An agreement between a company and a new, wholly owned subsidiary for the sale of that business to the subsidiary.

Injunction An inhibitory writ by which a court stops or prevents an illegal or inequitable act being committed.

Judicial Committee of the Privy Council Hears appeals from courts in certain Commonwealth countries.

Lands Tribunal Assesses compensation for compulsory purchase of land, and the variation and discharge of land obligations.

Misfeasance The doing of a lawful act in a wrongful manner.

Novation The substitution of a new document of debt with the consent of the creditor, for an earlier document of debt.

Personal relationship company A company which is in essence a partnership between a few persons all of whom have management rights.

Power of attorney A document by which one person authorises another to act for him.

Shadow director Defined by section 741 (1) of the Companies Act 1985 as a 'person in accordance with whose directions or instructions the directors of the company are accustomed to act'.

Void Without legal effect

Voidable Capable of being avoided (by legal action).

SCOTTISH LEGAL TERMS

Arrestment Attaches assets in the hands of a third party in satisfaction of a debt owed by a debtor to a creditor.

Action of Furthcoming   Court action by which funds or property belonging to a debtor which have been arrested in the hands of a third party are made available to the creditor.

Declarator   Court action seeking a decree confirming or denying the existence of a right.

Diligence   The process by which, *inter alia*, court decrees are implemented through the attachment of assets belonging to the debtor.

Interdict   A prohibitory order of a court to prevent a wrongful act or breach of contract occurring.

Judicial factor   Trustee appointed by a court to administer estates to provide protection to the beneficiaries against loss or injustice.

Table of cases

1. Legal personality

Summary

1. Sources of the law

The legal personality of an incorporated company is largely a doctrine of case law, whereby, insofar as it is capable of bearing them, a company is accredited with similar rights and obligations in law as those of a natural person. The principle of separate legal personality was clearly established by *Salomon* v. *Salomon & Co. Ltd.* [1897]. See also *Macaura* v. *Northern Assurance Co. Ltd.* [1925]; and *Lee* v. *Lee's Air Farming Ltd.* [1961]. There are, however, some statutory provisions on the subject in the Companies Act 1985 and related legislation, and also in other statutes, where in particular circumstances the separate legal personality of the company will be ignored.

2. The attributes of separate legal personality

An incorporated company has the following attributes:

(i)   It can hold property in its corporate name;
(ii) It can sue and be sued in its corporate name;
(iii) It can be debtor and creditor in its own name, and even of its own members;
(iv) Insolvency of the company need not bring about the bankruptcy of its members;
(v)   It has perpetual succession, so that the membership may change, without affecting the legal personality of the company;
(vi) It can make contracts in the corporate name, to the limit of the objects clause of the memorandum of association. Contracts beyond those limits can be ratified, and will generally be binding on the company under ss. 35, 35A, 35B and 711A of the Companies Act 1985 (see Chapter 3 below);
(v)   It can commit crimes which do not involve *mens rea* such as road

traffic offences. Crimes involving *mens rea* can also be committed if the person who was instrumental in causing the crime to be committed was in a senior management position within the company, such that he can be considered to be the *alter ego* (other self) of the company. See *Tesco Supermarkets Ltd.* v. *Nattrass* [1972]. In Scotland, the *alter ego* doctrine was not accepted as part of the law in **Dean* v. *John Menzies (Holdings) Ltd.* [1981] JC 23; [1981] SLT (JC) 50, but in **Purcell Meats (Scotland) Ltd.* v. *Mcleod* 1987 the High Court of Justiciary appeared to accept the doctrine. The position is therefore unclear in Scotland.

(vi) It can commit torts (*delicts), either through the instrumentality of its officers or its employees. The company can be vicariously liable for acts of employees committed in the course of employment. See, for example, *Conway* v. *George Wimpey Ltd.* [1951] 2 KB 266.

3. Lifting the veil of incorporation

Notwithstanding the general principle that a company once incorporated has separate legal personality, there are instances where the legislature and the courts have disregarded it in the interests of justice. These cases are therefore exceptions to the general rule of separate legal personality. The following are some instances where separate legal personality has been disregarded:

(a) Taxation

Legislation requires the maintenance of group accounts by holding companies, despite the separate legal personality of every member company in the group.

The Inland Revenue applies a 'management and control' test to determine the residence of a company: see *Unit Construction Co. Ltd.* v. *Bullock (Inspector of Taxes)* [1960].

(b) Companies Act 1985 and related legislation

There are many instances where this legislation imposes liability on members or directors for acts of, or in relation to, the company. For example, section 24 of the Companies Act 1985 imposes personal liability jointly and severally with the company on a sole member of a company who allows the company to carry on business with only one member for more than six months, in respect of debts incurred during that period; section 349 of the Companies Act 1985 imposes personal liability on officers of the company who sign or authorise the signature of a bill of exchange, promissory note, cheque or order for money or goods on which the name of the company is not correctly stated: see *Rafsanjan Pistachio Producers Co-operative* v. *Reiss* [1990]; **Scottish & Newcastle Breweries Ltd.* v. *Blair* 1967 SLT (OH) 72. Further, section 117 of the Companies Act 1985 imposes joint and several liability on the directors of public companies incorporated as such which do not obtain a trading certificate, and which enter into transactions which they fail to fulfil within twenty-one days of being called upon to do so; sections 213 and 214 of the Insolvency Act 1986 impose liability on any person, in the case of section 213, and on directors and shadow directors, in the case of section 214, for fraudulent and wrongful trading activities (see Chapter 14 below); section 15 of the Company Directors Disqualification Act 1986 imposes personal liability for the company's debts on a person who is involved with the management of the company while disqualified by the court or while an undischarged bankrupt (see Chapter 8 below).

(c) The public interest

In some cases the public interest has dictated that the veil of incorporation be lifted by the judges in order to apply some other principle. This is seen in time of war, where the status of a company as an enemy alien has been determined according to the nationality of members and directors, rather than according to the nationality of the company—the location of the registered office would be the normal determining factor for nationality: see *Daimler Co. Ltd.* v. *Continental Tyre and Rubber Co. (Great Britain) Ltd.* [1916] 2 AC 307.

(d) Economic entity

On occasion, depending on the facts of an individual case, the courts will lift the veil of incorporation to recognise a group entity among a group of companies, rather than regarding them as separate legal entities. This was done in *D.H.N. Food Distributors Ltd.* v. *Tower Hamlets London Borough Council* [1976]. However, the companies were not regarded as an economic entity in **Woolfson* v. *Strathclyde Regional Council* 1978, or in *National Dock Labour Board* v. *Pinn & Wheeler Ltd. and others* (1989).

(e) Evasion of contractual obligations

The courts have, on occasion, lifted the veil of incorporation in the interests of justice to prevent the evasion of a contractual obligation, as in the case of *Gilford Motor Co. Ltd.* v. *Horne* [1933], where

Horne's company was treated as a party to a contract that had been entered into between the Gilford Motor Co. Ltd. and Horne personally, in order to prevent injustice arising.

(f) Implied agency

Occasionally, a company has been regarded as transparent, and treated as the agent of another person or company. This was the argument in *Salomon* v. *Salomon & Co. Ltd.* [1897] that was disapproved by the decision in the House of Lords. It has, however, succeeded in other cases, for example, *Re F.G. (Films) Ltd.* [1953] 1 All ER 615, where a company incorporated in the United Kingdom was held to be a nominee of an American company and therefore not entitled to produce films as British films under the Cinematograph Act 1938.

Salomon v. Salomon & Co. Ltd.

[1897] AC (HL) 22; [1895–9] All ER 33
House of Lords

Salomon had operated an unincorporated business as a leather merchant and wholesale boot manufacturer. He later transferred the business to a registered company in which, apart from his wife, daughter and four sons who each held one share, the entire issued share capital was held by Salomon. The business was solvent at the time when it was taken over. Part of the payment for the business was made in the form of debentures forming a floating security issued by the company to Salomon. A Mr Broderip had advanced money to Salomon on the security of his debentures, and new debentures were issued to Broderip in place of Salomon's debentures. Salomon defaulted on payment of interest on the debentures, and Broderip then sued to enforce his security against the company. The company was put into liquidation at the instance of unsecured creditors. If Broderip's claim were accepted, there would be nothing left for the unsecured creditors. The liquidator sought to rescind the purchase agreement and have Salomon pay back all sums received by him from the company on the grounds that the assets were overvalued and that the formation of the company constituted a fraud on the creditors. In the court of first instance, Vaughan Williams, J. granted an order in terms of which Salomon was to indemnify the liquidator against the whole unsecured debts of the company, and entitling the liquidator to a lien for the amount of the indemnity over all sums that might be payable by the company in respect of the debentures. The company was held to be the agent of Salomon himself. The case was appealed to the Court of Appeal which dismissed the appeal. A further appeal was made to the House of Lords. By this time Broderip had been paid off and therefore ceased to be a party to the action.

HELD that the company once incorporated was an entirely separate legal person from Salomon himself and, therefore, Salomon was not liable to indemnify the company against the creditors' claims; that there had been no fraud committed on the creditors or shareholders; and that the company was not entitled to rescind the original purchase agreement.

LORD HALSBURY, L.C. My Lords, the important question in this case, I am not certain it is not the only question, is whether the respondent company was a company at all—whether in truth that artful creation of the legislature had been validly constituted in this instance; and in order to determine that question it is necessary to look at what the statute itself has determined in that respect. I have no right to add to the requirements of the statute, nor to take from the requirements thus enacted. The sole guide must be the statute itself.

Now, that there were seven actual living persons who held shares in the company has not been doubted. As to the proportionate amounts held by each I will deal presently; but it is important to observe that the first condition of the statute is satisfied, and it follows as a consequence that it would not be competent to any one—and certainly not to these persons themselves—to deny that they were shareholders.

I must pause there to point out that the statute enacts nothing as to the extent or degree of interest which may be held by each of the seven or as to the proportion of interest or influence possessed by one or the majority of the shareholders over the others. One share is enough. Still less is it possible to contend that the motive of becoming shareholders or of making them shareholders is a field of inquiry which the statute recognises as legitimate. If they are shareholders, they are shareholders for all purposes; and even if the statute was silent as to the recognition of trusts, I should be prepared to hold that if six of them were the *cestuis que trust* of the seventh, whatever might be their rights *inter se*, the statute would have made them shareholders to all intents and purposes with their respective rights and liabilities, and, dealing with them in relation to the company, the only relations which I believe the law would sanction would be that they were corporators of the corporate body.

I am simply here dealing with the provisions of the statute, and it seems to me to be essential to the artificial creation that the law should recognise only that artificial existence—quite apart from the motives or conduct of individual corporators. In saying this, I do not at all mean to suggest that if it could be established that this provision of the statute to which I am adverting had not been complied with, you could not go behind the certificate of incorporation to shew that a fraud had been committed upon the officer entrusted with the duty of giving the certificate, and that by some proceeding in the nature of *scire facias* you could not prove the fact that the company had no real legal existence. But short of such proof it seems to me impossible to dispute that once the company is legally incorporated it must be treated like any other independent person with its rights and liabilities to itself, and that the motives of those who took part in the promotion of the company are absolutely irrelevant in discussing what those rights and liabilities are.

. . . My Lords, the truth is that the learned judges (in the High Court and Court of Appeal) have never allowed in their own minds the proposition that the company has a real existence. They have been struck by what they have considered the inexpediency of permitting one man to be in influence and authority of the whole company; and, assuming that such a thing could not have been intended by the legislature, they have sought various grounds upon which they might insert into the Act some prohibition of such a result. Whether such a result be right or wrong, politic or impolitic, I say, with the utmost deference to the learned judges, that we have nothing to do with that question if this company has been duly constituted by law; and, whatever may be the motives of those who constitute it, I must decline to insert into that Act of Parliament limitations which are not to be found there. . . . The result is that I move your Lordships that the judgment appealed from be reversed . . .

LORD HERSCHELL. It is to be observed that both Courts treated the company as a legal entity distinct from Salomon and the members who composed it, and therefore as a validly constituted corporation. This is, indeed, necessarily involved in the judgment which declared that the company was entitled to certain rights as against Salomon. Under these circumstances, I am at a loss to understand what is meant by saying that A. Salomon & Co., Limited, is but an "alias" for A. Salomon. It is not another name for the same person; the company is *ex hypothesi* a distinct legal persona. As little am I able to adopt the view that the company was the agent of Salomon to carry on his business for him. In a popular sense, a company may in every case be said to carry on business for and on behalf of its shareholders; but this certainly does not in point of law constitute the relation of principal and agent between them or render the shareholders liable to indemnify the company against the debts which it incurs. Here, it is true, Salomon owned all the shares except six, so that if the business were profitable he would be entitled, substantially, to the whole of the profits. The other shareholders, too, are said to have been "dummies", the nominees of Salomon. But when once it is conceded that they were individual members of the company distinct from Salomon, and sufficiently so to bring into existence in conjunction with him a validly constituted corporation, I am unable to see how the facts to which I have just referred can affect the legal position of the company, or give it rights as against its members which it would not otherwise possess.

LORD MACNAGHTEN. The company had a brief career: it fell upon evil days. Shortly after it was started there seems to have come a

period of great depression in the boot and shoe trade. There were
strikes of workmen too; and in view of that danger contracts with
public bodies, which were the principal source of Mr Salomon's profit,
were split up and divided between different firms. The attempts made
to push the business on behalf of the new company crammed its
warehouses with unsaleable stock. Mr Salomon seems to have done
what he could: both he and his wife lent the company money; and then
he got his debentures cancelled and reissued to a Mr Broderip, who
advanced him £5000, which he immediately handed over to the
company on loan. The temporary relief only hastened ruin. Mr
Broderip's interest was not paid when it became due. He took
proceedings at once and got a receiver appointed. Then, of course,
came liquidation and a forced sale of the company's assets. They
realised enough to pay Mr Broderip, but not enough to pay the
debentures in full; and the unsecured creditors were consequently left
out in the cold.

. . . When the memorandum is duly signed and registered, though
there be only seven shares taken, the subscribers are a body corporate
"capable forthwith", to use the words of the enactment, "of
exercising all the functions of an incorporated company". Those are
strong words. The company attains maturity on its birth. There is no
period of minority—no interval of incapacity. I cannot understand how
a body corporate thus made "capable" by statute can lose its
individuality by issuing the bulk of its capital to one person, whether
he be a subscriber to the memorandum or not. The company is at law
a different person altogether from the subscribers to the memorandum;
and, though it may be that after incorporation the business is precisely
the same as it was before, and the same persons receive the profits, the
company is not in law the agent of the subscribers or trustee for them.
Nor are the subscribers as members liable, in any shape or form,
except to the extent and in the manner provided by the Act. That is, I
think, the declared intention of the enactment. If the view of the
learned judge were sound, it would follow that no common law
partnership could register as a company limited by shares without
remaining subject to unlimited liability.

. . . I am of opinion that the appeal ought to be allowed, and the
counter-claim of the company dismissed with costs, both here and below.

Macaura v. Northern Assurance Co. Ltd. and others

[1925] AC 619; [1925] All ER 51
House of Lords
Macaura (M.), the owner of a timber estate sold all the timber to a registered company, the Irish Canadian Sawmills Ltd., in exchange for shares in that company. The timber continued to be insured in M.'s name personally, rather than in the name of the company. M. was also the company's largest unsecured creditor. A fire destroyed the bulk of the timber on the estate. M. sued the insurance companies which refused to pay on the ground that M. had no insurable interest in the timber. The matter was referred to arbitration, and the arbitrator ruled that the claimant had no insurable interest. The case was appealed from the Court of Appeal in Northern Ireland to the House of Lords.

HELD that neither as shareholder nor as creditor did M. have an insurable interest in the timber; and that, having allowed the arbitrator to consider the question of insurable interest, it was not open to M. to question the arbitrator's authority to make a ruling on it.

LORD BUCKMASTER. The appellant could only insure either as a creditor or as a shareholder in the company. And if he was not entitled in virtue of either of these rights he can acquire no better position by reason of the fact that he held both characters. As a creditor his position appears to me quite incapable of supporting the claim. If his contention were right it would follow that any person would be at liberty to insure the furniture of his debtor, and no such claim has ever been recognised by the Courts. . . .

. . . Turning now to his position as a shareholder, this must be independent of the extent of his share interest. If he were entitled to insure holding all the shares in the company, each shareholder would be equally entitled, if the shares were all in separate hands. Now, no shareholder has any right to any item of property owned by the company, for he has no legal or equitable interest therein. He is entitled to a share in the profits while the company continues to carry on business and a share in the distribution of the surplus assets when the company is wound up. If he were at liberty to effect an insurance against loss by fire of any item of the company's property, the extent of his insurable interest could only be measured by determining the extent to which his share in the ultimate distribution would be diminished by the loss of the asset—a calculation almost impossible to make. There is no means by which such an interest can be definitely measured and no standard which can be fixed of the loss against which the contract of insurance could be regarded as an indemnity.

LORD SUMNER. It is clear that the appellant had no insurable interest in the timber described. It was not his. It belonged to the Irish Canadian Sawmills Ltd., of Skibbereen, Co. Cork. He had no lien or security over it and, though it lay on his land by his permission, he had no responsibility to its owner for its safety, nor was it there under any contract that enabled him to hold it for his debt. He owned almost all the shares in the company, and the company owed him a good deal of money, but, neither as creditor nor as shareholder, could he insure the company's assets. The debt was not exposed to fire nor were the shares, and the fact that he was virtually the company's only creditor, while the timber was its only asset, seems to me to make no difference.

Lee v. Lee's Air Farming Ltd.

[1961] AC 12; [1960] 3 All ER 420
Privy Council
Lee had formed a company, Lee's Air Farming Ltd., for the purpose of carrying out top-dressing of crops from the air. He was the controlling shareholder, governing director of the company, and its chief pilot. The company operated in New Zealand. The company held insurance against liability to pay compensation to Lee. While carrying out his duties, the aeroplane crashed and Lee was killed. His widow claimed compensation from the company on the grounds that he was a 'worker' employed by the company within the meaning of the New Zealand Workers' Compensation Act 1922, which obliged an employer to pay compensation for personal injuries arising out of and in the course of employment. The New Zealand Court of Appeal had held in a case stated from the Compensation Court of New Zealand that Lee could not be employed by a company in which he was governing director. The case was appealed to the Privy Council.

HELD that the deceased was a 'worker' within the meaning of the statute. He and the company were separate legal persons who had entered into a valid contract of employment.

LORD MORRIS OF BORTH-Y-GEST. The substantial question which arises is, as their Lordships think, whether the deceased was a "worker" within the meaning of the Workers' Compensation Act 1922, and its amendments. Was he a person who had entered into or worked under a contract of service with an employer? The Court of Appeal thought that his special position as governing director precluded him from being a servant of the company. On this view it is difficult to know what his status and position was when he was performing the arduous and skilful duties of piloting an aeroplane which belonged to the company and when he was carrying out the operation of top-dressing farm lands from the air. The company kept a wages book in which these were recorded. The work that was being done was being done at the request of farmers whose contractual rights and obligations were with the company alone. It cannot be suggested that when engaged in the activities above referred to the deceased was discharging his duties as governing director. Their Lordships find it impossible to resist the conclusion that the active aerial operations were performed because the deceased was in some contractual relationship with the company. That relationship came about because the deceased as one legal person was willing to work for and to make a contract with the company which was another legal entity. A contractual relationship could only exist on the basis that there was consensus between the two contracting parties. It was never suggested (nor, in their Lordships' view could it reasonably have been suggested) that the company was a sham or a mere simulacrum. It is well established that the mere fact that someone is a director of a company is no impediment to his entering into a contract to serve the company. If, then, it be accepted that the respondent company was a legal entity their Lordships see no reason to challenge the validity of any contractual obligations which were created between the company and the deceased.

    . . . Nor in their Lordships' view were any contractual obligations invalidated by the circumstance that the deceased was sole governing director in whom was vested the full government and control of the company. Always assuming that the company was not a sham then the capacity of the company to make a contract with the deceased could not be impugned merely because the deceased was the agent of the company in its negotiation.

. . . *Ex facie* therefore there was a contract of service. Their Lordships conclude, therefore, that the real issue in the case is whether the position of the deceased as sole governing director made it impossible for him to be the servant of the company in the capacity of chief pilot of the company. In their Lordships' view, for the reasons which have been indicated, there was no such impossibility. There appears to be no greater difficulty in holding that a man can give orders to himself in another capacity than there is in holding that a man acting in one capacity can make a contract with himself in another capacity. The company and the deceased were separate legal entities. The company has the right to decide what contracts for aerial top-dressing it would enter into. The deceased was the agent of the company in making the necessary decisions. Any profits earned would belong to the company and not to the deceased. If the company entered into a contract with a farmer, then it lay within its right and power to direct its chief pilot to perform certain operations. The right to control existed even though it would be for the deceased in his capacity as agent for the company to decide what orders to give . . . . Their Lordships consider, therefore, that the deceased was a worker and that the question posed in the case stated should be answered in the affirmative.

Tesco Supermarkets Ltd. v. Nattrass

[1972] AC 153; [1971] 2 All ER 127; [1971] 2 WLR 1166
House of Lords

Tesco Supermarkets Ltd. were accused of an offence under section 24(2) of the Trade Descriptions Act 1968 (now section 20 of the Consumer Protection Act 1987). It was alleged that they had offered to supply goods at a price less than the price at which they were in fact being offered. A packet of Radiant washing powder bearing the statement 'Radiant 1s. off Giant Size 2s. 11d.' had been sold to a customer at the full price of 3s. 11d. There was evidence that the defendants intended the special offer only to apply to those packs which were marked as such. The Act contained a defence in section 24 under which it could be proved that the commission of the offence was due to the act or default of another person, and that the defendants had taken all reasonable precautions and exercised due diligence to avoid the commission of the offence. The defendants raised this defence, and sought to transfer the liability to the store manager of the branch where the offence was committed. The trial justices found that the defendants had set up a proper system to prevent such offences occurring, in terms of the defence, and that the manager had failed to fulfil his part in the operation of the system, the offence being due to his failure of supervision. However, the justices held that the defence failed because the store manager could not be 'another person' in terms of the statutory defence. They accordingly convicted the defendants.

The defendants appealed to the Court of Appeal. The Court of Appeal dismissed the appeal, but on different grounds, holding that although the manager could be a separate person from the company itself at law, nevertheless the company had not set up a proper system to prevent the offence occurring. The company appealed to the House of Lords.

HELD (1) that the store manager was 'another person' within the meaning of section 24, since any person could fit the section, provided that where the defendant was an individual, the person was someone other than the defendant, and where the defendant was an incorporated company, the person was not one of the persons named in section 20 (director, manager, secretary or similar officer); and (2) the company had set up an efficient system to avoid offences under the Act in terms of section 24, and had not delegated to the store managers the task of ensuring that the system was carried out. Accordingly, the appeal was allowed.

LORD REID. Where a limited company is the employer difficult questions do arise in a wide variety of circumstances in deciding which of its officers or servants is to be identified with the company so that his guilt is the guilt of the company.

I must start by considering the nature of the personality which by a fiction the law attributes to a corporation. A living person has a mind which can have knowledge or intention or be negligent and he has hands to carry out his intentions. A corporation has none of these: it must act through living persons, though not always one and the same person. Then the person who acts is not speaking or acting for the company. He is acting as the company and his mind which directs his acts is the mind of the company. There is no question of the company being vicariously liable. He is not acting as a servant, representative, agent or delegate. He is an embodiment of the company or, one could say, he hears and speaks through the persona of the company, within his appropriate sphere, and his mind is the mind of the company. If his is a guilty mind then that guilt is the guilt of the company. It must be a question of law whether, once the facts have been ascertained, a person in doing particular things is to be regarded as the company or merely as the company's servant or agent. In that case any liability of the company can only be a statutory or vicarious liability.

In *Lennard's Carrying Case Co. Ltd.* v. *Asiatic Petroleum Co. Ltd.* [1915] AC 705 the question was whether damage had occurred without the "actual fault or privity" of the owner of a ship. The owners were a company. The fault was that of the registered managing owner who managed the ship on behalf of the owners and it was held that the company could not dissociate itself from him so as to say that there was no actual fault or privity on the part of the company. Viscount Haldane L.C. said, at pp. 713, 714:

> "For if Mr. Lennard was the directing mind of the company, then his action must, unless a corporation is not to be liable at all, have been an action which was the action of the company itself within the meaning of section 502. . . . It must be upon the true construction of that section in such a case as the present one that the fault or privity is the fault or privity of somebody who is not merely a servant or agent for whom the company is liable upon the footing *respondeat superior*, but somebody for whom the company is liable because his action is the very action of the company itself."

Reference is frequently made to the judgment of Denning L.J. in *H.L. Bolton (Engineering) Co. Ltd.* v. *T.J. Graham & Sons Ltd.* [1957] 1 QB 159. He said, at p. 172:

> "A company may in many ways be likened to a human body. It has a brain and nerve centre which controls what it does. It also has hands which hold the tools and act in accordance with directions from the centre. Some of the people in the company are mere servants and agents who are nothing more than hands to do the work and cannot be said to represent the mind or will. Others are directors and managers who represent the directing mind and will of the company, and control what it does. The state of mind of these managers is the state of mind of the company and is treated by the law as such."

Normally the board of directors, the managing director and perhaps other superior officers of a company carry out the functions of management and speak or act as the company. Their subordinates do not. They carry out orders from above and it can make no difference that they are given some measure of discretion. But the board of directors may delegate some part of their functions of management giving to their delegate full discretion to act independently of instructions from them. I see no difficulty in holding that they have thereby put such a delegate in their place so that within the scope of the delegation he can act as the company. It may not always be easy to draw the line but there are cases in which the line must be drawn. *Lennard's* case [1915] AC 705 was one of them. . . . In my judgment the appellants established the statutory defence. I would therefore allow the appeal.

LORD MORRIS OF BORTH-Y-GEST. Within the scheme of the Act now being considered an indication is given (which need not necessarily be an all-embracing indication) of those who may personify "the directing mind and will" of the company. The question in the present case becomes a question whether the company as a company took all reasonable precautions and exercised all due diligence. The magistrates so found and so held. The magistrates found and held that "they" (i.e. the company) had satisfied the provisions of section 24(1)(b). The reason why the Divisional Court felt that they could not accept that finding was that they considered that the company had delegated its duty to the manager of the shop. The manager was, they thought, "a person to whom the appellants had delegated in respect of that particular shop their duty to take all reasonable precautions and exercise all due diligence to avoid the commission" of an offence. Though the magistrates were satisfied that the company had set up an efficient system there had been "a failure by someone to whom the duty of carrying out the system was delegated properly to carry out that function".

My Lords, with respect I do not think that there was any feature of delegation in the present case. The company had its responsibilities in regard to taking all reasonable precautions and exercising all due diligence. The careful and effective discharge of those responsibilities required the directing mind and will of the company. A system had to be created which could rationally be said to be so designed that the commission of offences would be avoided. There was no delegation of the duty of taking precautions and exercising diligence. There was no such delegation to the manager of a particular store. He did not function as the directing mind or will of the company. His duties as manager of one store did not involve managing the company. He was the one who was being directed. He was one who was employed but he was not a delegate to whom the company passed on its responsibilities. He had certain duties which were the result of the taking by the company of all reasonable precautions and of the exercising by the company of all due diligence. He was a person under the control of the company and on the assumption that there could be proceedings against him, the company would by section 24(1)(b) be absolved if the company had taken all proper steps to avoid the commission of an offence by him. To make the company automatically liable for an offence committed by him would be to ignore the subsection. He was, so to speak, a cog in the machine which was devised: it was not left to him to devise it. Nor was he within what has been called the ''brain area'' of the company. If the company had taken all reasonable precautions and exercised all due diligence to ensure that the machine could and should run effectively then some breakdown due to some action or failure on the part of ''another person'' ought not to be attributed to the company or to be regarded as the action or failure of the company itself for which the company was to be criminally responsible. The defence provided by section 24(1) would otherwise be illusory.

LORD PEARSON. Section 24 requires a dividing line to be drawn between the master and any other person. The defendant cannot disclaim liability for an act or omission of his ego or alter ego. In the case of an individual defendant, his ego is simply himself, but he may have an alter ego. For instance, if he has only one shop and he appoints a manager of that shop with full discretion to manage it as he thinks fit, the manager is doing what the employer would normally do and may be held to be the employer's alter ego. But if the defendant has hundreds of shops he could not be expected personally to manage each one of them and the manager of one of his shops cannot in the absence of exceptional circumstances be considered his alter ego. In the case of a company, the ego is located in several persons, for example, those mentioned in section 20 of the Act or other persons in a similar position of direction or general management. A company may have an alter ego, if those persons who are or have its ego delegate to some other person the control and management, with full discretionary powers, of some section of the company's business. In the case of a company, it may be difficult, and in most cases for practical purposes unnecessary, to draw the distinction between its ego and its alter ego, but theoretically there is that distinction.

Mr Clement, being the manager of one of the company's several hundreds of shops, could not be identified with the company's ego nor was he an alter ego of the company. He was an employee in a relatively subordinate post. In the company's hierarchy there were a branch inspector and an area controller and a regional director interposed between him and the board of directors.

LORD DIPLOCK. My Lords, a corporation incorporated under the Companies Act 1948 owes its corporate personality and its powers to its constitution, the memorandum and articles of association. The obvious and the only place to look to discover by what natural persons its powers are exercisable, is in its constitution. The articles of association, if they follow Table A, provide that the business of the company shall be managed by the directors and that they may "exercise all such powers of the company" as are not required by the Act to be exercised in general meeting. Table A also vests in the directors the right to entrust and confer upon a managing director any of the powers of the company which are exercisable by them. So it may also be necessary to ascertain whether the directors have taken any action under this provision or any other similar provision providing for the co-ordinate exercise of the powers of the company by executive directors or by committees of the directors and other persons, such as are frequently included in the articles of association of companies in which the regulations contained in Table A are modified or excluded in whole or in part.

In my view, therefore, the question: what natural persons are to be treated in law as being the company for the purpose of acts done in the course of its business, including the taking of precautions and the exercise of due diligence to avoid the commission of a criminal offence, is to be found by identifying those natural persons who by the memorandum and articles of association or as a result of action taken by the directors, or by the company in general meeting pursuant to the articles, are entrusted with the exercise of the powers of the company.

Unit Construction Co. Ltd. v. Bullock (Inspector of Taxes)

[1960] AC 351
House of Lords
A company resident for tax purposes in the United Kingdom had three subsidiaries which were registered in Kenya. In terms of their memorandum and articles of association, the subsidiary companies' management was in the hands of its directors, whose meetings could

take place anywhere outside the United Kingdom. In fact, contrary to the memorandum and articles of association, the companies were managed and controlled by the parent company in the United Kingdom. The appellant company, which was another wholly owned subsidiary, attempted to deduct payments made to the Kenyan subsidiaries in computing its profits for the purpose of assessment to income tax. If the Kenyan subsidiaries were 'resident in the United Kingdom' within the meaning of section 20(9) of the Finance Act 1953, the payments were tax deductible. The Court of Appeal had earlier dismissed an appeal from an order of the Chancery Division, whereby an appeal by way of case stated by the Commissioners for the Special Purposes of the Income Tax Acts was sustained.

HELD that the residence of a company for the purposes of income tax was determined by the actual place of management of a company, and not by the place from which it ought to have been managed in terms of its memorandum and articles of association. The companies were therefore resident in the United Kingdom within the meaning of section 20(9) of the Finance Act 1953.

VISCOUNT SIMONDS. It has been trite law for two generations or more that a limited company "resides for the purposes of income tax where its real business is carried on" and that its "real business is carried on where the central management and control actually abides". This test has not only been reasserted and applied over and over again in judicial decisions; it has now also received legislative recognition, see section 468(7) of the Income Tax Act 1952. It cannot be questioned by your Lordships. The familiar words that I have cited come from Lord Loreburn's speech in *de Beers Consolidated Mines Ltd.* v. *Howe* [1906] AC (HL) 455, 458. At that time the possibility of an artificial legal person such as a limited company residing in two countries at one and the same time had not been fully examined. Twenty years later, in *Swedish Central Railway Co. Ltd.* v. *Thompson* (1923) 9 TC 343, 352, Rowatt J. saw no difficulty in such a concept and, indeed, found it easier for a corporation to have two residences than for a natural person.

. . . The business is not the less managed in London because it ought to be managed in Kenya. Its residence is determined by the solid facts, not by the terms of its constitution, however imperative. If, indeed, I must disregard the facts as they are, because they are irregular, I find a company without any central management at all. For, though I may disregard existing facts, I cannot invent facts which do not exist and say that the company's business is managed in Kenya. Yet it is the place of central management, which, however much of little weight ought to be given to other factors, essentially determines its residence. I come, therefore to the conclusion, though truly no precedent can be found for such a case, that it is the actual place of management, not that place in which it ought to be managed, which fixes the residence of a company. If it were not so, the result to the Revenue would be serious enough. In how many cases would a limited company register in a foreign country, prescribe by its articles that its business should be carried on by its directors meeting in that country, and then claim that its residence was in that country though every act of importance was directed from the United Kingdom?

In my opinion, Wynn-Parry J. and the Court of Appeal have adopted a wrong test in this admittedly difficult case. I would allow this appeal and restore the determination of the commissioners. The respondents must pay the appellants' costs here and below.

Rafsanjan Pistachio Producers Co-operative v. Reiss

[1990] BCLC 352; [1990] BCC 730
Queen's Bench Division

Five post-dated cheques were issued to the plaintiffs on temporary cheque forms which did not give the name of the company, but only the account number. The payment was in respect of a debt due to the plaintiffs by the company, Firegreen Ltd. for which the plaintiffs had obtained judgment. The cheques were issued by the defendant, who was a director of Firegreen Ltd. The defendant did not indicate in what capacity she had signed the cheques. After the first two cheques were presented and paid, the remaining three were dishonoured and the company went into receivership. The plaintiffs sued the defendant, relying on section 349(4) of the Companies Act 1985 which provides for personal liability of officers of the company in respect of failure to give the name of the company or to state it correctly on cheques. The defendant argued that the plaintiffs were estopped from making her personally liable, by their acceptance of the cheques in the form they were issued, and by their presentation of two of them for payment, and that she should be allowed to rectify the cheques to insert the name of the company.

HELD that the plaintiffs were not estopped by their actions from making the defendant personally liable; and that to allow the insertion of the name of the company into the cheques would be to negate the purpose of section 349(4) of the Companies Act 1985 which was to impose statutory liability as a quasi-penalty.

POTTER, J. Clearly in a large number of cases to which section 349 applies, there will exist a common mistake between the original parties as to the form and effect of the bill concerned, coupled with an absence of any contemporary intention that the signatory be personally liable. Even assuming that it is not in principle too late to permit rectification after the cheque has been delivered, presented and dishonoured, to do so would in my view be to negate the plain intention of the Act by depriving the recipient of the cheque of the benefit of a statutory liability imposed upon the signatory as a quasi-penalty. The unfortunate fact that in many cases the effect of the statutory provision will be to create considerable personal hardship on a director innocent of any moral blame in the matter must have been apparent to the legislature when the provision was first created. Again, sympathy for the plight of such a defendant does not enable me to hold that any defence arises to the claims of the plaintiffs in this case.

I therefore hold that the defendant's personal liability has been established and there will be judgment for the plaintiffs upon the three cheques.

D.H.N. Food Distributors Ltd. v. Tower Hamlets London Borough Council

[1976] 3 All ER 462; [1976] 1 WLR 852
Court of Appeal
The claimants were D.H.N. Food Distributors Ltd. (D.H.N.) and two wholly owned subsidiaries which together ran a grocery business. One of the subsidiary companies (Bronze) held freehold properties from which D.H.N. traded; another subsidiary (Transport) operated a fleet of vehicles. In 1969 Tower Hamlets London Borough Council made a compulsory purchase order for the property. Under section 5 of the Land Compensation Act 1961 compensation was paid to the subsidiary which held title to the land for 'the value of the land'. However,

because D.H.N. and the transport subsidiary could find no alternative premises, they were forced to cease trading, and were themselves not paid compensation for disturbance. An application was made to the Lands Tribunal on a preliminary question of law to ascertain whether D.H.N. and the transport subsidiary were entitled to compensation for disturbance. The tribunal held that the only compensation for disturbance to which D.H.N. was entitled was the value of the unexpired interest of a yearly tenant. The matter was appealed to the Court of Appeal.

HELD that the appeal should be allowed: the veil of incorporation should be lifted, and the group of companies treated as a single economic entity, entitling D.H.N. to claim compensation for disturbance; if the companies had to be treated as separate entities, D.H.N. would still be entitled to claim compensation for disturbance, on the ground that they had an irrevocable licence to occupy the premises for as long as they wished; and (*per* Goff and Shaw, JJ.) that the subsidiary holding the title to the property held it in trust for D.H.N. which therefore had an equitable interest in the premises sufficient to give it a right to compensation for disturbance.

LORD DENNING, M.R. The question is: what is the effect of the firm being in truth the three companies? The acquiring authority say that the owners of the land were Bronze Investments Ltd., and that company are entitled to the value of the land £360,000. They have actually been paid it. But the acquiring authority say that the company are not entitled to compensation for disturbance because they were not disturbed at all. The authority admit that D.H.N. (who ran the business) and the Transport subsidiary (who owned the vehicles) were greatly disturbed in their business. But the acquiring authority say that those two companies are not entitled to any compensation at all, not even for disturbance, because they had no interest in the land, legal or equitable. They say that in 1970 D.H.N. were only licensees of Bronze, the subsidiary which owned the land: and D.H.N. being licensees only, with no interest in the land, their only claim was under section 20(1) of the Compulsory Purchase Act 1965. That section says that if a person has no greater interest than a tenant from year to year in the land, then he is only entitled to compensation for that lesser interest. Seeing that a licensee can be turned out on short notice, the compensation payable to D.H.N. would be negligible.

The strange thing about this case is, that the acquiring authority admit that at any time from February 1970, during the local inquiry and afterwards (right up to the time in October 1970 when the council gave notice to treat) the people running these three companies could have put their house in order so as to make the claim impregnable. All they had to do was to take a very simple step. Being in control of all three companies, they could have arranged for Bronze to convey the land to D.H.N. No stamp duty would be payable because it would be exempt under section 42 of the Finance Act 1930. And D.H.N., being owners, could also claim conpensation for disturbance. So at any time up to October 30, 1970, this group of three companies could have put themselves in an unassailable position to claim not only the value of the land but also compensation for disturbance. But that was not done. The acquiring authority say that, by failing to do it, the group have missed the boat. They are left behind on the quay because of the technical provisions of our company law whereby each of the three companies is in law a separate person. Each of its interests must be considered separately. D.H.N. had no interest in the land. It was only a licensee. So it cannot claim compensation for disturbance.

. . . We all know that in many respects a group of companies are treated together for the purpose of general accounts, balance sheet, and profit and loss account. They are treated as one concern. Professor Gower in *Modern Company Law* 3rd ed. (1969), p. 216 says:

> "there is evidence of a general tendency to ignore the separate legal entities of various companies within a group, and to look instead at the economic entity of the whole group."

This is especially the case when a parent company owns all the shares of the subsidiaries—so much so that it can control every movement of the subsidiaries. These subsidiaries are bound hand and foot to the parent company and must do just what the parent company says. A striking instance is the decision of the House of Lords in *Harold Houldsworth & Co. (Wakefield) Ltd.* v. *Caddies* [1955] 1 WLR 352. So here. This group is virtually the same as a partnership in which all the three companies are partners. They should not be treated separately so as to be defeated on a technical point. They should not be deprived of the compensation which should justly be payable for disturbance. The three companies should, for present purposes, be treated as one, and the parent company D.H.N. should be treated as that one. So D.H.N. are entitled to claim compensation accordingly. It was not necessary for them to go through a conveyancing device to get it.

I realise that the President of the Lands Tribunal in view of the previous cases, felt it necessary to decide as he did. But now that the matter has been fully discussed in this court, we must decide differently from him. These companies as a group are entitled to compensation not only for the value of the land, but also compensation for disturbance. I would allow the appeal accordingly.

GOFF, L.J. This is a case in which one is entitled to look at the realities of the situation and to pierce the corporate veil. I wish to safeguard myself by saying that so far as this ground is concerned, I am relying on the facts of this particular case. I would not at this juncture accept that in every case where one has a group of companies one is entitled to pierce the veil, but in this case the two subsidiaries were both wholly owned; further, they had no separate business operations whatsoever; thirdly, in my judgment, the nature of the question involved is highly relevant, namely, whether the owners of this business have been disturbed in their possession and enjoyment of it.

★ Woolfson and another v. Strathclyde Regional Council

1978 SC (HL) 90; 1978 SLT 159

House of Lords

Campbell Ltd. (C. Ltd.) carried on a retail business in a chain of bridal shops, three of which were owned by Woolfson and the other two by Solfred Ltd. (S. Ltd.). Woolfson owned all but one of the shares of C. Ltd., the remaining share being held by his wife. Woolfson and his wife between them also owned the entire issued share capital of S. Ltd. C. Ltd. paid rent for the premises to both Woolfson and S. Ltd., although leases had never been executed. C. Ltd. kept its own accounts, paid its own tax, and was registered in the valuation roll as the occupier of the premises. The local authority compulsorily acquired the premises for development of the Inner Ring Road in Glasgow, in terms of the Land Compensation (Scotland) Act 1963. Under that statute, compensation would be paid for disturbance to an occupier or to an owner occupier, but not to an owner which was not an occupier. Both Woolfson and S. Ltd. sought compensation for disturbance through the Lands Tribunal for Scotland on the grounds that they formed one economic entity with C. Ltd. Both the Lands Tribunal for Scotland and the Second Division of the Court of Session refused to award compensation to them on the ground that C. Ltd.

alone was the occupier and had a separate legal persona. Woolfson and S. Ltd. appealed to the House of Lords.

HELD there was no basis for lifting the corporate veil to consider Woolfson as the beneficial owner of C. Ltd.'s business or of the assets of S. Ltd., since Woolfson's wife held one share in C. Ltd. and the evidence did not show that she held it as Woolfson's nominee, and that any losses suffered by Woolfson would be in his capacity as shareholder of C. Ltd. and not as owner of the land. The appeal was accordingly dismissed.

LORD KEITH. I can see no grounds whatever, upon the facts found in the special case, for treating the company structure as a mere façade, nor do I consider that the *D.H.N. Food Distributors* case [1976] 1 WLR 852 is, on a proper analysis, of assistance to the appellants' argument. . . . I consider the *D.H.N. Food* case to be clearly distinguishable on its facts from the present case. There the company that owned the land was the wholly owned subsidiary of the company that carried on the business. The latter was in complete control of the situation as respects anything which might affect its business, and there was no one but itself having any kind of interest or right as respects the assets of the subsidiary. Here, on the other hand, the company that carried on the business, Campbell, has no sort of control whatever over the owners of the land, Solfred and Woolfson. Woolfson holds two-thirds only of the shares in Solfred and Solfred has no interest in Campbell. Woolfson cannot be treated as beneficially entitled to the whole shareholding in Campbell, since it is not found that the one share in Campbell held by his wife is held as his nominee. In my opinion there is no basis consonant with principle upon which on the facts of this case the corporate veil can be pierced to the effect of holding Woolfson to be the true owner of Campbell's business or of the assets of Solfred.

NOTE
It is interesting to compare the decisions in *D.H.N. Food Distributors Ltd.* v. *Tower Hamlets London Borough Council* [1976] 1 WLR 852 (reported on page 20 above) with the decision in this case. In *D.H.N.*, Goff, L.J. was careful to point out that the decision of the Court of Appeal was dependent on the facts of that case. Although the facts of these two cases are very similar, the differences between them were sufficient for the House of Lords in *Woolfson* to come to an opposite

conclusion. The major difference between them is that in *D.H.N.* the company that operated the business from the premises that were compulsorily acquired was the parent company, and was in complete control of the other two companies, whereas in the *Woolfson* case, the company which occupied the premises, Campbell Limited, had no control over the owners of the premises, who were Solfred Limited and Woolfson. In addition, it was relevant to the decision that Woolfson's wife held one share in the occupying company, C. Ltd., which meant that Woolfson could not be held to be beneficially entitled to the entire share capital of C. Ltd. Note also that *Woolfson* was decided by the House of Lords whereas *D.H.N.* was decided by the Court of Appeal. Being a Scottish case, the *Woolfson* judgment is only of persuasive authority in England and Wales. It has, however, been followed in *National Dock Labour Board* v. *Pinn & Wheeler Ltd. and others* [1989] reported below.

For further cases on this point see:

Tunstall v. *Steigman* [1962] 2 QB 593;

Smith, Stone & Knight Ltd. v. *Birmingham Corporation* [1939] 4 All ER 116;

Revlon Inc. v. *Cripps & Lee Ltd.* [1980] FSR 85;

* *Harold Houldsworth & Co. (Wakefield) Ltd.* v. *Caddies* 1955 SC (HL) 27: [1955] 1 All ER 725; [1955] 1 WLR 352;

* *City of Glasgow District Council* v. *Hamlet Textiles Ltd.* 1986 SLT 415.

National Dock Labour Board v. Pinn & Wheeler Ltd. and others

15 March 1989 (LEXIS transcript)
Court of Appeal
The National Dock Labour Board appealed against the decision of an industrial tribunal that three companies within a group (Pinn & Wheeler, K. & B. Forest Products Ltd. and Sabah) were 'waterside manufacturers' for the purpose of determining, under section 51(3) of

the Docks and Harbours Act 1966 and the Dock Workers Employment Scheme 1967, 'whether any work is dock work'. Under the terms of the Dock Workers Employment Scheme for the City of London, 'dock work' did not include work carried out by 'waterside manufacturers', which could be carried out by unregistered dock workers. The work in question was unloading by the employees of Pinn & Wheeler (who were not registered dock workers) of a cargo owned by Sabah. Pinn & Wheeler had a wharf at which the goods were unloaded, whence they were taken to K. & B.'s mill to be processed. The mill was not actually on the waterside but was nearby. There was a threatened strike of dock workers which had led to an injunction restraining the applicants from having cargo unloaded by unregistered dock workers. The tribunal had treated the three companies as one economic entity and had held that the three applicants together qualified as waterside manufacturers. Macpherson, J. held in the High Court, reversing the decision of the industrial tribunal, that it was only in exceptional circumstances that the veil of incorporation should be lifted, when the corporate form was a mere façade concealing the true facts; where separate companies were set up for good commercial reasons there was no reason to lift the veil; further, even if the veil of incorporation were to be lifted, in any event the manufacturing work was not 'waterside' within the meaning of the Docks and Harbours Act 1966 and the Dock Workers Employment Scheme 1967. The appeal was therefore allowed. A further appeal was made to the Court of Appeal.

HELD, dismissing the appeal, that the four companies possessed separate legal identities, and accordingly the corporate veil should not be lifted.

MAY, L.J. On the substantive appeal from the Industrial Tribunal's decision to the Divisional Court, in addition to the point with which we have already dealt in the context of the corporate re-organisation, it was argued that the Industrial Tribunal had been wrong (as it was expressed) to pierce the corporate veil clothing all four limited companies. It was submitted to the learned judge that the Industrial Tribunal had had to deal with the companies as they were and in respect of one as a wharfinger and in respect of another as a manufacturer.

Being different legal entities, it was wrong of the Industrial Tribunal to coalesce the two particularly relevant companies and conclude that together they constituted a waterside manufacturer and thus entitled to the exemption. With that submission the learned judge agreed. He expressed his decision in this way:

> "It is only in special circumstances which indicate that there 'is a mere façade concealing the true facts' that it is appropriate to pierce the corporate veil . . ."

In my judgment there was (to quote Lord Keith's words) "no basis consonant with principle" upon which on the facts of this case "the corporate veil can be pierced". It does indeed seem to me perhaps to be unseemly that the three companies should be allowed to unveil themselves in order to try to avoid the effect of the Dock Labour Scheme.

It was argued in support of this particular aspect of the appeal to us from the decision of the Divisional Court that, contrary to the view taken by the learned judge below, the Industrial Tribunal were indeed justified in the circumstances of the instant case in not paying strict regard to the separate corporate identities of the respective companies and were correct in their common sense and, as was suggested, realistic approach in looking at the commercial reality of the situation. There was, Mr Field (counsel for the appellants) submitted, sufficient identity between at least the two material companies in a commercial sense, to entitle the Industrial Tribunal to consider the two together as constituting a waterside manufacturer. Indeed it was in the context of the whole scheme and the creation of this particular exemption that one should really look at the commercial reality of the situation and not allow oneself to be circumscribed by any strict adherence to the legal principle that the companies were each separate legal entities. Alternatively it was submitted that the Industrial Tribunal would have been correct to go behind the corporate veil and identify one particular company about which it could be said, construing the scheme realistically and from a commercial point of view, that it was a waterside manufacturer, and in the circumstances of this particular case it would have been the manufacturing company, K & B Forest Products Ltd.

In support of these submissions we were referred to two authorities. First, *D.H.N. Food Distributors Ltd.* v. *Tower Hamlets London Borough Council* [1976] 1 WLR 852, 32 P & CR 240 and to various passages from the judgments of the court in that case. For present purposes I do not think it necessary to rehearse those passages in this judgment because we were also referred to a later decision in which that earlier decision was considered, namely *Woolfson* v. *Strathclyde Regional Council* 38 P & CR 521. It was unnecessary to go through the facts of that case, but in delivering the principal speech in the

House of Lords, with which the remainder of their Lordships agreed, Lord Keith of Kinkel at 38 P & CR 521 page 525 referred to the *D.H.N. Food Distributors Ltd.* case and at page 526, in relation to the decision of the Court of Appeal in that case, said this:

> "I have some doubts whether in this respect the Court of Appeal properly applied the principle that it is appropriate to pierce the corporate veil only where special circmstances exist indicating that it is a mere façade concealing the true facts."

In my judgment, on this and other authorities to which I have taken the opportunity of looking, that is the basic principle by which one should be guided in deciding whether or not the corporate veil, enveloping separate corporate identities in law, should be pierced and that one should look at the realities of the situation, rather than the legal niceties. In the instant case there were no special circumstances which indicated that the separate companies were a mere façade concealing the true facts. There were originally, as I understand the situation, commercial and subsequently at least historical reasons why the four companies were retained in existence.

In those circumstances I respectfully agree with the learned judge that the Industrial Tribunal, although seeking very properly in other cases to look at the commercial reality of the situation, erred in law in this case in failing to recognise and separate the different legal corporate identities of the four companies concerned.

Accordingly, for those reasons I would dismiss the appeal against the learned judge on this particular point.

Gilford Motor Co. Ltd. v. Horne
[1933] 1 Ch 935
Court of Appeal

The defendant was appointed as managing director of the plaintiff company under a contract which contained a restrictive covenant which prohibited the defendant from soliciting the customers of the plaintiff company, both while he was employed by the company and afterwards within a radius of three miles from any premises where the business of the company was carried on. The business of the plaintiff company was the manufacture of vehicles and the supply of spare parts and servicing. The defendant's employment with the plaintiff company was terminated, and shortly thereafter he formed a limited company trading in the same line of business, supplying spare parts for all the Gilford vehicles. The directors and shareholders were the defendant's wife and an associate of the defendant. The plaintiff company raised an action to implement the restrictive covenant by injunction. Farwell, J. in the High Court held that the covenant was too wide and therefore unenforceable, as the defendant would not, as managing director of the plaintiff company, come into contact with the customers. The case was appealed to the Court of Appeal.

HELD, reversing the decision of Farwell, J., that the covenant was no wider than was necessary to protect the plaintiff company's business and therefore was enforceable.

LORD HANWORTH, M.R. In these circumstances the appeal must be allowed; and . . . I think the injunction must go against the company. Sir Walter Greaves-Lord admitted that if the company were such as is indicated by Lindley L.J. in *Smith.* v. *Hancock* [1894] 2 Ch 377, 385, it would not be possible to object to the injunction going against the company. Lindley L.J. indicated the rule which ought to be followed by the Court: "If the evidence admitted of the conclusion that what was being done was a mere cloak or sham, and that in truth the business was being carried on by the wife and Kerr for the defendant, or by the defendant through his wife for Kerr, I certainly should not hesitate to draw that conclusion, and to grant the plaintiff relief accordingly." I do draw that conclusion; I do hold that the company was "a mere cloak or sham"; I do hold that it was a mere device for enabling Mr E.B. Horne to continue to commit breaches of clause 9, and under those circumstances the injunction must go against both defendants, the appeal must be allowed with costs here and below, and the injunction will be in the terms asked in the prayer in the statement of claim.

LAWRENCE, L.J. I am of opinion that the evidence amply justified the learned judge in drawing the inference that the company was a mere cloak or sham for the purpose of enabling the defendant to commit a breach of his covenant against solicitation. I need not recall the facts, but it seems to me that the evidence as to the formation of the company and as to the position of its shareholders and directors leads to that inference. Of course, that inference might have been displaced by evidence adduced on the part of the defendants, but although the issue was plainly raised on the pleadings, no such evidence was forthcoming. In these circumstances, I agree with the finding by the learned judge that the defendant company was a mere channel used by the defendant Horne for the purpose of enabling him, for his own benefit, to obtain the advantage of the customers of the plaintiff company, and that therefore the defendant company ought to be restrained as well as the defendant Horne.

I agree that this appeal ought to be allowed, with the consequences stated by the Master of the Rolls.

2. Incorporation, promotion and pre-incorporation contracts

Summary

1. Sources of the law

The law on incorporation is found in sections 1–21 of the Companies Act 1985. The law relating to promotion and pre-incorporation contracts is found in section 36C of the Companies Act 1985, and in case law.

2. Incorporation

Section 1(1) of the Companies Act 1985 states:

> Any two or more persons associated for a lawful purpose may, by subscribing their names to a memorandum of association and otherwise complying with the requirements of this Act in respect of registration, form an incorporated company, with or without limited liability.

Although there are two other methods of incorporation—incorporation by special Act of Parliament and incorporation by royal charter—the Companies Act 1985 is concerned with incorporation by registration.

From the words of the section, it is not competent to form a company for an unlawful purpose, and such a company can have its registration removed by application to court by the Attorney General (*Lord Advocate). See *R.* v. *Registrar of Companies, ex parte Attorney General* [1991].

To register a company the following documents must be registered at Companies House:

(1) The memorandum and articles of association (see Chapter 3);

(2) A statement giving details of the first directors and secretary and the intended location of the first registered office;

(3) A statutory declaration of compliance with the registration requirements of the Companies Act 1985.

A fee is payable in respect of incorporation.

Provided that the objects of the company are legal and that the incorporation papers have been correctly completed, the Registrar of Companies issues a certificate of incorporation, which is conclusive evidence that the registration requirements of the Companies Act 1985 have been complied with, and that if the certificate states that the company is a public company, that it is such a company. From the date of the certificate, the company exists as an independent legal person. See *Official Receiver and Liquidator of Jubilee Cotton Mills Ltd.* v. *Lewis* [1924].

3. Promoters

Promoters are persons who are responsible for the creation of the company: they may do any of a range of tasks, such as forming the company; finding potential shareholders, directors, secretaries and employees; arranging contracts in the name of the company both before and after incorporation; and arranging share issues on behalf of the company.

Promoters occupy an anomalous position in relation to the company as regards work undertaken before the company was formed, when they are not the agents of the company. For further information in relation to their liability on pre-incorporation contracts see section 4 of this Chapter below.

However, it has been decided by case law that promoters owe fiduciary duties towards the company (duties of loyalty and good faith) similar to those of a director. The principal duties are to disclose any personal interest in a company contract, and not to make a secret profit on a company contract. See *Erlanger* v. *The New Sombrero Phosphate Co.* (1878), and *Gluckstein* v. *Barnes* [1900]. Promoters also owe a duty to take reasonable skill and care in the conduct of the promotion.

4. Pre-incorporation contracts

When promoters enter into a contract on behalf of a company before it has been granted a certificate of incorporation, such a contract is binding personally on the promoter under section 36C of the Companies Act 1985, which states:

(1) A contract which purports to be made by or on behalf of a company at a time when the company has not been formed has effect, subject to any agreement to the contrary, as one made with the person purporting to act for the company or as agent for it, and he is personally liable on the contract accordingly.

(2) Subsection (1) applies—
   (a) to the making of a deed under the law of England and Wales, and

   (b) to the undertaking of an obligation under the law of Scotland as it applies to the making of a contract.

Section 36C was first enacted as section 9(2) of the European Communities Act 1972 following an EEC Council Directive of 9 March 1968 (68/151/EEC). By necessary implication from the statute, the promoter is the person with title to sue on a pre-incorporation contract. See *Phonogram Ltd.* v. *Lane* [1982] and *Cotronic (UK) Ltd.* v. *Dezonie* [1991].

The statutory law simplifies the previous common law provisions. The common law is still relevant in relation to the ratification of a pre-incorporation contract: the position is that a pre-incorporation contract cannot be ratified so as to make it binding on both the company and the party with whom the contract was made, and so as to release the party who made the contract for the company prior to incorporation. Such a contract can, however, be novated, i.e. a new contract can be entered into between the company after incorporation and the other party. In the absence of novation, by implication from section 36C of the Companies Act 1985, the promoter will be the person with title to sue for breach of contract under a pre-incorporation contract: see *Tinnevelly Sugar Refining Co. Ltd.* v. *Mirrlees Watson & Yaryan Co. Ltd.* [1894].

R. v. Registrar of Companies, ex parte Attorney General

[1991] BCLC 476

Queen's Bench Division

Lindi St Claire, a prostitute, formed a company to carry out the service of prostitution. She had attempted to call her company Prostitute Ltd., Hookers Ltd., and Lindi St Claire (French Lessons) Ltd., all of which were rejected as unsuitable names by the Registrar of Companies. Finally the company was registered under the name of Lindi St Claire (Personal Services) Ltd. The objects of the company were stated to be 'to carry on the business of prostitution'. Ms St Claire, who was one of the directors of the company, had described her occupation as 'prostitute'. An application was made for judicial review on the ground that the Registrar of Companies had acted *ultra vires* or misdirected himself or otherwise erred in law in allowing the company to be registered, as the company was not formed for a lawful purpose as required by section 1(1) of the Companies Act 1948 (now section 1(1) of the Companies Act 1985).

HELD that the court would grant judicial review of the decision of the Registrar of Companies, and would strike the company off the register.

ACKER L.J. It is well settled that a contract which is made upon a sexually immoral consideration or for a sexually immoral purpose is against public policy and is illegal and unenforceable. The fact that it does not involve or may not involve the commission of a criminal offence in no way prevents the contract being illegal, being against public policy and therefore unenforceable. Here, as the documents clearly indicate, the association is for the purpose of carrying on a trade which involves illegal contracts because the purpose is a sexually immoral purpose and as such against public policy.

. . . I would order that the registration be therefore quashed.

NOTE

This case follows *Bowman* v. *The Secular Society Ltd.* [1917] AC 406.

Jubilee Cotton Mills Ltd. v. Lewis

[1924] AC 958
House of Lords

The respondent, Lewis, was the promoter of a company formed for the purpose of purchasing a cotton mill which was to operate the business of cotton spinners. Although the certificate of incorporation was dated 6 January 1920, in fact it was not signed by the Registrar of Companies until 8 January. However, on 6 January the company, without filing a statement in lieu of prospectus as required by the Companies (Consolidation) Act 1908, had issued a large number of fully paid shares and debentures to the vendor, apparently as consideration for the purchase, but really to provide for promotion profits. The bulk of the shares and debentures were transferred to the respondent, who made a profit on their sale. The company was liquidated, in the course of which the official receiver and liquidator issued a misfeasance summons against the respondent to make him liable for secret profits made as a promoter in respect of the shares and debentures. The respondent defended on the ground that the issue of the shares and debentures was invalid as the company had not been in existence on 6 January when the issue had been made and the shares were, therefore, worthless. The High Court had found that the respondent was a promoter, and that his secret profit amounted to £35,390. On appeal, the Court of Appeal had, by majority, reversed this decision. An appeal was made to the House of Lords.

HELD that the certificate of incorporation was conclusive evidence as to the date of incorporation within the meaning of section 16(2) of the Companies Act 1908 (now section 13(7) of the Companies Act 1985), and therefore the allotment of shares was not void on that ground; but (by majority) assuming that the allotment was void because it was made without filing a statement in lieu of prospectus, the respondent as promoter was in any event liable to account for the secret profit made by him.

LORD SUMNER. It is reasonably clear that in fact the registrar did not actually sign the certificate of incorporation till January 8, certain formalities not having been completed till that day, but the certificate itself, which bears date January 6, 1920, certifies that the company was incorporated on the 6th; and section 17 of the Act of 1908 makes the statement conclusive evidence ''that all the requirements of this

Act in respect of registration and of matters precedent and incidental thereto have been complied with.''

It is true that the section does not add ''on and from this date'', but I do not think this is necessary, for section 16 sub-section 1, provides, ''that on the registration . . . the registrar shall certify . . . that the company is incorporated,'' and, by sub-section 2, ''from the date of incorporation mentioned in the certificate of incorporation, the subscribers . . . shall be a body corporate . . . capable forthwith of exercising all the functions of an incorporated company.'' I think it is now well settled that in a statute such as this ''from the date of incorporation mentioned in the certificate'' means (in the present case) ''from some part of January 6'' and not ''from no part of that date but from the earliest part of the next day'', and that the law does not in this connection divide a day into hours and minutes, but means by a day, the date of which is given, the whole of that day. We must accordingly take it that the company was, from the commencement of January 6, ''a body corporate . . . capable forthwith of exercising all the functions of an incorporated company'' limited by shares, and must be taken to have been already born at the moment of allotment, whatever the actual fact may have been.

Erlanger and others v. The New Sombrero Phosphate Co. and others

(1878) 3 App. Cas. 1218; [1874–80] All ER 271
House of Lords

A syndicate bought the lease of an island—Sombrero in the West Indies—reputed to contain valuable phosphate mines. Erlanger, who headed the syndicate, promoted a company to take over the island and work the mines. He appointed the directors, who were, apart from one, all subject to Erlanger's control. The island was acquired by the company, at double its true market value. A prospectus was issued, and many shares were sold. The real circumstances of the purchase of the island by the syndicate and its resale to the company were not disclosed to the shareholders, who began to hear rumours relating to the prices at which these sales had taken place. A committee of investigation was appointed, and the directors were removed from office, and replaced by a new board. Eventually proceedings were brought to have the contract with the company rescinded. In the High

Court the proceedings were dismissed, without costs. The Court of Appeal reversed the decision, and ordered the contract to be rescinded. An appeal was then made to the House of Lords.

HELD that the contract was voidable, and could be rescinded. The Lord Chancellor, however, expressed his (minority) view that there had been substantial delay on the part of the company in seeking to rescind the contract, sufficient to render the company estopped by acquiescence from rescinding the contract, which was only voidable and not void. OBSERVED (*obiter*) that persons who purchase property and then create a company to purchase that property from them, stand in a fiduciary relationship to the company, and must disclose all material facts to that company.

LORD CAIRNS, L.C. In the whole of this proceeding up to this time the syndicate, or the House of *Erlanger* as representing the syndicate, were the promoters of the company, and it is now necessary that I should state to your Lordships in what position I understand the promoters to be placed with reference to the company which they proposed to form. They stand, in my opinion, undoubtedly in a fiduciary position. They have in their hands the creation and moulding of the company; they have the power of defining how, and when, and in what shape, and under what supervision, it shall start into existence and begin to act as a trading corporation. If they are doing all this in order that the company may, as soon as it starts into life, become, through its managing directors, the purchaser of the property of themselves, the promoters, it is, in my opinion, incumbent upon the promoters to take care that in forming the company they provide it with an executive, that is to say, with a board of directors, who shall both be aware that the property which they are asked to buy is the property of the promoters, and who shall be competent and impartial judges as to whether the purchase ought or ought not to be made. I do not say that the owner of property may not promote and form a joint stock company, and then sell his property to it, but I do say that if he does he is bound to take care that he sells it to the company through the medium of a board of directors who can and do exercise an independent and intelligent judgment on the transaction, and who are not left under the belief that the property belongs, not to the promoter, but to some other person.

LORD O'HAGAN. The original purchase of the island of *Sombrero* was perfectly legitimate—and it was not less so because the object of the purchase was to sell it again, and to sell it by forming a company which might afford them a profit on the transaction. The law permitted them to take that course, and provided the machinery by which the transfer of their interest might be equitably and beneficially effected for themselves and those with whom they meant to deal. But the privilege given them for promoting such a company for such an object, involved obligations of a very serious kind. It required, in its exercise, the utmost good faith, the completest truthfulness, and a careful regard to the protection of the future shareholders. The power to nominate a directorate is manifestly capable of great abuse, and may involve, in the misuse of it, very evil consequences to multitudes of people who have little capacity to guard themselves. Such a power may or may not have been wisely permitted to exist. I venture to have doubts upon the point. It tempts too much to fraudulent contrivance and mischievous deception; and, at least, it should be watched with jealousy and restrained from employment in such a way as to mislead the ignorant and the unwary. In all such cases the directorate nominated by the promoters should stand between them and the public, with such independence and intelligence, that they may be expected to deal fairly, impartially, and with adequate knowledge in the affairs submitted to their control. If they have not those qualities, they are unworthy of trust. They are the betrayers and not the guardians of the company they govern, and their acts should not receive the sanction of a Court of justice.

Now . . . I think that the promoters in this case failed to remember the exigencies of their fiduciary position, when they appointed directors who were in no way independent of themselves, and who did not sustain the interests of the company with ordinary care and intelligence. . . .

The value of the island was ascertained by a learned Judge to be £55,000, and, a few days after, circumstances remaining wholly unchanged, a contract for the sale of it, at £110,000, was confirmed, in the absence of M. *Drouyn de Lhuys* and Mr *Eastwick* by three of the five directors . . . Apparently, there was no inquiry as to the enormous advance in the price beyond that which the Vice-Chancellor had accepted on his judicial responsibility, no consideration of the state of the property—and no intelligent estimate of its capabilities and prospects. If the directors had been nominated merely to ratify any terms the promoters might dictate, they discharged their function; if it was their duty, as it certainly was, to protect the shareholders, they never seem to have thought of doing it . . . I concur in, I believe, the unanimous opinion of your Lordships that such a transaction ought not to be allowed to stand.

Gluckstein v. Barnes (Official Receiver and Official Liquidator of Olympia Ltd.)

[1900] AC 240

House of Lords

A syndicate including Gluckstein (G.), raised a fund which was held by trustees, and used it to buy the Olympia Exhibition Hall in London for £140,000. They promoted a limited company, Olympia Ltd., of which they were the only directors, and resold the hall to it for £180,000. Securities on the property were also acquired by the promoters at a discount, which were later realised at face value, making a profit of £20,000. A prospectus was issued, which disclosed the profit of £40,000 made by the promoters on the sale of the property to the company, but not the £20,000 profit on the realisation of the securities. Shares were issued, but the company shortly thereafter went into liquidation. An action was raised by the Official Receiver and Official Liquidator of the company for recovery of the £20,000 as a secret profit. The summons was dismissed by the trial judge, but the decision was reversed by the Court of Appeal. G. appealed to the House of Lords.

HELD that the trustees ought to have disclosed the profit of £20,000, and the fact that the company was in liquidation and could not rescind the contract was no bar to relief; G. as one of the trustees was bound to repay that portion of the £20,000 which had been paid to the trustees as their share.

EARL OF HALSBURY, L.C. When they did afterwards sell to a company, they took very good care there should be no one who could ask questions. They were to be sellers to themselves as buyers, and it was a necessary provision to the plan that they were to be both sellers and buyers, and as buyers to get the money to pay for the purchase from the pockets of deluded shareholders.

My Lords, I decline to discuss the question of disclosure to the company. It is too absurd to suggest that such a disclosure to the parties to this transaction is a disclosure to the company of which these directors were the proper guardians and trustees. They were there by the terms of the agreement to do the work of the syndicate, that is to say, to cheat the shareholders; and this, forsooth, is to be treated as a disclosure to the company, when they were really there to hoodwink the shareholders, and so far from protecting them, were to obtain from them the money, the produce of their nefarious plans.

LORD MACNAGHTEN. These gentlemen set about forming a company to pay them a handsome sum for taking off their hands a property which they had contracted to buy with that end in view. They bring the company into existence by means of the usual machinery. They appoint themselves sole guardians and protectors of this creature of theirs, half-fledged and just struggling into life, bound hand and foot while yet unborn by contracts tending to their private advantage, and so fashioned by its makers that it could only act by their hands and only see through their eyes. They issue a prospectus representing that they had agreed to purchase the property for a sum largely in excess of the amount which they had, in fact, to pay. On the faith of this prospectus they collect subscriptions from a confiding and credulous public. And then comes the last act. Secretly, and therefore dishonestly, they put into their own pockets the difference between the real and the pretended price. After a brief career the company is ordered to be wound up. In the course of the liquidation the trick is discovered. Mr Gluckstein is called upon to make good a portion of the sum which he and his associates had misappropriated. Why Mr Gluckstein alone was selected for attack I do not know any more than I know why he was only asked to pay back a fraction of the money improperly withdrawn from the coffers of the company.

LORD ROBERTSON. In the normal case, where the directors are truly and not merely in name the executive of the company, it may be assumed that they will be vigilant and critical of the particulars of a bargain of such paramount importance as the purchase of the property to be traded with, and that, dealing at arm's length, they will examine into anything bearing on that matter that does not tell its own story on its face. But, in the present case, the company was paralysed so far as vigilance and criticism were concerned; for the board-room was occupied by the enemy. Now, the question whether adequate disclosure has been made to a company by a vendor bound to do so must necessarily depend upon the intelligence brought to bear on the information. And if, by his own act, the promoter has weakened, or, as here, has annulled the directorate, his case on disclosure becomes extremely arduous—for he has to make out such disclosure to shareholders as makes directors unnecessary.

Phonogram Ltd. v. Lane

[1982] QB 938; [1981] 3 All ER 182; [1981] 3 WLR 736

Court of Appeal

A company to be called Fragile Management Ltd. was to be formed to manage a pop group to be called Cheap, Mean and Nasty. Phonogram Ltd. had agreed to finance the pop group up to £12,000, payable in two instalments. The first cheque was sent to the defendant, an artistes' manager, stating that the money was sent to him in anticipation of a contract being entered into between Phonogram Ltd. and Fragile Management Ltd., and that the money was repayable if the contract was not entered into within a specified period. The cheque was made out for administrative reasons to a company, Jelly Music Ltd. (J. Ltd.), of which the defendant was a director. The defendant, as requested by the plaintiffs, signed a copy of the letter 'for and on behalf of Fragile Management Ltd.' which was returned to the plaintiffs. Fragile Management Ltd. was never formed. The contract was not entered into and, therefore, the £6,000 became repayable. It was not, however, repaid, and the plaintiffs sued the defendant, Lane. The trial judge held that the defendant was not subject to the contract with the plaintiffs but that he was, nevertheless, personally liable to make repayment of the £6,000 under section 9(2) of the European Communities Act 1972 (now section 36C of the Companies Act 1985). The defendant appealed on the ground that section 9(2) was intended (as evidenced by EEC Council Directive 68/151) to apply to a company that was already in the course of formation, which was not the case with Fragile Management Ltd. Further, that the phrase 'a contract *purporting* to be made by a person as agent of a company' meant that there had to be a representation that the unformed company was already in existence and, finally, that a company could be the 'person' who purported to contract on behalf of the unformed company, and that J. Ltd., could be that 'person'.

HELD that the defendant was personally liable to repay the £6,000 to the plaintiffs on the following grounds: (1) only the spirit and intent of an EEC Directive was binding on a member state, and section 9(2) of the European Communities Act 1972 did accord with the spirit and intent of Directive 68/151, therefore it could apply to a company which was not yet in the process of formation; (2) under section 9(2) there did not have to be a representation that the company was already in existence; (3) J. Ltd. had not contracted with the plaintiffs as agent for Fragile Management Ltd. and, therefore, it could not be liable under section 9(2).

OBSERVED (*obiter*) that under section 9(2), an 'agreement to the contrary', i.e. to the effect that the person contracting for the unformed company is not to be personally liable on the contract, is not to be inferred by the fact that the person signed expressly as agent for the company, and that there would have to be an express exclusion of liability; and that since the passing of section 9(2), the distinction found in earlier case law between the effect of a signature as 'agent for' and 'for and on behalf of' an unformed company had been removed. (See *Kelner* v. *Baxter* (1866) LR 2 CP 174, and *Newborne* v. *Sensolid (Great Britain) Ltd.* [1953] 1 All ER 708.

LORD DENNING, M.R. I reject the submission of counsel for Mr Lane. I do not think we should go by the French text of the directive. It was drafted with regard to a different system of company law from that in this country. We should go by section 9(2) of our own statute, the European Communities Act 1972. Under article 189 of the EEC Treaty, these directives are to be binding only in so far as the spirit and intent are concerned. Article 189 says:

> "A directive shall be binding, as to the result to be achieved, upon each Member State to which it is addressed, but shall leave to the national authorities the choice of form and methods."

Section 9(2) is in accordance with the spirit and intent of the directive. We should go by our own statute, and not by the directive.

That brings me to the second point. What does "purports" mean in this context? Counsel for Mr Lane suggests that there must be a representation that the company is already in existence. I do not agree. A contract can purport to be made on behalf of a company, or by a company, even though that company is known by both parties not to be formed and that it is only about to be formed.

The third point made by counsel for Mr Lane was that a company can be a "person" within the meaning of that expression where it first occurs in section 9(2). He says that Jelly Music Ltd. was a "person" which was purporting to contract on behalf of Fragile Management Ltd. I do not agree. Jelly Music Ltd. were not entering into a contract. Mr Lane was purporting to do so.

So all three points made by Mr Lane's counsel fail.

But I would not leave the matter there. This is the first time the section has come before us. It will have much impact upon the common law. I am afraid that before 1972 the common law had adopted some fine distinctions. As I understand *Kelner* v. *Baxter* (1866) LR 2 CP 174, it decided that, if a person contracted on behalf of a company which was non-existent, he himself would be liable on the contract. Just as, if a man signs a contract for and on behalf "of his horses", he is personally liable. But, since that case was decided, a number of distinctions have been introduced by *Hollman* v. *Pullin* (1884) Cab & El 254, *Newborne* v. *Sensolid (Great Britain) Ltd.* [1953] 1 All ER 708, [1954] 1 QB 45 and *Black* v. *Smallwood* (1965) 117 CLR 51 in the High Court of Australia. Those three cases seem to suggest that there is a distinction to be drawn according to the way in which an agent signs a contract. If he signs as "agent for X company", or "for and on behalf of X company", and there is no such body as X company, then he himself can be sued on it. On the other hand, if he signs it as X company *per pro* himself the managing director, then the position may be different; because he is not contracting personally as an agent. It is the company which is contracting.

. . . In my opinion the distinction has been obliterated by section 9(2) of the European Communities Act 1972. We now have the clear words, "Where a contract purports to be made by a company, or by a person as agent for a company, at a time when the company has not been formed." That applies whatever formula is adopted. The person who purports to contract for the company is personally liable.

Cotronic (UK) Ltd. v. Dezonie and others
[1991] BCLC 721; [1991] BCC 200
Court of Appeal

Proceedings were brought by Cotronic (UK) Ltd. against Dezonie and Wendaland Builders Ltd. for payment for the cost of installation of an alarm, lighting, and a nurse-call system supplied by them at a residential home for the elderly. Cotronic (UK) Ltd. was not involved in this appeal. The background was that the work was carried out by Cotronic (UK) Ltd. as subcontractors for Wendaland Builders Ltd. The contract for building work had been made between Mrs Osbourne (the third party) and Wendaland Builders Ltd., and was signed by Dezonie for and on behalf of Wendaland Builders Ltd. However, Wendaland Builders Ltd. had, unknown to Dezonie, in fact been struck off the register and dissolved by the Registrar of Companies five years before the purported contract had been made. Two years after the purported contract was made, Dezonie realised that the company had been struck off and dissolved, and thereafter incorporated a new company, also called Wendaland Builders Ltd. Third party proceedings were instigated in which the defendants claimed indemnity from Mrs Osbourne for the amount of the plaintiff's claim, and the balance due under the building agreement. Mr Registrar Hargreaves ordered that the third party proceedings be struck out. An appeal was made to the Court of Appeal.

HELD that the appeal should be dismissed: the contract between Mrs Osbourne and Wendaland Builders Ltd. signed by Dezonie was a pre-incorporation contract and was a nullity; Dezonie could not sue on the contract personally, because the contract was not subject to section 36(4) of the Companies Act 1985 (now section 36C of the Companies Act 1985), because Dezonie was not aware that the old company was not in being, and intended the old company to be bound by the contract; however, Dezonie could sue *quantum meruit* for the work done, and this was not affected by section 34 of the Companies Act 1985 (which imposes criminal liability if a person trades using the word 'limited' in a company name, when the liability of the company is in fact unlimited), because that section did not prevent enforcement of contracts.

DILLON, L.J. There is no doubt at all, in the light of such cases as *Newbourne* v. *Sensolid (Great Britain) Ltd.* [1953] 1 All ER 708, [1954] 1 QB 45 that, as a matter of common law where there is before the incorporation of a company a contract to which the company is ostensibly a party, the contract is void unless a fresh contract is made by the company after incorporation with the other party to the contract to adopt it as a fresh contract. That situation was felt to create difficulties when, in 1973, the United Kingdom joined the European Community and provision was made about it in the European Communities Act 1972, s. 9. That provision was taken across into the Companies Act 1985 as s. 36(4). It provides as follows (it is now actually to be found elsewhere but this is the term which was relevant at the date of this agreement):

> "Where a contract purports to be made by a company, or by a person as agent for a company, at a time when the company has not been formed, then subject to any agreement to the contrary, the contract has effect as one entered into by the person purporting to act for the company or as agent for it, and he is personally liable on the contract accordingly."

The judge in his judgment referred to a passage in *Gore-Brown on Company Law* (44th edn, 1986) where it is suggested that, if that section applies, then any person who is liable to be sued under a contract as having signed it on behalf of a company not yet formed can equally sue on it and he reached the view therefore that Mr Dezonie was able to enforce, in the right of the new Wendaland Builders Ltd. (the second company) the terms of the contract. I do not agree with this approach since I do not regard section 36(4) as applicable in this case. At the time of the 1986 building agreement no one had thought about forming a new company at all. Accordingly it is not possible to say that the contract purports to be made by the new company which was not actually formed until March 1988. No one thought of the new company because Mr Dezonie thought that the original company was still in being. The original company, however, does not fit the wording ''where the contract purports to be made by a company or by a person as agent for a company at a time when the company has not been formed'', because it had been formed long before. The problem was not one to which the European Communities Act 1972 was directed.

★ Tinnevelly Sugar Refining Co. Ltd. and others v. Mirrlees, Watson & Yaryan Co. Ltd.

(1894) 21R 1009; (1894) 2 SLT 149
Court of Session

Messrs Darley & Butler ordered machinery from Mirrlees Watson & Yaryan Co. Ltd. (Mirrlees), on behalf of the Tinnevelly Sugar Refining Co. Ltd. (Tinnevelly), a company which had not been incorporated at the time the contract was made. Messrs Darley & Butler were large shareholders in Tinnevelly, who paid for the machinery. Tinnevelly sued Mirrlees on the ground that the machinery did not meet the specification in the contract; accordingly they had suffered damage which they assessed at £23,000. The defence was that the pursuers had no title to sue, because the contract was a pre-incorporation contract. The Lord Ordinary allowed a proof before answer. The defenders sought a ruling from the Inner House of the Court of Session as to whether there was title to sue.

HELD the pursuers had not established title to sue as Darley & Butler could not contract as agents so as to bind the pursuers before the pursuers were incorporated.

LORD PRESIDENT. They [the pursuers] begin by saying that when Darley & Butler contracted with the defenders they were acting, and were known by the defenders to be acting, as agents for the Tinnevelly Company. This is the basis for the pursuers' case. It is in law an untenable proposition, for Darley & Butler could not be the agents of a non-existent company. I should infer from the record that the persons acting for the company had not realised this. Accordingly, it is quite consistent with the record to suppose that the persons acting for the company were unaware that if the company was to take the place of Darley & Butler it required—that is to say, the shareholders or the executive required—consciously to do so. In place of any such overt action on the part of the company things were allowed to rest on the original contract between Darley & Butler and the defenders, which was erroneously believed to bind the company. I do not pronounce this to have been the true state of the facts, having no occasion to do so; all I say is that the pursuers' record says nothing to the contrary, and much to this effect.

Well, now, the law applicable to such a case seems to be tolerably clear. First of all, where there is no principal there can be no agent, there having been no Tinnevelly Company at the date of this contract, Darley & Butler were not agents of that company in entering into the contract. The next point is that, in order to bind the company to a contract not incumbent on it, it is necessary that the company should voluntarily so contract; and it is not equivalent to this if the company merely acts as if, contrary to the fact, the contract had from the beginning been obligatory on it.

. . . I am for finding that the pursuers have not set forth any title in the Tinnevelly Sugar Refining Company Limited, to sue; that there are no relevant averments to support the conclusions in so far insisted in by Darley & Butler; and that the action should be dismissed.

NOTE

This case was decided before the enactment of what is now section 36C of the Companies Act 1985. However, by implication from the statutory provision, the position nowadays would be the same as in this case, and the promoter would be the only party with title to sue, unless the company had expressly novated the contract after incorporation with the approval of the other party to the contract. On this point, the law is the same in England and Wales and in Scotland.

3. The memorandum of association

Summary

1. Sources of the law

The law is found in sections 1–6, 10–21, 25–34, 35, 35A and 35B of the Companies Act 1985, and also in the case law.

2. Contents of the memorandum

The memorandum of association is part of the written constitution of a registered company. It sets rules for the external dealings of the company. The contents of the memorandum of association are prescribed in sections 2 and 3 of the Companies Act 1985. Styles of memoranda for different types of company are provided in the Companies (Tables A–F) Regulations 1985 (SI 1985 No. 805). A company must have in its memorandum of association each of the clauses appropriate to the particular type of company. For example, the clauses which the memorandum of association of a public company must contain are set out in Table F and are:

* Name clause;
* Public company clause;
* Registered office clause;
* Objects clause;
* Limitation of liability clause;
* Capital clause;
* Clause of association.

The compulsory clauses of the memorandum of association of a private company limited by shares are set out in Table B and are:

* Name clause;
* Registered office clause;

* Objects clause;
* Limitation of liability clause;
* Capital clause;
* Clause of association.

3. Purpose of the memorandum

The memorandum of association reveals to persons who may deal with the company what kind of enterprise they are dealing with, and particularly whether the members have limited liability for company debts. It also sets out the objects of the company, and hence the extent of the company's contractual capacity (but see section 6 below). The memorandum and articles of association together constitute a contract between the members and the company and also among the members (see Chapter 4 below).

4. The name clause

The name of a company is controlled by sections 25–34 of the Companies Act 1985. These rules restrict choice of name, to prevent the public being misled as to the nature of a company's business. Companies House can refuse to register certain names. In certain circumstances the Secretary of State for Trade and Industry can require a company to change its name (sections 28 and 32 of the Companies Act 1985). In addition, a passing off action can be maintained at common law if one enterprise chooses a name which suggests a business connection with another pre-existing enterprise. In such cases, an injunction (*interdict) may be granted to forbid the use of the name by the newly established business, and damages may be awarded. Factors which are important in a passing off action are the degree of similarity of the name; whether there was an intention to deceive (*Chill Foods (Scotland) Ltd. v. Cool Foods Ltd. 1977); whether the name incorporates the name of the owner of the business or principal shareholder, as the courts will tend to allow a party to trade under his/her real name where possible; and whether the two enterprises trade in the same geographical location or are in the same line of business. See Ewing v. Buttercup Margarine Co. Ltd. [1917], Exxon Corporation and others v. Exxon Insurance Consultants International Ltd. [1982], *Salon Services (Hairdressing Supplies) Ltd. v. Direct Salon Services Ltd. 1988 SLT June 10, 44. Passing off actions may be used by and against all types of business, incorporated and unincorporated.

A company may change its name voluntarily by special resolution (section 28(1) of the Companies Act 1985). This has no effect on the legal personality of the company. See section 28(7) of the Companies Act 1985, and *Oshkosh B'Gosh Incorporated* v. *Dan Marbel Ltd. and another* (1988).

5. The registered office clause

The registered office clause states whether the registered office of the company is situated in England and Wales or in Scotland. The registered office is the official address of the company. It is normally the address where the registers of the company are kept (for example, the register of members), and is the address at which documents such as court writs may be served. The location of the registered office normally determines the nationality and domicile of the company. It also determines jurisdiction. However, in *Re Baby Moon (UK) Ltd.* (1985) a company with a registered office in Scotland, which had been wrongly registered in England, was held subject to the jurisdiction of the English courts for the purposes of winding up. The location of the registered office can be changed by whatever method the articles provide, but information on the new location must be filed at Companies House (section 287(3) of the Companies Act 1985). The location of the company can only be moved from Scotland to England or vice versa only by special Act of Parliament. The nationality of the company cannot be changed.

6. Objects clause

By section 2(1)(c) of the Companies Act 1985, the memorandum of association must contain an objects clause which sets limits to the contractual capacity of the company. The clause is intended to protect members and creditors, who invest in a company relying on its expertise in certain defined activities. The *ultra vires* doctrine used to hold that if a company exceeded its objects, the contract could be challenged in court either by the company or its members, or by the other party to the contract, and the contract could be held to be void. See *Ashbury Railway Carriage & Iron Co. Ltd.* v. *Riche* (1875) LR7 HL 653. Generally such a challenge arose in the course of the liquidation of the company. The doctrine was amended by section 9 of the European Communities Act 1972, following the First Council Directive 1968, after the United Kingdom's entry into the European Communities in 1972. It has since been amended again by sections

108–12 of the Companies Act 1989, which insert amended provisions into the Companies Act 1985 (principally sections 3A, 35, 35A and 35B). Under these rules the *ultra vires* doctrine is all but abolished. The third party is not required to have constructive notice of the contents of the memorandum (section 35B of the Companies Act 1985). A transaction made in the name of the company cannot be challenged on the ground that it is not authorised by the memorandum. The third party dealing in good faith with the directors, or with persons authorised by them to deal is protected from the contract being held to be *ultra vires* the memorandum or the articles of association. Such a transaction may still be beyond the powers of the directors, which may render them liable in damages to the company. Such a transaction may be prohibited in advance by a member or members by injunction (*interdict), but they have no power to prohibit such a transaction from being fulfilled after it has been made (section 35A(4)). Transactions outside the objects clause may now be ratified by special resolution, and breach of duty by the directors in causing such a transaction to be entered into may also be ratified by special resolution (section 35(3)). Transactions involving the directors themselves as parties to the contract are not given the same protection (see section 322A of the Companies Act 1985).

Section 3A of the Companies Act 1985 provides for simplified objects clauses for general commercial companies, where 'the object of the company is to carry on any trade or business whatsoever'. Such companies would avoid any vestigial challenge to their contracts for being *ultra vires* by members seeking injunctions. However, it is thought that such companies will be rare, as banks tend to prefer to lend to companies with detailed objects.

When it was a more far-reaching doctrine than it is now, strategies were devised for drafting objects clauses to avoid problems of *ultra vires*. Such strategies included: drafting very lengthy objects clauses; making every sub-clause into an independent main objects clause (see *Cotman* v. *Brougham* [1918]); including general words at the end of the objects (see *In re New Finance and Mortgage Co. Ltd. (In Liquidation)* [1975]); including a provision allowing the directors to trade in any business which could in the discretion of the board of directors advantageously be carried on as ancillary to the general business of the company (see *Bell Houses Ltd.* v. *City Wall Properties Ltd.* [1966]).

The objects clause can now be altered freely by special resolution, with a right to members holding at least 15 per cent of the issued shares to take their objections to the change to the courts (section 4 of the Companies Act 1985).

The question of whether a contract is binding on the company as coming within the objects clause, or because of the statutory rules of outsider protection outlined above, is a separate question from the power of the directors to make the contract on behalf of the company. If they do not have that power, contracts they make will generally be valid under sections 35, 35A and 35B of the Companies Act 1985, and also under the rule in *Royal British Bank* v. *Turquand* [1955] (see Chapter 4), unless the obligation is also a breach of fiduciary duty, and that fact is known to the other party to the obligation, when the obligation may be voidable. See *Rolled Steel Products (Holdings) Ltd.* v. *British Steel Corporation* [1986].

Where a company gives away assets for no consideration, for example, the provision of a pension scheme, or an inter-company guarantee, questions may arise as to whether the company can competently enter such an obligation. In such a case, the obligation will be *intra vires* if the objects permit the obligation, whether or not the obligation is for the good of the company. See *In re Horsley & Weight Ltd.* [1982]. If the obligation constitutes a breach of fiduciary duty, as being a use of a corporate power for an improper purpose, the obligation may be voidable. See *Rolled Steel Products (Holdings) Ltd.* v. *British Steel Corporation* [1986].

Companies may ultimately be wound up on the just and equitable ground (section 122(1)(g) of the Insolvency Act 1986) at the instance of their members where the substratum or basis on which the company was formed has disappeared. See *In re German Date Coffee Co.* (1882). This ground of winding up is discussed further in Chapter 14.

★ Chill Foods (Scotland) Ltd. v. Cool Foods Ltd.

1977 SLT (OH) 38

Court of Session

Murray and Dick had together run a company called S. & J. (Catering Products) Ltd. (S. & J.), which had acquired another company called Chill Foods (Scotland) Ltd. (Chill Foods). Without consulting Murray, Dick formed a new company called Cool Foods Ltd. which traded in areas served by both S. & J., and all three companies traded in frozen foodstuffs. Petitions were presented to the Outer House of the Court of Session by Dick, S. & J. and Chill Foods for interdicts and interim interdicts to prevent Dick participating in any similar business to that of S. & J. within a radius of 50 miles of the registered office of S. & J., to prevent Dick and another party, Maxwell, from using information obtained from the records of S. & J., and to prevent Cool Foods Ltd. from trading under that name, unless they clearly dissociated themselves from the petitioners.

HELD, granting some of the interim interdicts: (1) that the similarity of the name between Chill Foods (Scotland) Ltd. and Cool Foods Ltd. was sufficient to give rise to considerable risk of confusion, and that the similarity gave rise to the prima facie inference that the similarity was motivated by an intention to mislead; (2) where breach of contract is alleged, especially a restrictive covenant, and where the existence of the contract is denied and cannot be proved, a very strong argument on the balance of convenience would be needed to justify interim interdict; (3) in questions of the balance of convenience with interim interdict the court would protect the long-established business against the interloper.

LORD MAXWELL. (Petition: *Chill Foods (Scotland) Ltd.* v. *Cool Foods Ltd*). In this case the interim interdict sought is against the respondent "trading in frozen foodstuffs under their company name unless and until they specifically dissociate and distinguish themselves from the petitioners in any canvassing for or soliciting of orders from and in any advertising of whatsoever nature directed at or which may be seen by persons or establishments which were, prior to August 1976, customers or suppliers of the petitioners."

This is in effect a "passing off" interdict in the broad sense of that expression. Counsel for the respondents argued that there was not sufficient similarity between the two names to justify restraint. He maintained that the two names were "descriptive names" and that, on the authority of *Office Cleaning Services Ltd.* v. *Westminster Cleaning Services Ltd.* (1946) 63 RPC 39, in such a case, small differences between the names would be enough to exclude restraint. I do not agree that the names are "descriptive" as opposed to "fancy" names within the meaning of that authority. It seems to me obvious that in common use the names will be abbreviated to "Chill Foods" and "Cool Foods" respectively and that, in the circumstances narrated in these petitions, there is a considerable risk of confusion. Counsel for the petitioners lodged a letter admittedly from a supplier, not a customer, showing that such confusion has already occurred.

Further, while it is well settled that intention to cause confusion is not an essential element of a "passing off" case, the existence of such intention will make proof of likelihood of passing off easier. In the circumstances of this case the promoters of Cool Foods Ltd., having selected a name for their company so similar to the petitioners', can hardly complain, if, at this stage, a deliberate intention to mislead is suspected.

Counsel for the respondents founded strongly on the fact that at present, according to him, the respondents and petitioners are not in direct competition, the respondents being wholesalers and the petitioners retailers. I do not attach great weight to this. The two companies are dealing with the same line of products and the connection between the petitioners and S. & J. (Catering Products) Ltd. is close and very likely well-known in the catering trade. Further, Dick and Maxwell who, together with others, promoted and run the respondents, have deleted the amendment from their answers to the petition at the instance of S. & J. (Catering Products) Ltd. an averment that they "do not at present have any intention of expanding into the retail frozen food market".

Counsel for the respondents complained that the form of the interdict is such that it might be impractical to comply with it without changing the respondents' name. The petitioners might perhaps have sought for a wider interdict but they have been guided as to its form by certain *dicta* in *Montgomery* v. *Thomson* [1891] AC 217. If the effect of the interdict is to force the respondents to change their name that might be no bad thing.

As to balance of convenience, I have no doubt that this lies with the petitioners, for much the same reasons as those I have mentioned in relation to the petition at the instance of S. & J. (Catering Products) Ltd. A change of name, if that is what will emerge, will be far less damaging, in my view, to a company which has only just started to trade than the damage to the petitioners which I consider can be anticipated if the respondents are not restrained.

I have accordingly granted interim interdict as craved.

NOTE

The relevant factors on which the court based this decision were: the similarity of the name, the similarity of the line of business, and intention to cause confusion.

In another Scottish passing off case, *Salon Services (Hairdressing Supplies) Ltd.* v. *Direct Salon Services Ltd.* 1988 SLT June 10, 414, interdicts were recalled on the grounds that the small difference of name was sufficient to differentiate the two businesses, which did not trade in the same geographical location, and had different brand names for their products. There was also no evidence that the petitioners had suffered economic loss.

Ewing v. Buttercup Margarine Co. Ltd.

[1917] 2 Ch 1

Court of Appeal

The plaintiff traded as a sole trader under the name of the Buttercup Dairy Co. as wholesalers and retailers of dairy products and margarine in Leith, Scotland. He also operated shops throughout Scotland and in the north of England, but not in the south of England. He had been in business since 1904. The business was popularly known as 'Buttercup'. The defendants set up in business in 1916, the objects of the company being the wholesale and retail trade in dairy products and margarine. The intention was, however, to manufacture margarine from a factory in London and to trade in it wholesale. The defendants operated in the south of England, although at the time of the proceedings they had not begun to manufacture margarine. The plaintiff issued a motion to restrain the defendants from using the name 'Buttercup Margarine Co. Ltd.', or any name colourably resembling the plaintiffs' trade name, or carrying on business under any description calculated to produce the belief that the defendants' business was that of the plaintiff or a branch of it. The Buttercup Margarine Co. Ltd. established that the word Buttercup was used by three other companies throughout the United Kingdom. The High

Court (Chancery Division) had granted the motion to restrain the defendant from using the name. The defendants appealed to the Court of Appeal.

HELD that the court had jurisdiction to restrain a defendant from using a trade name colourably resembling that of the plaintiff even if innocently adopted, if it is nevertheless calculated to deceive either (a) by diverting customers from the plaintiff to the defendant or (b) by causing confusion between the two businesses.

LORD COZENS-HARDY, M.R. In a case like that, where the plaintiff is the owner of a business which has been established since 1904 and has a turnover of half a million a year, and must be regarded as an old-established business none the less because its actual sphere of operations is mainly in Scotland and the North of England, what should I expect the defendants as honest men or honest representatives of a newly formed company to do? I should expect them to say: "We are very sorry; we were not aware of your existence in Scotland, but as you object to our name we will change it so as not in any way to interfere with you." Instead of doing that they assert their right to use the name and file a mass of affidavits in support of their claim to do what they have threatened and continued to do; and they seek to justify their name on the ground that the arm of the Court is not long enough to reach a defendant who takes a name similar to that of the plaintiff, unless it can be shown that such a name is calculated to deceive in the sense that a person desiring to be a customer of the plaintiff is induced thereby to become a customer of the defendant. And they say that there can be no deception here because they are wholesale people while the plaintiff is a retailer, that it is true that they have the fullest possible power under the memorandum and articles of association to carry on a retail business, but that at the present moment they have no such intention. . . . I know of no authority, and I can see no principle, which withholds us from preventing injury to the plaintiff in his business as a trader by a confusion which will lead people to conclude that the defendants are really connected in some way with the plaintiff or are carrying on a branch of the plaintiff's business.

BANKES, L.J. If the court accepts the view put forward by these witnesses [for the plaintiff, proving that the defendant would manufacture margarine which would lead to confusion in the mind of the public]—and it seems to me to be the natural view—a case is plainly made out for the injunction; and it is perfectly immaterial for the defendants to say that they are wholesale dealers.

WARRINGTON, L.J. Looking at those two names, it seems to me obvious that a trader or a customer who has been in the habit of dealing with the plaintiff might well think that the plaintiff had adopted the name of the Buttercup Margarine Company Limited as his own name for the purposes of the margarine branch of his business, or for the purposes, if you will, of doing what it is said the defendants are going to do, namely, to make their own margarine instead of buying it in the market.

Exxon Corporation and others v. Exxon Insurance Consultants International Ltd.

[1982] 1 Ch 119; [1981] 2 All ER 495

Court of Appeal

The plaintiffs raised the action seeking to claim a copyright in the word 'Exxon' as being an 'original literary work' in terms of section 2 of the Copyright Act 1956. They sought an injunction to restrain the defendants from infringing their copyright in the word, and from using the word so as to pass their business off as connected with that of the plaintiffs, and also sought an order compelling the defendant company to change its name to remove the word 'Exxon'. The defendant company did not lodge a defence. The judge granted the injunction to restrain the passing off by the continued use of the word 'Exxon' and ordered that the company must change its registered name. However, he refused to grant the injunction to restrain breach of copyright, on the ground that the word 'Exxon', was not an 'original literary work' within the Copyright Act 1956. The plaintiffs appealed to the Court of Appeal.

HELD, dismissing the appeal, that a literary work must afford information, instruction or pleasure in the form of literary enjoyment, and that the word 'Exxon', being a combination of four letters which served for identification purposes, did not come within the statutory definition of an 'original literary work'.

Oshkosh B'Gosh Incorporated v. Dan Marbel Incorporated Ltd. and another

(1988) 4 BCC 795

Court of Appeal

Oshkosh B'Gosh Incorporated sued Dan Marbel Incorporated Ltd. and one of its directors for US $192,666.93 in respect of goods supplied to Dan Marbel Incorporated Ltd. The director had acquired the company off the shelf when it was called Egormight Ltd. The company resolved to change its name to Dan Marbel Incorporated Ltd. in 1981, but the certificate of incorporation on change of name was not issued until 1985. The goods supplied by the plaintiffs had been contracted for at a time when the name of the defendant company was Egormight Ltd., although the contract was entered into using forms bearing the name Dan Marbel Incorporated Ltd. The second defendant had authorised the forms to be completed, but the writing did not include the company name or the name of any individual. The plaintiffs claimed that the second defendant should be personally liable under section 9(2) of the European Communities Act 1972 (now section 36C of the Companies Act 1985) on the ground that the contract was made at a time when the company had not been formed, or alternatively, that the second defendant should be personally liable under section 108(4) of the Companies Act 1948 (now section 349 of the Companies Act 1985) for authorising the signing of orders for goods on behalf of the company on which the correct name of the company was not mentioned. At first instance the plaintiff obtained judgment in full, in default of substantive defences. Later the court of first instance set aside the judgment against the first defendant (the company) but upheld it against the second defendant. The judgment was appealed by the second defendant to the High Court (Queen's Bench Division), where the appeal was dismissed. A further appeal was made to the Court of Appeal.

HELD that the appeal by the second defendant should be allowed: (1) that the contract had not been made at a time when the company had not been formed within section 9(2) of the European Communities Act 1972, because although the company was not trading under its correct name, it was in fact incorporated at the time the contract was made. The effect of the certificate of incorporation on change of name was not to re-incorporate the company; (2) the argument based on section 108(4) of the Companies Act 1948 also failed on the ground that the statute required there to be an individual affixation of the company name in affirmation of an individual order, and that had not occurred in the case.

NOURSE, L.J. Section 13(1) [of the Companies Act 1948] . . . shows that the company was formed or incorporated on the date mentioned in the certificate of incorporation. On one reading of the words "shall be a body corporate by the name contained in the memorandum" it might be possible to argue that the retention of the name under which it was incorporated was essential to the company's continued existence. But that point has not been taken by Mr Fawls and cannot anyway stand with the much clearer provisions of sec. 18 to which I now turn.

I have already read sec. 18(1) and (3), each of which, as did sec. 18(2), referred to the company changing "its" name, thus recognising the continued existence of the company, notwithstanding the change. Moreover, sec. 18(3) provided that the registrar should enter the new name on the register in place of the former name and should issue "a certificate of incorporation altered to meet the circumstances of the case". None of that is consistent with the view that the issue of the altered certificate effects the reformation or re-incorporation of the company. More compelling still are the terms of sec. 18(4):

"A change of name by a company under this section shall not affect any rights or obligations of the company or render defective any legal proceedings by or against the company, and any legal proceedings that might have been continued or commenced against it by its former name may be continued or commenced against it by its new name."

It is difficult to think of a provision which could be drafted so as more clearly to recognise the continued existence of the company.

. . . This argument [based on section 108(4) of the Companies Act 1948] also fails. It is no doubt true that the act which is sufficient to constitute a signature may vary according to the context in which the requirement is found, but I am not aware that it has ever been suggested that a document can be signed without there being written on or otherwise affixed to it a name or some mark to represent a name.

NOTE
A similar Scottish case is *Victor Spence Associates* v. *Balchin* 1990 SLT 10.

Re Baby Moon (UK) Ltd.

(1985) 1 BCC 99, 298

Chancery Division

Baby Moon (UK) Ltd. was formed in 1981. The memorandum of association stated that the registered office of the company was situated in England. The company was registered at Companies House in Cardiff. However, the address of the registered office supplied to Companies House was in Livingston, Scotland. When a petition was presented to an English court for the winding up of the company, the court initially would not hear the petition on the ground that it had no jurisdiction over a company apparently registered in Scotland.

HELD that the English court did have jurisdiction to wind up this company because its certificate of incorporation under section 3 of the Companies Act 1980 (now section 13 of the Companies Act 1985) was conclusive evidence that the company had fulfilled the statutory requirements for registration. Leave to serve out of the jurisdiction was granted, and an adjournment was granted to allow the matter to be properly served and advertised.

HARMAN, J. I have before me a petition in the matter of Baby Moon (UK) Ltd. Upon the matter first being called before me, it appears from para. 2 of the petition that the registered office was situate in Scotland, I intimated to counsel that I could have no jurisdiction over a company registered in Scotland. It now appears that a most extraordinary state of affairs exists in relation to this company, the like of which I certainly have never seen and I am quite sure was never intended to be allowed under any of the machinery of the Companies Acts.

It is the duty of the Registrar of Companies to register a company in England, pursuant to section 12 of the 1980 Act, if the memorandum of association so states. In this instance a copy of the memorandum of the company has been produced to me in two forms, one dated 7 September 1981, with the company's registration stamp, which plainly states in para. 2 that the registered office will be situate in England, and a further one, probably on a change of objects although the date of it does not appear, which again in para. 2 states that the registered office shall be situate in England. Thus the company should have been and, as I understand, according to its number was registered in England.

The address of the registered office was filled in on the form simply as Rennie Square, Brucefield Industrial Park, Livingston, with no country being referred to. The address which is in the petition shows that in fact that place is in Scotland and is thus not a proper registered office for a company registered in England. However, Mrs Hill points out to me, correctly, that this court has jurisdiction under section 218(1) of the Companies Act 1948 [now section 117 of the Insolvency Act 1986] to wind up any company registered in England. The certificate of the registrar is conclusive under section 3 of the 1980 Act. That certificate shows that the company was registered in England, and thus I have jurisdiction. It is quite plain that though companies registered in England ought never to have a registered office in Scotland, in this case the impossible has occurred. How that has happened nobody on the part of the petitioner can explain, but in my judgment the jurisdiction is plainly founded and it is right that this company should answer in this court for whatever obligations it may have.

Extract from the First Council Directive of March 1968

(68/152/EEC)

Article 9

1. Acts done by the organs of the company shall be binding upon it even if those acts are not within the objects of the company, unless such acts exceed the powers that the law confers or allows to be conferred on those organs.

   However, Member States may provide that the company shall not be bound where such acts are outside the objects of the company, if it proves that the third party knew that the act was outside those objects or could not in view of the circumstances have been unaware of it; disclosure of the statutes shall not of itself be sufficient proof therof.

2. The limits on the powers of the organs of the company, arising under the statutes or from a decision of the competent organs, may never be relied on as against third parties, even if they have been disclosed.

3. If the national law provides that authority to represent a company may, in derogation from the legal rules governing the subject, be

conferred by the statutes on a single person or on several persons acting jointly, that law may provide that such a provision in the statutes may be relied on as against third parties on condition that it relates to the general power of representation; the question whether such a provision in the statutes can be relied on as against third parties shall be governed by Article 3.

NOTE

Article 3 is concerned with disclosure of information about companies in a public register which in the United Kingdom takes the form of registration at Companies House. 'Statutes' in the Directive means, in the context of United Kingdom law, the memorandum and articles of association.

'The organ of the company' means in this context the board of directors.

Cotman v. Brougham

[1918] AC HL (E) 514

House of Lords

The company, Essequibo Rubber and Tobacco Estates Ltd. (Essequibo), had an objects clause in its memorandum of association which enabled it to carry on almost every conceivable kind of business. The last sub-clause contained a declaration that every sub-clause should be construed as a substantive clause and not be limited or restricted by reference to any other sub-clause or by the name of the company, and that none of the sub-clauses should be deemed to be subsidiary or auxilliary to the principal object. The principal object of the company was to acquire rubber and tobacco estates. However, the Essequibo company underwrote certain shares in another company (company A). £14,456 remained outstanding on the shares in respect of unpaid calls. Essequibo transferred the shares to a third company, which failed to pay for them in full. The company whose shares had been underwritten was wound up. Essequibo and the third company were also wound up. Essequibo was put on the B list of contributories in respect of the outstanding sum due in respect of the unpaid calls on the shares of company A. The appellant sought to vary the B list of contributories by excluding Essequibo, on the ground that the application for the shares was *ultra vires* the objects clause of the memorandum of association. The trial judge held that the underwriting was *intra vires*, and that decision was affirmed by the Court of Appeal. The appellant appealed to the House of Lords.

HELD that the memorandum must be construed according to its literal meaning, and the underwriting as *intra vires*. The decision of the Court of Appeal was affirmed.

LORD FINLAY, L.C. Warrington L.J. [in the Court of Appeal] expressed some doubt in his judgment in this case whether a memorandum setting out such a profusion of objects was a compliance with the Act, and it is possible that in some future case the question may arise on application for a *mandamus* if the registrar should refuse registration, taking the ground that the Act requires that the memorandum should be in such a form that the real objects of the company are made intelligible to the public.

. . . The question depends on the interpretation to be put upon the 3rd clause of the memorandum of association. This clause has 30 heads dealing with a multitude of objects and powers. . . . I agree with both Courts below in thinking that it is impossible to say that the acquisition of these powers was *ultra vires* of the Essequibo Company.

It is well worthy of consideration whether, if it should appear that the law as it stands is not sufficient to cope with such abuses as are exemplified in the memorandum now in consideration, the Companies Act should not be amended so as to bring the practice into conformity with what must have been the intention of the framers of the Act. But the only question before us now is the construction of the memorandum as it stands, and in my opinion this appeal must be dismissed with costs.

LORD PARKER OF WADDINGTON. Clause 3, sub-clauses 8 and 12, of the memorandum are in their terms amply wide enough to cover the transaction in question, and the concluding words of sub-clause 30 were clearly introduced to preclude the operation of these (among other) sub-clauses being cut down by considerations such as arose in *Stephens* v. *Mysore Reefs (Kangundy) Mining Co.* [1902] 1 Ch 745.

. . . I think the appeal should be dismissed with costs.

LORD WRENBURY. There has grown up a pernicious practice of registering memoranda of association which, under the clause relating to objects, contain paragraph after paragraph not specifying or delimiting the proposed trade or purpose, but confusing power with purpose and indicating every class of act which the corporation is to have power to do. . . . It has arrived now at a point at which the fact is that the function of the memorandum is taken to be, not to specify, not to disclose, but to bury beneath a mass of words the real object or objects of the company with the intent that every conceivable form of activity shall be found included somewhere within its terms. The present is the very worst case of the kind that I have seen. Such a memorandum is not, I think, a compliance with the Act.

. . . The Essequibo Company have been put upon the B list of contributories. They, by their liquidator (for they are also in liquidation), applied to vary the B list by excluding their name therefrom. The ground of that application was that the transaction was *ultra vires* the Essequibo Company. The only question open on this appeal is whether upon the construction of the memorandum of association the transaction was *ultra vires*.

The construction of the instrument does not admit of reasonable doubt. Clause 3, sub-clauses 8 and 12, are in terms so wide that an obligation in a contingent event to take up shares falls within them. The language of clause 3, sub-clause 30, is such that I cannot say that such a transaction was *ultra vires*, because it was not ancillary to or connected with or in furtherance of something which I find elsewhere in the company's memorandum to have been "its business". Upon the narrow question, upon which alone it is unfortunately within the competence of this House to determine, I think the decision below was right. It follows that this appeal must be dismissed with costs.

In re New Finance and Mortgage Co. Ltd. (In Liquidation)

[1975] 1 Ch 420; [1975] 2 WLR 443
Queen's Bench Division

The objects clause of the memorandum of association of a company, contained a sub-clause allowing it to carry on business 'as financiers, capitalists, concessionaires, bankers, commercial agents, mortgage brokers, financial agents and advisers, exporters and importers of goods and merchandise of all kinds, and merchants generally'. As well as operating as financiers, the company ran two garages and associated shops. The company went into voluntary liquidation. The applicants,

Total Oil (Great Britain) Ltd., lodged a proof in the winding up founding on a judgment debt which related to the sale of motor fuel to the company. The liquidator rejected the proof on the ground that the transaction for the purchase of the oil was *ultra vires*.

HELD that the words 'and merchants generally' in sub-clause 3(a) of the objects clause were broad enough to make all commercial operations *intra vires*, and therefore the purchase of motor fuel was *intra vires*, and the applicants' proof should be allowed by the liquidator.

GOULDING, J. The oldest judicial authority cited by counsel on the meaning of 'merchant' was a passage in *Hamond* v. *Jethro* (1611) 2 Brownl. 97, 99:

> '. . . It was agreed by all the justices, that by the law of merchants, if two merchants joyn in trade; that of the increase of that, if one dye, the other shall not have the benefit by survivor: see Fitzherbert's Natura brevium, Accompt. 38 Ed.3. And so of two joynt shopkeepers, for they are merchants: for as Coke saith, there are four sorts of merchants, that is, merchant adventurers, merchants dormants, merchants travelling, and merchants residents, and amongst them all there shall be no benefit by survivor. *Jus accrescendi inter Mercatores locum non habet.*'

The authority of that passage as a matter of law is incontestable. On the meaning of the words I think it is now too remote to be a safe guide to recent usage.

. . . Dictionaries of different date that I have examined are by no means uniform in their interpretation of the term "merchant". Dr. Johnson (1755) defined a merchant as "one who trafficks in remote countries".

. . . *Webster's Dictionary* vol. 1. (1890) p. 913, contains the following definition: "1. One who traffics on a large scale, especially with foreign countries; a trafficker; a trader." Item 2 is irrelevant: "3. One who keeps a store or shop for the sale of goods; a shopkeeper. [U.S. & Scot.]."

Finally, *Chambers Dictionary* (1972), p. 819, defines a merchant as "a trader, esp. wholesale: a shopkeeper". *Chambers* may be suspect because of its Scottish origins, but the current edition is careful to distinguish Doricisms where they occur and does not qualify the definition that I have just read.

In my own experience, the word "merchant" is now rarely used without qualification, except in the economic sense already mentioned where it distinguishes the trader from any other species of entrepreneur, for example, a manufacturer. Where it is qualified it may signify, according to the qualification, either a wholesale or a retail trader. Thus coal merchants and wine merchants, as the *New English Dictionary* recognises, are commonly retailers. A provision merchant may be a wholesaler but frequently is, or at any rate was in my youth, much the same as a retail grocer. A paper merchant on the other hand is commonly a wholesaler; paper is sold by a stationer. Sometimes it is necessary to indicate expressly the limits of the term by the word "wholesale" or "retail". For example, in the *London Classified Telephone Directory* I find a heading of "Fish Merchants—Wholesale", the retailers being classed as "Fishmongers". There are other groups, such as builders' merchants who are in a sense retailers, but retailers to a special section of the public carrying on a particular trade. . . . The real choice, as I see it, is either to read the words " . . . and merchants generally", as adding nothing to the preceding reference to " . . . exporters and importers of goods and merchandise of all kinds"; or, on the other hand, to extend them to all purely commercial operations. The former follows Dr Johnson's old definition; the latter embraces all the current uses of "merchant" in different contexts.

On the whole, it is the latter that I prefer, and not only because it coincides with my first impression. Even in this memorandum of association I should be slow to dismiss words as unnecessary surplusage; and I also think that the word "generally" here points to a wide construction of the word that precedes it.

In my judgment, therefore, an authorisation to carry on business as "exporters and importers of goods and merchandise of all kinds, and merchants generally" was wide enough to cover the company's business as proved by the evidence. I must, accordingly, reverse the liquidator's decision and allow Total's proof.

Bell Houses Ltd. v. City Wall Properties Ltd.

[1966] 2 QB 656; [1966] 2 WLR 1323
Court of Appeal

The plaintiff company's principal objects were the acquisition of land

and the erection of houses. Sub-clause (c) of the objects clause allowed it 'to carry on any other trade or business whatsoever which can, in the opinion of the board of directors, be advantageously carried on by the company in connection with or as ancillary to any of the above businesses or the general business of the company'. Sub-clause (q) allowed the company 'to . . . turn to account . . . any of the property and assets for the time being of the company for such consideration as the company may think fit . . . ', while sub-clause (u) allowed the company 'to do all such other things as are incidental or conducive to the above objects or any of them'.

The plaintiff company had acquired expertise in the sources of finance for property development. The plaintiff company sued the defendants for a fee for the introduction to the defendants of a financier who provided finance to them for property development. The defendants alleged that the transaction was *ultra vires* the plaintiffs. The trial judge dismissed the action on the grounds that the transaction was *ultra vires*. The plaintiffs appealed to the Court of Appeal.

HELD that the appeal should be allowed, on the grounds (1) that the objects clause allowed the directors to carry on any trade or business which they considered could be advantageously carried on in connection with or as ancillary to the main business, and that it was not necessary for the additional business to have an objective connection with the main business, and therefore the transaction was *intra vires* under sub-clause (c); and (2) the chairman was turning to account his expertise in capital broking, which was an asset of the company in terms of sub-clause (q), and therefore the transaction was *intra vires* under that sub-clause also. Salmon, L.J. considered that the contract was also valid under sub-clause (u).

DANCKWERTS, L.J. The judge considered a line of authorities: *Ashbury Railway Carriage & Iron Co. Ltd.* v. *Riche* (1875) LR 7 HL 653; *Joint Stock Discount Co.* v. *Brown* (1866) LR 3 Eq. 139; *In re German Date Coffee Co.* (1882) 20 Ch 169; *London Financial Association* v. *Kelk* (1884) 26 Ch 107, *In re Crown Bank* (1890) 44 Ch 634; *Cotman* v. *Brougham* [1918] AC 514; (1918) 34 TLR 410 (HL) (E); *Keren Kayemeth Le Jisroel Ltd.* v. *Inland Revenue Commissioners* [1931] 2 KB 465; (1931) 47 TLR, 461; *Oxford Group* v. *Inland Revenue Commissioners* [1949] WN 343, [1949] 2 All ER 537; *Associated Artists Ltd.* v. *Inland Revenue Commissioners* [1956] 1 WLR 752, [1956] 2 All ER 583.

. . . The result of these authorities, in my opinion, is to establish that a clause on the lines of sub-clause 3(c) in the present case is able to make the *bona fide* opinion of the directors sufficient to decide whether an activity of the company is *intra vires*. There was, in the present case, no resolution of the board of directors expressing the opinion of the board. But I do not think that such a resolution was necessary and I do not understand that it was contended that a resolution was necessary. In fact, the chairman managed the operation of the company and exercised by delegation the functions of the board of directors, as he was entitled to do, by virtue of the resolution of the board of directors of June 10, 1955.

. . . In my opinion, the appeal should be allowed . . .

SALMON, L.J. I come to the conclusion, both on what appears to be the clear meaning of the words and on authority, that under clause 3(c) of the plaintiff company's memorandum of association the contract here sued upon was *intra vires* if it constituted carrying on business which in the opinion of the plaintiffs' board of directors could be advantageously carried on by the plaintiffs in connection with or as ancillary to their general business. It was conceded by the defendants that entering into the contract did constitute carrying on business within the meaning of sub-clause (c) and also that it would be sufficient for the purposes of sub-clause (c) if the plaintiff company's chairman alone had formed the opinion there referred to, since the powers of the board had been properly delegated to him. Mr Templeman did, however, argue, although faintly, that there was nothing to show that the chairman had formed such an opinion and that this court should, therefore, come to the conclusion that he had not. I cannot accept this argument. There was ample evidence that he had formed the necessary opinion. Moreover, the onus is on the defendants to make out their defence that the contract was *ultra vires* the plaintiff company. It was for the defendants to prove that he had not formed the necessary opinion, but when he gave evidence at the trial, it was not even suggested to him in cross-examination by counsel then appearing for the defendants that he had not genuinely formed the opinion that the contract sued upon constituted business which could be advantageously carried on by the plaintiff company in connection with or as ancillary to its general business. It follows that, in my view, the contract was clearly *intra vires* sub-clause (c).

Moreover, in my judgment, the plaintiff company is also entitled to succeed under sub-clause (u) of clause 3, for the making of the contract was in fact as well as in the chairman's opinion "incidental and conducive" to the plaintiffs' objects of carrying on the business of building and land development. Finance for the acquisition of land was vital to the plaintiff company. . . . By introducing the trust to the defendants at a time when the trust was looking for an outlet for £1,000,000 by way of a development project, the plaintiff company was cementing its good relations with the trust, and thereby increasing the prospect of the trust advancing money in the future for the purpose of the company's development projects.

. . . I agree that this appeal should be allowed.

In Re Horsley & Weight Ltd.

[1982] Ch 442; [1982] 3 All ER 1045; [1982] 3 WLR 431
Court of Appeal

The respondent was a director of the company. The company had been run informally, with no board meetings. When he retired, he was told that the company was purchasing a pension policy on his behalf for £10,000. The purchase of the policy was approved by the two shareholders of the company. The objects of the company included power to grant pensions to present and past directors and to employees. The memorandum of association contained an independent main objects clause. Shortly after the respondent retired the company was wound up. The liquidator sought a declaration that the purchase of the pension policy was *ultra vires*, and that the respondent was guilty of misfeasance and breach of trust under section 333 (1) of the Companies Act 1948 [now section 212 of the Insolvency Act 1986] by having the company take out the policy on his behalf. Oliver J. held that the company had power to take out the pensions policy, and rejected the misfeasance claim. The liquidator appealed to the Court of Appeal.

HELD, dismissing the appeal: (1) that the power to grant a pension was a substantive power in the memorandum of association, and not an ancillary power, and therefore it was irrelevant whether the exercise of the power benefited the company: the grant of the pension to the respondent was therefore *intra vires* and valid; and (2) that in the absence of misfeasance, a company and its directors could use the company's issued capital for any purpose that was *intra vires*, and although the purchase of the pension scheme had not been approved by the directors or the company in general meeting, nevertheless it had been ratified after the event by the consent of the company's only shareholders (who themselves made up the board of directors). The pension scheme, accordingly, did not form an asset in the winding up. Dictum of Eve, J. in *In re Lee, Behrens & Co. Ltd.* [1932] 2 Ch 46, 52, and *In re W. & M. Roith Ltd.* [1967] 1 WLR 432 doubted.

BUCKLEY, L.J. Mr Evans-Lombe [counsel for the liquidator], relying principally on the judgment of Eve, J. in *In re Lee, Behrens & Co. Ltd.* [1932] 2 Ch 46, submits that, properly construed, paragraph (o) [of the objects clause] should be read as conferring merely an ancillary power. In that case the directors of a company procured that the company should enter into a deed of covenant to pay to the widow of a former director a life annuity. The company subsequently went into liquidation and the annuitant lodged a proof in the winding up for the capitalised value of the annuity. The liquidator rejected the proof on, among other grounds, the ground that the deed was *ultra vires* the company. Eve, J. held that, although the company's memorandum contained an express power to pension widows of ex-employees of the company, this did not extend to pensioning widows of ex-directors. Accordingly the transaction in question had to be justified, if at all, under an implied power to pension widows of ex-directors. Eve, J. said, at pp 51–52:

> "But whether they be made under an express or an implied power, all such grants involve an expenditure of the company's money, and that money can only be spent for purposes reasonably incidental to the carrying on of the company's business, and the validity of such grants is to be tested, as is shown in the authorities, by the answers to three pertinent questions: (i) Is the transaction reasonably incidental to the carrying out of the company's business? (ii) Is it a *bona fide* transaction? (iii) Is it done for the benefit and to promote the prosperity of the company? . . . "

. . . Mr Evans-Lombe, however, submits that the decision indicates that a capacity to grant pensions to employees or ex-employees, or to directors or ex-directors, is of its nature a power enabling the company to act as a good employer in the course of carrying on its business, and as such is an incidental power which must be treated as though it were expressly subject to a limitation that it can only be exercised in circumstances in which a grant of a pension will benefit the company's business. I do not feel able to accept that contention. Paragraph (o) must be read as a whole. It includes not only pensions and other disbursements which will benefit directors, employees and their dependants, but also making grants for charitable benevolent or public purposes or objects. The objects of a company do not need to be commercial; they can be charitable or philanthropic, indeed, they can be whatever the original incorporators wish, provided that they are legal. Nor is there any reason why a company should not part with its funds gratuitously or for non-commercial reasons if to do so is within its declared objects. . . . . It is a misapprehension to suppose that the directors of a company owe a duty to the company's creditors to keep the contributed capital of the company intact. The company's creditors are entitled to assume that the company will not in any way repay any paid-up share capital to the shareholders except by means of a duly authorised reduction of capital. They are entitled to assume that the company's directors will conduct its affairs in such a manner that no unauthorised repayment will take place. It may be somewhat loosely said that the directors owe an indirect duty to the creditors not to permit any unlawful reduction of capital to occur, but I would regard it as more accurate to say that the directors owe a duty to the company in this respect and that, if the company is put into liquidation when paid-up capital has been improperly repaid, the liquidator owes a duty to the creditors to enforce any right to repayment which is available to the company. On the other hand, a company and its directors acting on its behalf, can quite properly expend contributed capital for any purpose which is *intra vires* the company. As I have already indicated, the purchase of the pension policy was, in my view, *intra vires* the company. It was not, however, within the powers of Mr Campbell-Dick and Mr Frank Horsley acting not as members of the board of directors but as individual directors. Unless the act was effectively ratified it cannot bind the company. They were, however, the only two shareholders. A company is bound in a matter which is *intra vires* the company by the unanimous agreement of its members (*per* Lord Davey in *Salomon* v. *Salomon & Co. Ltd.* [1897] AC 22, 57; and see *In re Express Engineering Works Ltd.* [1920] 1 Ch 466) even where that agreement is given informally: *Parker & Cooper Ltd.* v. *Reading* [1926] Ch 975.

. . . . For these reasons this appeal in my view fails and should be dismissed.

TEMPLEMAN, L.J. There remains the question whether the grant of the pension was in the circumstances a misfeasance committed by the two directors who procured the grant and by the respondent, the director who accepted the grant. If the company had been doubtfully solvent at the date of the grant to the knowledge of the directors, the grant would have been both a misfeasance and a fraud on the creditors for which the directors would remain liable. But the good faith of the directors is not impugned.

In the absence of fraud there could still have been negligence on the part of the directors. If the company could not afford to spend £10,000 on the grant of a pension, having regard to problems of cash-flow and profitability, it was negligent of the directors to pay out £10,000 for the benefit of the respondent at that juncture. There could have been gross negligence, amounting to misfeasance.

. . . The findings of the judge are sufficient to support the suspicion that the company could not afford to pay out £10,000 for the benefit of the respondent, but this suspicion is largely based on hindsight. The accounts show that business was expanding, that there were no discernible cash-flow problems and that past profits were sufficient to absorb half of the payments for the pension, leaving the other half to be absorbed in the future. There seemed to be every indication that with the profits anticipated, and the possibility of reducing directors' salaries if necessary, the remainder of the payment for the pension could be absorbed by the company. In these circumstances it is difficult to convict the directors of negligence.

. . . I would dismiss the appeal on the grounds that the payment was *intra vires* the company and on the grounds that misfeasance by the directors was not proved.

In re German Date Coffee Co.

[1882] 20 Ch 169

Court of Appeal

The objects clause of the memorandum of association of a company stated that it had been formed to work a German patent for the manufacture of coffee from dates, and for obtaining other patents to improve or extend the invention, and to acquire or purchase other inventions for similar purposes, and to import and export all descriptions of produce for the purpose of food, and to acquire or lease buildings for the purposes of the company. A prospectus had been issued in which it was stated that a German patent was to be purchased and worked. The German patent was never granted, but the company purchased a Swedish patent, and set up works in Hamburg from which they made and sold coffee made from dates without a patent. Many of the shareholders left the company on learning that the German patent could not be obtained, but the majority of the shareholders wanted to continue the company, which was solvent. A petition was brought by two shareholders for the winding up of the company on the grounds that its objects had failed. Kay, J. had granted the winding up order on the ground that the substratum of the company had failed. An appeal was made to the Court of Appeal.

HELD, affirming the decision of Kay, J., that the order should be granted on the ground that the substratum of the company had failed, and therefore it was just and equitable that the company be wound up.

KAY, J. In this case a petition is presented by two shareholders of the company, one of whom holds 100 shares and the other ten, for a winding up of the company, and it is supported by a sufficient number of shareholders to make me quite sure that the application is a thoroughly *bona fide* one. On the other hand, it is opposed by the company and a considerable body of shareholders.

. . . The law so far is established . . . that if the whole substratum of the company is gone, it is within section 79 [now section 122(1)(g) of the Insolvency Act 1986] "just and equitable" that the company should be wound up.

. . . Where on the fact of the memorandum you see there is a distinct purpose which is the foundation of the company, then, although the memorandum may contain other general words which include the doing of other objects, those general words must be read as being ancillary to that which the memorandum shews to be the main purpose, and if the main purpose fails and fails altogether, then . . . the substratum of the association fails.

With that understanding of the law I come to the question which I have to decide here, which is a question so near the line that it is a little troublesome to decide upon which side of the line it comes. In this case the name of the company is the *German Date Coffee Company Limited*, and the name seems to me to be rather material in determining what the real object and purpose of the company was. The memorandum states the objects of the company to be "to acquire and purchase, and to use, exercise, and vend certain inventions for manufacturing from dates a substitute for coffee, for which a patent has or will be granted by the Empire of *Germany*".

. . . I cannot really doubt that the meaning of this memorandum is that the first purpose, the main object of the company, is to acquire an invention patented in *Germany*, and to work that invention, and that it is not to acquire an invention which is not patented.

. . . But then it is said another patent has been obtained, namely, the Swedish patent. It seems almost ludicrous to imagine that the *German company*, a company formed for the purpose of carrying on business in *Germany*, can say that it has taken any steps towards the accomplishment of that object by obtaining a Swedish patent for the same invention. . . . I therefore think the whole substratum of the company has failed . . . . I therefore make the usual winding-up order.

The company appealed to the Court of Appeal.

JESSEL, M.R. It appears to me that this memorandum, when fairly read, and, notwithstanding the rather loose use of general words, is simply to buy this patent, and to work it either with or without improvements. That is the substance of the whole thing.

Now what happened was this. I have no reason to doubt that the framers of the memorandum and articles believed that they would obtain the German patent, for they said "for which a patent has or will be granted by the Empire of *Germany*". But they were a little too sanguine, and they cannot complain if, like other prophets, their prophesies are sometimes not verified by the results. It turned out that the German Empire would not grant the patent. When that happened what ought they to have done? Surely they ought to have said, "We cannot carry on business, and we must wind up"; and that is exactly what Mr Justice *Kay* ordered to be done.

. . . It seems to me that the learned Judge in the Court below has arrived at the right conclusion, and that this appeal ought to be dismissed. If the full effect of the general words is allowed they might carry on any business whatever.

BAGGALLAY, L.J. Now, is there an impossibility in carrying on the business of the company? It appears to me from the evidence that there is. Not only is there very strong evidence that the obtaining of these letters patent was contemplated by all the parties who took shares, but the holders of 27,000 shares, being more than one quarter of all shares in the company, had their names removed from the register of shareholders, on the ground that they had been deceived by a statement in the prospectus that the patent had been already obtained.

It appears to me beyond all question that there is an impossibility of carrying on the business of the company, and I think that the order Mr Justice *Kay* made is quite correct.

LINDLEY, L.J. In construing this memorandum of association, or any other memorandum of association in which there are general words, care must be taken to construe those general words so as not to make them a trap for unwary people. General words construed literally may mean anything; but they must be taken in connection with what are shewn by the context to be the dominant or main objects. It will not do under general words to turn a company for manufacturing one thing into a company for importing something else, however general the words are. Taking that as the governing principle, it appears to me plain beyond all reasonable dispute that the real object of this company, which, by the by, is called the *German Date Coffee Company Limited*, was to manufacture a substitute for coffee in *Germany* under a patent, valid according to German law. It is what the company was formed for, and all the rest is subordinate to that. The words are general, but that is the thing for which the people subscribe their money.

. . . It appears to me, therefore, that the judgment of Mr Justice *Kay* was perfectly correct, and that the facts warrant the judgment be pronounced, and the application ought to be dismissed with costs.

NOTE

In this case, the judges were influenced in their decision by the following factors: the terms of the principal objects clause of the memorandum of association which placed emphasis on the working of a German patent; the name of the company; the terms of the prospectus; and the fact that a sizeable minority had left the company on learning that a German patent was not to be granted.

If a case on the same facts were to be considered by a court today, it might be that it would have a different outcome. Since that time there has been specific legislative provision for a type of objects clause which allows the company to carry on any trade or business whatsoever, and if such objects were used, it would be impossible to establish that the substratum of the company had failed (section 3A of the Companies Act 1985). The *ultra vires* doctrine has been virtually abolished by sections 35, 35A and 35B of the Companies Act 1985. Also, the remedies under sections 459–61 of the Companies Act 1985 could be used in circumstances such as occurred in *Re German Date Coffee Co.* ('unfairly prejudicial conduct'), as a result of which the court might order the purchase of the shares of the petitioning shareholders either by the company or by other shareholders (section 461(2)(d)). Compare *Re Abbey Leisure Ltd.* (1989) 5 BCC 183 (see Chapter 14 page 281 below).

4. The articles of association

Summary

1. Sources of the law

The law relating to the articles of association of a company is found in sections 7–9 of the Companies Act 1985 and in case law. The Companies (Tables A to F) Regulations 1985 (SI 1985 No. 805) provide styles of articles of association for different forms of company in Tables A (private and public companies limited by shares), Table C (company limited by guarantee without a share capital), Table D (public and private companies limited by guarantee with a share capital), and Table E (unlimited company with a share capital). There is provision in section 128 of the Companies Act 1989 for the creation in the future of a Table G to provide a form of articles of association for a partnership company, (a company in which the shares are held substantially by the employees).

2. The contents of the articles of association

The articles of association contain the internal rules of the company: in them will be found, for example, the rules governing the extent of the directors' powers, rules on transfer of shares, rules on calls on shares, rules for the payment of a dividend, and rules on voting at general meetings. A company is free to adopt verbatim the styles provided in the Tables A to F Regulations, or to adapt the styles, or to adopt completely different articles. Of these styles, Table A is the style in most frequent use, since in most companies liability is limited by shares.

3. Registration of the articles of association

The articles, together with the memorandum of association, must be filed with Companies House at registration, together with the other incorporation papers (see Chapter 2 above).

4. Alteration of the articles of association

A company has a limited right to alter the articles of association, provided in section 9 of the Companies Act 1985, which states:

> Subject to the provisions of this Act and to the conditions contained in its memorandum, a company may by special resolution alter its articles.

They can also be altered by unanimous written resolution in a private company under section 381A of the Companies Act 1985.

Alterations are subject to the following restrictions:

(1) An alteration cannot effectively provide for an article to be unalterable, because section 9 does provide for alteration. However, they may *in effect* be unalterable, if the memorandum or articles of association provide for weighted votes: see *Bushell* v. *Faith* [1970] (see Chapter 8 below).

(2) Any alteration which is inconsistent with the Companies Act 1985 will not be valid: section 9. In particular, any alteration of the articles which obliges a member to subscribe for more shares than he originally contracted for or to increase his liability will be invalid by section 16 of the Companies Act 1985.

(3) Any alteration which is inconsistent with the memorandum of association will be invalid: section 9.

(4) The alteration must be *bona fide* for the benefit of the company as a whole. See *Allen* v. *The Gold Reefs of West Africa Ltd.* [1900].

An alteration of the articles of association, although legal, may constitute a breach of contract by the company: see *Southern Foundries Ltd.* v. *Shirlaw* [1940] (see Chapter 8 below).

5. Section 35A and 35B of the Companies Act 1985

The rules in these sections, which were stated with reference to the memorandum of association in Chapter 3 above, also apply to the articles of association (see page 50; and *TCB Ltd.* v. *Gray* [1986]. In relation to the articles, these rules largely supersede the rule of indoor management, associated with the case of *Royal British Bank* v. *Turquand* (1856).

6. Legal effect of the memorandum and articles of association

By section 14 of the Companies Act 1985, the memorandum and articles of association when registered bind the company and its members to the same extent as if they had been signed and sealed by each member and contained covenants on the part of each member to observe all the provisions of the memorandum and the articles. The memorandum and articles of association accordingly constitute a double contract between each member and the company, and among all the members, whether or not they were themselves subscribers to the memorandum and articles. They do not constitute a contract with outside parties other than members. See *Eley* v. *The Positive Government Security Life Assurance Co. Ltd.* (1876); and *Rayfield* v. *Hands and others* [1960].

Allen v. The Gold Reefs of West Africa Ltd.

[1900] 1 Ch 656

Court of Appeal

The articles of association of the company stated that the company had a lien for all debts and liabilities of any member to the company 'upon all shares (not being fully paid) held by such member'. Zuccani (Z.), who was the only holder of fully paid shares in the company, also held shares which were not fully paid. He had acquired his fully paid shares as consideration for property conveyed by him to the company. At his death he had arrears of unpaid calls, but his assets were insufficient to meet these. The company by special resolution under section 50 of the Companies Act 1862 altered the articles by omitting from the provision regarding the lien the words 'not being fully paid', creating a lien also on the fully paid shares. This was challenged in court. The trial judge, Kekewich, J., had granted an injunction restraining the defendants from enforcing a lien on paid-up shares belonging to the deceased Z.

HELD by the Court of Appeal that the company had power to alter the articles in this way; held also (Vaughan Williams, L.J. dissenting) that the extended lien, being made in good faith, was enforceable against Z.'s fully paid shares, since he took them subject to the original articles and subject to the company's power to alter them under section 50 of the Companies Act 1862 and did not make any special or implied bargain that they should not be affected by any subsequent alteration of the articles; and that the fact of those shares being vendor's shares allotted in payment for the property purchased by the company instead of being shares paid for in cash, was immaterial.

LINDLEY, M.R. The power thus conferred on companies to alter the regulations contained in their articles is limited only by the provisions contained in the statute and the conditions contained in the company's memorandum of association. Wide, however, as the language of section 50 is, the power conferred by it must, like all other powers, be exercised subject to those general principles of law and equity which are applicable to all powers conferred on majorities and enabling them to bind minorities. It must be exercised, not only in the manner required by law, but also *bona fide* for the benefit of the company as a whole, and it must not be exceeded. These conditions are always implied, and are seldom if ever, expressed. But if they are complied with, I can discover no ground for judicially putting any other restrictions on the power conferred by the section than those contained in it. How shares shall be transferred, and whether the company shall have any lien on them, are clearly matters of regulation properly prescribed by a company's articles of association. . . . But, although the regulations contained in a company's articles of association are revocable by special resolution, a special contract may be made with the company in the terms of or embodying one or more of the articles, and the question will then arise whether an alteration of the articles so embodied is consistent or inconsistent with the real bargain between the parties. A company cannot break its contracts by altering its articles, but when dealing with contracts referring to revocable articles, and especially with contracts between a member of the company and the company respecting his shares, care must be taken not to assume that the contract involves as one of its terms an article which is not to be altered.

. . . After carefully considering the whole case, and endeavouring in vain to discover the grounds for holding that there was some special bargain differentiating Zuccani's shares from others, I have come to the conclusion that the appeal from the decision of the learned judge, so far as it relates to the lien created by the altered articles, must be allowed.

Royal British Bank v. Turquand

(1856) 6 E & B 327

Exchequer Chamber

The plaintiff sued Turquand, who was the manager of a coal mining and railway company, on a bond which the company had issued to the plaintiff for £2,000. The bond had been signed by two directors under the seal of the company. In fact, under the constitution, the granting of bonds had to be authorised by a general resolution of the company, and in this case there had been no such authorisation. The company therefore averred that the bond was invalid as having been given without the authority of the shareholders. The Court of Queen's Bench had held the company bound by the bond. The plaintiffs appealed to the Court of Exchequer Chamber.

HELD that the bond was valid because, in the absence of facts putting the plaintiff on its inquiry, the bank had a right to presume that there had been a resolution at a general meeting authorising the borrowing of the money on bond.

JERVIS, C.J. I am of opinion that the judgment of the Court of Queen's Bench ought to be affirmed. I incline to think that the question which has been principally argued both here and in that court does not necessarily arise, and need not be determined. My impression is (though I will not state it as a fixed opinion) that the resolution set forth in the replication goes far enough to satisfy the requisites of the deed of settlement. The deed allows the directors to borrow on bond such sum or sums of money as shall from time to time, by a resolution passed at a general meeting, authorising the directors to borrow on bond such sums for such periods and at such rates of interest as they might deem expedient, in accordance with the deeds of settlement and the Act of Parliament; but the resolution does not otherwise define the amount to be borrowed. That seems to me to be enough. If that be so, the other question does not arise. But whether it be so or not we need not decide; for it seems to us that the plea, whether we consider it was a confession and avoidance or a special *non est factum*, does not raise any objection to this advance as against the company. We may now take for granted that the dealings with these companies are not like dealings with other partnerships, and that the parties dealing with them are bound to read the statute and the deed of settlement. But they are not bound to do more. And the party here, on reading the deed of settlement, would not find a prohibition from borrowing, but a permission to do so on certain conditions. Finding that the authority might be made complete by a resolution, he would have a right to infer the fact of a resolution authorising that which on the face of the document appeared to be legitimately done.

Eley v. Positive Government Security Life Assurance Co. Ltd.

(1876) 1 Exch D 20, 88
Court of Exchequer
Eley was named as company solicitor by the articles of association of

a company, in which it was stated that he was only removable on grounds of misconduct. He had not been appointed by any board resolution, or by any instrument bearing the common seal of the company. After a time, the directors ceased to employ him as solicitor and used other firms, although there was no formal resolution not to employ him. Eley sued the company for breach of contract. It was held in the Exchequer Division that there was no contract between the plaintiff and the company, since the articles of association constituted a contract between the shareholders one with another, and were not a contract with outsiders such as the plaintiff. The plaintiff appealed to the Court of Appeal.

HELD that the appeal should be dismissed and the decision of the Exchequer Division affirmed.

LORD CAIRNS, L.C. This case was first rested in the 118th Article. Articles of association, as is well known, follow the memorandum, which states the objects of the company, while the articles state the arrangement between the members. They are an agreement *inter socios*, and in that view . . . it [article 118] becomes a covenant between the parties to it that they will employ the plaintiff. Now, so far as that is concerned, it is *res inter alios acta*, the plaintiff is no party to it. No doubt he thought that by inserting it he was making his employment safe as against the company; but his relying on that view of the law does not alter the legal effect of the articles. This article is either a stipulation which would bind the members, or else a mandate to the directors. In either case it is a matter between the directors and shareholders, and not between them and the plaintiff.

The matter has been put in another way. It is said, this, though not an agreement in itself, is at all events a statement of what had been agreed upon; it must have been intended to be brought to the plaintiff's knowledge, he has accepted and acted upon it, and therefore it is evidence of another agreement on which he can rely. Now it may be considered that Article 118 would have warranted the directors in entering into an agreement with the plaintiff by which they should contract to employ the plaintiff; but I ask, was such a contract ever made? A joint stock company may act under their seal, or by the signature of their directors, which may have equal effect as their seal, or possibly by a resolution of the board. Nothing of the kind exists here; and if the article is not an agreement on which the plaintiff can rely, there is nothing in the case before us but the fact of his employment, and that would entitle him to remuneration only for the work he has done. This seems to us to dispose of the whole case; and I think that . . . the judgment of the Court below must be affirmed.

TCB Ltd. v. Gray

[1986] 1 Ch 621; [1986] 2 WLR 517
Chancery Division

Loans were advanced by TCB Ltd., a secondary bank, to two companies in which Gray was the principal shareholder and director. One of the companies, Link Service Stations Ltd. (Link), was to grant a debenture, and Gray was to provide a personal guarantee. Gray provided a guarantee with a limitation of liability clause which had not been agreed between the parties, and the clause was deleted by Gray's solicitor, acting under a power of attorney from Gray. The debenture was executed by the solicitor as attorney for Gray, and by the company secretary, and sealed with the common seal of the company. In fact, the power of attorney should have been sealed in terms of section 1(1) of the Powers of Attorney Act 1971, and the debenture, although sealed, was not sealed in terms permitted by the articles of association. The two companies went into liquidation, and the security was insufficient to pay the lenders in full. An action was raised against Gray under the personal guarantee by TCB Ltd. Gray defended by claiming that both the guarantee and the debenture were invalid because they had not been properly executed.

HELD that both documents were valid: the power of attorney was valid because Gray intended it to be relied on and therefore he was estopped from denying that it was sealed, and that the transaction was protected by section 9(1) of the European Communities Act 1972 (now sections 35, 35A and 35B of the Companies Act 1985); accordingly Gray was liable to an unlimited extent on the personal guarantee.

SIR NICHOLAS BROWNE-WILKINSON, V.-C. Mr Gray has executed a document drafted as a deed and which says that he has thereunto set his hand and seal. The document states in terms that it was signed, sealed and delivered in the presence of Mr McGuinness. There is therefore a representation of the fact that it was in fact sealed. Mr Gray executed the document with the intention that it should be relied on as a power of attorney and knowing that TCB were going to rely on it as such. TCB in fact relied on it to their detriment, since they advanced money in reliance on documents executed under the power. The case therefore has all the necessary elements of a classic estoppel.

. . . Under the old law, a person dealing with a corporation was required to look at the company's memorandum and articles to satisfy himself that the transaction was within the corporate capacity of the company and was to be carried through in accordance with the requirements of its articles. The rigour of those requirements was only tempered to the extent that the rule in *Royal British Bank* v. *Turquand* (1856) 6 E & B 327 allowed third parties to assume that acts of internal management had been properly carried out. It has been generally assumed that the old law has to a large extent been swept away by section 9(1) of the Act of 1972.

. . . Section 9(1) of the Act of 1972 was passed to bring the law of England into line with article 9 of Council Directive 68/151/EEC. In approaching the construction of the section, it is in my judgment relevant to note that the manifest purpose of both the directive and the section is to enable people to deal with a company in good faith without being adversely affected by any limits on the company's capacity or its rules for internal management. Given good faith, a third party is able to deal with a company through its "organs" (as the directive describes them) or directors. Section 9(1) achieves this in two ways: first it "deems" all transactions to be authorised; second, it deems that the directors can bind the company without limitations. The second part of the subsection reinforces this by expressly abolishing the old doctrine of constructive notice of the contents of the company's memorandum and articles. It being the obvious purpose of the subsection to obviate the commercial inconvenience and frequent injustice caused by the old law, I approach the construction of the subsection with great reluctance to construe it in such a way as to reintroduce, through the back door, any requirement that a third party acting in good faith must still investigate the regulating documents of a company.

Mr Brodie, whilst accepting that TCB had no actual or imputed knowledge of any irregularity in the execution of the debenture, at first submitted that TCB did not act "in good faith" within the meaning of the section since TCB was put on inquiry by the unusual manner in which the debenture had been executed. He said that TCB should have looked at the articles and would then have discovered the irregularity. Accordingly, he submitted, they were not acting "in good faith". On further consideration Mr Brodie abandoned this argument, to my mind rightly. The last words of the second part of section 9(1) expressly provide that good faith is to be presumed: the second part further provides that the person dealing with the company is not bound to inquire as to the limitations on the powers of the directors. In my judgment, it is impossible to establish lack of "good faith" within the meaning of the subsection solely by alleging that inquiries ought to have been made which the second part of the subsection says need not be made.

Mr Brodie's next submission was that, in order for section 9(1) to apply at all, the first requirement is that there must be a transaction by the company. Since Link never sealed the debenture in the only way authorised by the articles, there was here no transaction by Link at all; the debenture was not the act of Link. If this argument is right, it drives a coach and horses through the section. In every dealing with the company the third party would have to look at its articles to ensure that the company was binding itself in an authorised manner. In my judgment the section does not have that effect. The section is dealing with purported actions by a company which, having regard to its internal documents, may be a nullity, e.g., acts outside its corporate capacity. In such a case under the old law the purported act of the company would not be the act of the company at all. Yet the first part of section 9(1) deems it so to be. Similarly a document under seal by the company executed otherwise than in accordance with its articles was not, under the old law, the act of the company: but section 9(1) deems it so to be since the powers of the directors are deemed to be free from limitations, i.e. as to the manner of affixing the company's seal. In my judgment, section 9(1) of the Act applies to transactions which a company purports to enter into and deems them to be validly entered into.

. . . It has to be borne in mind that I have to determine whether a valid debenture was granted by Link. In my judgment Link, having put forward the minutes of the meeting of 25 January as one of the completion documents on the basis of which TCB made the loan, could not be heard to challenge the validity of that minute by denying that such a meeting ever took place. Therefore the minute stands as irrefutable evidence against Link that the grant of the debenture was a "transaction decided on by the directors". Accordingly the necessary basis for section 9(1) of the Act of 1972 to apply, as between Link and TCB, exists. It follows that the debenture was valid, and Mr Gray's second line of defence also fails.

. . . I accordingly hold that Mr Gray is liable without limit on his personal guarantee.

NOTE

Before the change in the law by the creation of what is now sections 35, 35A and 35B and section 711A of the Companies Act 1985 (at the time of this case, section 9 of the European Communities Act 1972) the transaction in *TCB Ltd.* v. *Gray* would not have been valid: it would not have been protected by the rule in *Royal British Bank* v. *Turquand* (1856) 6 E & B 327 because the defects in the debenture would have been detectable by the bank by comparison with the articles of association. The stautory rules remove the need for comparison of the transaction with the articles of association.

Rayfield v. Hands and others

[1960] 1 Ch 1; [1958] 2 All ER 194; [1958] 2 WLR 851

Chancery Division

The plaintiff, a shareholder, sued the directors for implement of the articles of association, which provided that a shareholder had to inform the directors when he wished to sell his shares, and that the directors 'will take the said shares equally between them at a fair value'. The plaintiff had notified the directors in terms of the provision, but they had declined to purchase his shares, on the ground that compliance with the provision was not obligatory on them.

HELD (1) that the articles did require the directors to purchase the shares at a fair valuation; (2) that the provision in the articles was concerned with the relationship between the plaintiff as a member and the defendants as members, and not as directors of the company; (3) the company did not need to be joined as a party in the proceedings.

VAISEY, J. The next and most difficult point taken by the defendants, as to which it would appear that there is no very clear judicial authority, is that article 11, as part of the company's articles of association, does not do what it looks like doing, that is, to create a contractual relationship between the plaintiff as shareholder and vendor and the defendants as directors and purchasers. This depends on section 20(1) of the Companies Act 1948, which reads as follows: "Subject to the provisions of this Act, the memorandum and articles shall, when registered, bind the company and the members thereof to the same extent as if they respectively had been signed and sealed by each member, and contained covenants on the part of each member to observe all the provisions of the memorandum and of the articles (now section 14 of the Companies Act 1985).

. . . Now the question arises at the outset whether the terms of article 11 relate to the rights of members *inter se* (that being the expression found in so many of the cases), or whether the relationship is between a member as such and directors as such. I may dispose of this point very briefly by saying that, in my judgment, the relationship here is between the plaintiff as a member and the defendants not as directors but as members. . . . I am of opinion, therefore, that this is in words a contract or quasi-contract between members, and not between members and directors.

NOTE

Such a decision would only be appropriate in companies where the directors are also members of the company, and where their directorship is viewed as one attribute of their membership, as in the case of a 'personal relationship' company.

5. Capital

Summary

1. Sources of the law

The law in this area is almost entirely statutory, and is found in the Companies Act 1985. Many of the modern statutory provisions derive from EC directives (for example, the Second Council Directive of 13 December 1976 on public limited liability companies 77/91 EEC).

The case law in this area is largely concerned with interpretation of statutory provisions, actions for implementation of statutory rights (see *Brady and another* v. *Brady and another* [1989]), or actions for implementation of rights relating to capital provided by the memorandum and articles of association. See **House of Fraser plc* v. *A.C.G.E. Investments Ltd.* [1987].

As the law is largely to be found in the Companies Act 1985, it is beyond the scope of this chapter to attempt to summarise all the statutory provisions on capital. Accordingly, the treatment given here is selective.

2. Raising and maintenance of capital

The Companies Act 1985 contains provisions to ensure that as far as possible, full money or money's worth is received by a company for the issue of share capital and, once raised, that the capital is maintained intact for the benefit of the creditors and is not returned to members without the sanction of the court. Many of the rules are relaxed for private companies. A company is now permitted to purchase or redeem its own shares, but the shares must be cancelled following the transaction and, if distributable profits are used, capital maintenance is achieved by the creation of a capital redemption reserve (see section 170 of the Companies Act 1985).

3. Variation of class rights

Sections 125–7 of the Companies Act 1985 are designed to ensure that members of minority classes among the shareholders do not have their rights defeated or eroded by decisions of the majority. Holders of class rights are given rights to approve changes to their rights, and to challenge changes in court. See *Cumbrian Newspapers Group Ltd.* v. *Cumberland & Westmorland Herald Newspaper & Printing Co. Ltd.* [1987]. However, it has been held that the statutory protections do not apply where class rights are being extinguished by resolutions passed by other shareholders. See *House of Fraser plc* v. *A.C.G.E. Investments Ltd.* [1987].

4. Financial assistance by a company for the purchase of its own shares

The giving of financial assistance by a company for the purchase of its own shares or those of its holding company is prohibited, with some exceptions, by section 151 of the Companies Act 1985. Breach is a criminal offence on the part of the company and its defaulting officers. The main exception arises where the main purpose of the financial assistance (whether given at the time of the acquisition or later, in order to extinguish liability), is not the acquisition of the shares, or the assistance is part of a larger purpose, and in both cases, the assistance must be given in good faith in the interests of the company. The rules are considerably relaxed for private companies. See *Brady and another* v. *Brady and another* [1989]; and *Neilson* v. *Stewart* 1991 SLT 523.

5. Listing particulars and prospectuses

The rules are mainly found in Part IV (listed securities) and Part V (unlisted securities) of the Financial Services Act 1986. At the time of writing, Part V has not yet come into force, and the rules for prospectuses for unlisted securities are still found in the Companies Act 1985. Companies seeking a Stock Exchange listing must follow the Rules for Admission of Securities to Listing published by the Council of the Stock Exchange (the 'Yellow Book').

Persons responsible for the issue of listing particulars/prospectuses containing errors or omissions which cause loss to those who subscribe for securities, are liable for compensation. See sections 150–2 and 166–8 of the Financial Services Act 1986. See also *Al-Nakib Investments (Jersey) Ltd.* v. *Longcroft* [1990].

6. Dividends

The rules on payment of dividends are largely statutory, and are found in Part VIII of the Companies Act 1985. There are generally also constitutional rules on the payment of dividends. See Table A regulations 102–8. Dividends are paid with reference to accounts showing a distributable profit. If a dividend is paid out of capital it is an unlawful distribution and recoverable from the shareholder if he knows or has reasonable cause for believing that it has been so made: section 277 of the Companies Act 1985. See *Precision Dippings Ltd.* v. *Precision Dippings Marketing Ltd.* [1986]; and *Re Cleveland Trust plc* [1991].

Brady and another v. Brady and another

[1989] AC 755; [1988] 2 All ER 617

House of Lords

The first plaintiff and first defendant were brothers who carried on a business as Brady Ltd. (B. Ltd.) and subsidiary companies, one of which was jointly owned by the second plaintiff and second defendant, who were both sons of the first defendant. The business operated in two areas: haulage and drinks. The brothers quarrelled. The first plaintiff petitioned the court under section 75 of the Companies Act 1980 (now sections 459–61 of the Companies Act 1985) for an order to buy out the shares of the first defendant, or for a winding-up order. An agreement was reached whereby one brother was to operate the haulage side and the other the drinks side of the business. The transaction involved the provision by B. Ltd. of financial assistance to an associated company, Motoreal Ltd. (M. Ltd.), to reduce its liability incurred in the purchase of shares in B. Ltd. However, the defendants refused to complete the transaction on the grounds that the assets had not been equally divided. The plaintiffs sued for specific performance. The defendants claimed that the agreement was *ultra vires* as it required B. Ltd. to (a) dispose of its assets without consideration, and (b) give unlawful financial assistance to reduce liability incurred in the purchase of its shares by M. Ltd., contrary to section 42(2) of the Companies Act 1981 (now section 151(1) and (2) of the Companies Act 1985). In the High Court the judge granted the order for specific performance on the ground that the financial assistance came within the larger purpose exception (now section 153(2) of the Companies Act 1985). The appeal was allowed by the Court of Appeal which held that the transaction was illegal. The case was appealed further to the House of Lords.

HELD (1) the transfer was *intra vires* the objects clause; (2) the proposed transfer was not a misfeasance on the part of B. Ltd's directors or a fraud on the creditors because the transfer had the support of the shareholders, and the company was solvent; (3) the reorganisation had been made in good faith in the interests of the company and therefore fell within section 153(2)(b) of the Companies Act 1985; (4) the financial assistance had not been part of a 'larger purpose' of the company within section 153(2)(a) and therefore *prima facie* it did not fall within the exception to the prohibition in section 151 of the Act against a company giving financial assistance for the acquisition of its own shares; but (5) allowing the appeal, this was a private company which could take advantage of relaxed rules in section 155(2) for financial assistance if assets were not thereby reduced or the financial assistance was provided out of distributable profits, if the directors could make a statutory declaration of solvency under section 156(2).

LORD OLIVER OF AYLMERTON. The question whether the proposed transfers of assets are *ultra vires* Brady and Athersmith [companies] can perhaps best be tested by postulating the following successive questions. First, does the express object enabling the company to dispose of its assets for such consideration as it thinks fit authorise a transfer in consideration of the promise of the transferee or of a third party to pay to the company the value of the assets transferred? The answer to that question must clearly be in the affirmative. Secondly, is this express object subject to some implied limitation excluding from the range of possible transferees or promisors either a company within the same group or a company which is the parent company of the transferor company? There can be no rational justification for any such implication and Mr Price has not contended that there is. Thirdly, if a promise of a parent or associated company is, in principle, an acceptable consideration, does it cease to be so because the promisor has, at the date of the promise, no other assets than the shares which it holds in the promisee? For my part, I can see no reason why, purely as a matter of the *vires* of the transferor company, it should do so, though of course there may be very good reasons for saying, according to the circumstances, that to enter into a contract on these terms may be ill-advised. But that, at any rate at this stage of the inquiry, is not the question.

. . . The proposed transfers are, in my judgment, clearly ones which are authorised by Brady's and Athersmith's corporate objects and are therefore *intra vires*, there being no suggestion whatever of fraud or ill-faith.

Then it is said that even if the transaction proposed is *intra vires* Brady and Athersmith, to carry it into effect will be a misfeasance on the part of the directors of those two companies which will render it either illegal or at least capable of being set aside. For my part I have been unable to see why this should be thought to be so. It is quite plain that at the date of the December letter the two companies were both solvent and possessed of a very comfortable surplus of assets over liabilities.

. . . My Lords, it follows from what I have said that if the appellants' claim is to be successfully resisted at all, it can only be on the ground that the transaction proposed infringes the provisions of section 151 of the Act of 1985.

. . . As already mentioned, the appellants' case failed in the Court of Appeal because the assistance given by Brady was not, in the view of the majority (albeit for different reasons), in the interests of the company and therefore failed to satisfy sub-paragraph (b) of the subsection.

. . . My Lords, I have found myself unable to share the views of the majority of the Court of Appeal with regard to sub-paragraph (b). The words "in good faith in the interests of the company" form, I think, a single composite expression and postulate a requirement that those responsible for procuring the company to provide the assistance act in the genuine belief that it is being done in the company's interest. In the circumstances of this case, where failure to implement the final stage of the scheme for the division of the two sides of Brady's business is likely to lead back to the very management deadlock that it was designed to avoid and the probable liquidation of Brady as a result, the proposed transfer is not only something which is properly capable of being perceived by Brady's directors as calculated to advance Brady's corporate and commercial interests and the interests of its employees but is indeed, viewed objectively, in the company's interest.

. . . Where I part company both from the trial judge and from the Court of Appeal is on the question of whether subpara. (a) can, on any reasonable construction of the subsection, be said to have been satisfied. . . . This much is clear, that subpara. (a) is contemplating two alternative situations. The first envisages a principal, and by implication, a subsidiary purpose. The inquiry here is whether the assistance given was principally in order to relieve the purchaser of shares in the company of his indebtedness resulting from the acquisition or whether it was principally for some other purpose—for instance, the acquisition from the purchaser of some asset which the company requires for its business. . . . That is not the case, for the purpose of the assistance here was simply and solely to reduce the indebtedness incurred by Motoreal on issuing the loan stock. The alternative situation is where it is not suggested that the financial assistance was intended to achieve any other object than the reduction or discharge of the indebtedness but where that result (i.e. the reduction or discharge) is merely incidental to some larger purpose of the company. . . . The trial judge found Brady's larger purpose to be that of freeing itself from the deadlock and enabling it to function independently and this was echoed in the judgment of O'Connor L.J. (1987) 3 BCC 535, at p. 540) where he observed that that answer "embraces avoiding liquidation, preserving its goodwill and the advantages of an established business". Croom-Johnson L.J. found the larger purpose in the reorganisation of the whole group. My Lords, I confess that I have not found the concept of a "larger purpose" easy to grasp, but if the sub-paragraph is to be given any meaning that does not in effect provide a blank cheque for avoiding the effective application of section 151 in every case, the concept must be narrower than that for which the appellants contend.

. . . The purpose and the only purpose of the financial assistance is and remains that of enabling the shares to be acquired and the financial or commercial advantages flowing from the acquisition, whilst they may form the reason for forming the purpose of providing assistance, are a by-product of it rather than an independent purpose of which the assistance can properly be considered to be an incident.

. . . The scheme of reorganisation was framed and designed to give Jack and Robert control of Brady for the best of reasons, but to say that the "larger purpose" of Brady's financial assistance is to be found in the scheme of reorganisation itself is to say only that the larger purpose was the acquisition of the Brady's shares on their behalf. For my part, I do not think that a larger purpose can be found in the benefits considered to be likely to flow or the disadvantages considered to be likely to be avoided by the acquisition which it was the purpose of the assistance to facilitate. The acquisition was not a mere incident of the scheme devised to break the deadlock. It was the essence of the scheme itself and the object which the scheme set out to achieve. In my judgment, therefore, subsection 2(a) of section 153 is not satisfied and if the matter rested there the appeal ought to fail on that ground.

[The second point] is simply this, that since all the companies concerned are private companies the transaction can be perfectly lawfully carried out in the manner contemplated without any departure from the agreed terms. . . . This can quite simply be done by operating the provisions of sections 155, 156 and 158 of the Act of 1985, which have the effect of disapplying the provisions of section 151. This is a matter which lies entirely in their hands and which does not involve the respondents in doing or concurring in the doing of anything which they have not agreed to do.

. . . If this is right, then there appears to be—and indeed, always to have been—a complete answer to the suggestion that the agreement is rendered unlawful by section 151 of the Act of 1985 and therefore incapable of specific performance, though clearly any decree of specific performance would have to contain appropriate conditions or undertakings to ensure that the provisions of sections 156 and 158 are complied with. Subject to this, therefore, I would allow the appeal but only on the terms previously indicated.

★ House of Fraser plc v. A.C.G.E Investments Ltd. and others

[1987] AC 387; [1987] 2 WLR 1083
Court of Session/House of Lords

The appellants held preference shares in House of Fraser plc. A petition had been presented to the Court of Session by the company seeking reduction of capital which included paying off the whole preference share capital as being unnecessary to the company's capital requirements. The special resolution authorising the reduction of capital under section 135 of the Companies Act 1985 was passed by the holders of the ordinary share capital only. The appellants, who were holders of preference shares, challenged this in court on the ground that the reduction of capital was an infringement of the preference shareholders' rights under the articles of association, and that it was a breach of their rights to approve a variation of class rights under section 125 of the Companies Act 1985. The Second Division rejected both arguments. In relation to the alleged infringement of the rights in section 125 of the Companies Act 1985 (whereby the class must be given an opportunity to consent to a proposed variation of its rights) the Inner House held that the protections in the section did not apply because in this case contractual rights were being fulfilled or satisfied, and consequently extinguished, but not varied. The appellants appealed to the House of Lords on the question of breach of the articles of association only.

HELD by the House of Lords that the appeal should be dismissed: the reduction of capital did not infringe the terms of the articles of association, but constituted a fulfilment of the rights of the preference shareholders rather than a variation of them.

LORD JUSTICE CLERK ROSS (Court of Session). In our opinion, the proposed cancellation of the preference shares would involve fulfilment or satisfaction of the contractual rights of the shareholders, and would not involve any variation of their rights. Variation of a right presupposes the existence of the right, the variation of the right, and the subsequent continued existence of the right as varied. A different situation obtains where a right is fulfilled and satisfied and thereafter ceases to exist. Moreover, although a right might be described as being abrogated or abolished where it is brought to an end without satisfaction or fulfilment of the right, in our opinion, there is no question of abrogation or abolition where the right is satisfied or fulfilled. Abolition or abrogation are not appropriate expressions to describe the situation where a right and its corresponding obligation have been extinguished by performance.

We are accordingly satisfied that the proposed cancellation of the preference shares did not amount to a variation (or abrogation) of the class rights of the holders in terms of section 125 of the Companies Act 1985.

Cumbrian Newspapers Group Ltd. v. Cumberland & Westmorland Herald Newspaper & Printing Co. Ltd.

[1987] 1 Ch 1; [1986] 2 All ER 816; [1986] 3 WLR 26
Chancery Division

A contract was entered into between the plaintiff and the defendant whereby the defendant acquired one of the plaintiff's newspapers and the plaintiff acquired 10 per cent of the defendant's issued share capital. The contract provided for the amendment of the defendant company's articles of association to grant to the plaintiff rights of pre-emption over the ordinary shares of the defendant company, rights in respect of unissued shares, and the right to appoint a director. The object sought by the plaintiff was to enable it to prevent a take-over of the defendant company. Some time later, the directors of the defendant company proposed to convene an extraordinary general meeting to pass a special resolution to cancel the articles conveying the special rights to the plaintiff. The plaintiff raised an action seeking a declaration that the rights were class rights which under section 125 of the Companies Act 1985 could not be abrogated without its consent, and an injunction restraining the defendant from holding the extraordinary general meeting.

HELD (1) that the rights were class rights within the meaning of the section, and accordingly the rights could not be varied or abrogated without the consent of the plaintiff; (2) that the adoption of the special articles, however, on the facts, was not a contractual term, nor could such a term be implied into the articles.

SCOTT, J. I turn to the critical question: are the plaintiff's rights under articles 5, 7, 9 and 12, rights attached to a class of shares?

Rights or benefits which may be contained in articles can be divided into three different categories. First, there are rights or benefits which are annexed to particular shares. Classic examples of rights in this character are dividend rights and rights to participate in surplus assets on a winding up. If articles provide that particular shares carry particular rights not enjoyed by the holders of other shares, it is easy to conclude that the rights are attached to a class of shares, for the purpose both of section 125 of the Act of 1985 and of article 4 of Table A. . . . The plaintiff's rights under articles 5, 7, 9 and 12 cannot, however, be brought within this first category. The rights were not attached to any particular shares. In articles 5, 7, and 9, there is no reference to any current shareholding by the plaintiff. The rights conferred on the plaintiff under article 12 are dependent on the plaintiff holding at least 10 per cent of the issued ordinary shares in the defendant. But the rights are not attached to any particular shares. Any ordinary shares in the defendant, if sufficient in number and held by the plaintiff, would entitle the plaintiff to exercise the rights.

A second category of rights or benefits which may be contained in articles (although it may be that neither "rights" nor "benefits" is an apt description), would cover rights or benefits conferred on individuals not in the capacity of members or shareholders of the company but, for ulterior reasons, connected with the administration of the company's affairs or the conduct of its business. *Eley* v. *Positive Government Security Life Assurance Co. Ltd.* (1875) 1 Exch D 20 was a case where the articles of the defendant company had included a provision that the plaintiff should be the company solicitor. The plaintiff sought to enforce that provision as a contract between himself and the company. He failed. The reasons why he failed are not here relevant, and I cite the case only to draw attention to an article which, on its terms, conferred a benefit on an individual but not in the capacity of member or shareholder of the company. It is, perhaps, obvious that rights or benefits in this category cannot be class rights. The plaintiff in *Eley* v. *Positive Government Security Life Assurance Co. Ltd.* was not a shareholder at the time the articles were adopted.

He became a shareholder some time thereafter.

. . . The evidence in this case has clearly established that the adoption by the defendant of articles 5, 7, 9 and 12, was inextricably connected with the issue to the plaintiff, and the plaintiff's acceptance, of the 280 ordinary £5 shares in the defendant. The purpose of the rights and privileges conferred on the plaintiff by those articles, was to enable the plaintiff, in its capacity as shareholder in the defendant, to obstruct an attempted take-over of the defendant. In my judgment, the plaintiff's rights under those articles do not fall within this second category.

That leaves the third category. This category would cover rights or benefits that, although not attached to any particular shares, were nonetheless conferred on the beneficiary in the capacity of member or shareholder of the company. The rights of the plaintiff under articles 5, 7, 9 and 12 fall, in my judgment, into this category. Other examples can be found in reported cases.

In *Bushell* v. *Faith* [1969] 2 Ch 438, affirmed by the House of Lords [1970] AC 1099, articles of association included a provision that on a resolution at a general meeting for the removal of any director from office, any shares held by that director should carry the right to three votes. The purpose of this provision was to prevent directors being removed from office by a simple majority of the members of the company. The validity of this article was upheld by the Court of Appeal and by the House of Lords; the reasons do not, for present purposes, matter. But the rights conferred by the article in question fall, in my view, firmly in this third category. They were not attached to any particular shares. On the other hand, they were conferred on the directors/beneficiaries in their capacity as shareholders. The article created, in effect, two classes of shareholders; namely, shareholders who for the time being were directors, on the one hand, and shareholders who were not for the time being directors, on the other hand.

The present case is, and *Bushell* v. *Faith* was, concerned with rights conferred by the articles. The other side of the coin is demonstrated by *Rayfield* v. *Hands* [1960] Ch 1. That case was concerned with obligations imposed on members by the articles. The articles of the company included an article entitling every member to sell his shares to the directors of the company at a fair valuation. In effect, the members enjoyed "put" options exerciseable against the directors. Vaisey J. held that the obligations imposed by the article on the directors for the time being were enforceable against them. He held that the obligations were imposed on the directors in their capacity as members of the company. It follows from his judgment that, as in

Bushell v. *Faith* [1970] AC 1099, there were in effect two classes of shareholders in the company. There were shareholders who were not for the time being directors and shareholders who were for the time being directors: the former had rights against the latter which the latter did not enjoy against the former. The two classes were identifiable not by reference to their respective ownership of particular shares, but by reference to the office held by the latter. But the rights of the former, and the obligations of the latter, required their respective ownership of shares in the company. Accordingly, as a matter of classification, the rights in question fall, in my view, into the third category.

In the present case, the rights conferred on the plaintiff under articles 5, 7, 9 and 12 were, as I have held, conferred on the plaintiff as a member or shareholder in the defendant. . . . The rights would not be enforceable by the plaintiff otherwise than as the owner of ordinary shares in the defendant. . . . Enforcement by the plaintiff of the rights granted under articles 5, 7, and 9, would require no more than ownership by the plaintiff of at least some shares in the defendant. . . . The question for decision is whether rights in this third category are within the meaning of the phrase in section 125 of the Companies Act 1985 and in article 4 of Table A, rights attached to a class of shares.

. . . A number of considerations lead me to the conclusion that the purpose of sections 125 and 127 of the act of 1985, and of section 32 of the Act of 1980 [Companies Act 1980], was to deal comprehensively with the manner in which class rights in companies having a share capital could be varied or abrogated. They are these: first, chapter II of part V of the Act (which included sections 125 to 129) is headed "Class Rights". The side note to section 125 reads "Variation of class rights". The language seems to treat "class rights" as synonymous with "rights attached to any class of shares", at any rate so far as companies with a share capital are concerned. Second, the use in section 17(2)(b) of the Act of 1985 of the expression "rights of any class of members" in connection both with companies having a share capital and companies having no share capital, underlines the point that the expression "rights attached to any class of shares" in section 125, must have been regarded by the legislature as synonymous with the former phrase, so far as companies with a share capital were concerned. Third, the evident intention of the legislature to protect rights attached to any class of shares against variation or abrogation by the mere alteration of articles, would, if coupled with an intention to provide no such protection against variation or abrogation of class rights of the third category, be anomalous and arbitrary. Fourth, if the variation or abrogation of third category rights are not dealt with by section 125, then the conclusion would seem to follow that if the rights were contained in the memorandum, the rights could not be varied or abrogated at all. The enabling provisions of section 125 of the Act of 1985 would obviously not apply, nor would the enabling provisions of section 17 of the Act of 1985. The terms of section 17, to my mind, strongly suggest a legislative belief that section 125 would deal with the variation or abrogation of any "special rights of any class of member" contained in the memorandum. Fifth, the combination of the considerations thirdly and fourthly abovementioned, leads to a further point. What sense could there be in the result under which third category rights contained in articles were more freely alterable than rights attached to any class of shares contained therein, but under which third category rights contained in the memorandum were less freely alterable than rights attached to any class of shares contained in the memorandum? The distinction would not be merely anomalous; it would, to my mind, be perverse.

For these reasons I conclude that section 125 of the Act of 1985 was intended by the legislature to cater for the variation or abrogation of any special rights given by the memorandum or articles of a company to any class of members—that is to say, not only rights falling into the first category I have described, but also rights falling into the third category. I must, therefore, construe section 125 so as to give effect to that legislative intention if the language of the section so permits. In my judgment, it does.

Subsection (1) refers to "the rights attached to any class of shares in a company whose share capital is divided into shares of different classes". In my judgment, if specific rights are given to certain members in their capacity as members or shareholders, then those members become a class. The shares those members hold for the time being, and without which they would not be members of the class, would represent, in my view, a "class of shares" for the purpose of section 125. The class would include those shares the ownership of which for the time being entitled the members of the company to the rights in question. For the purposes of section 125, the share capital of a company is, in my judgment, divided into shares of different classes, if shareholders, *qua* shareholders, enjoy different rights.

. . . In my judgment, a company which, by its articles, confers special rights on one or more of its members in the capacity of member or shareholder thereby constitutes the shares for the time being held by that member or members, a class of shares for the purposes of section 125. The rights are class rights. I have already expressed the opinion that the rights conferred on the plaintiff under articles 5, 7, 9 and 12, were conferred on the plaintiff as member or shareholder of the defendant. It follows that, in my judgment, the shares in the defendant for the time being held by the plaintiff constitute a class of shares for the purpose of variation or abrogation of those rights.

The conclusion I have reached on the plaintiff's first point disposes of this action.

NOTE

For a fuller treatment of *Bushell* v. *Faith* [1970] AC 1099 and *Rayfield* v. *Hands and others* [1960] Ch 1, mentioned in the judgment of Scott, J., see Chapter 8 page 145 and Chapter 4 page 86 respectively.

Al-Nakib Investments (Jersey) Ltd. and another v. Longcroft and others

[1990] All ER 321

Chancery Division

C.T. plc developed an electronic information storage system and decided to float the shares of its subsidiary, M., which was formed to exploit the new development, on the unlisted securities market. A prospectus was issued inviting the shareholders of C.T. plc to subscribe for shares in C.T. plc and M. by way of a rights issue. The plaintiff subscribed for 400,000 M. shares, and later made further purchases of both M. and C.T. plc shares through the stock market. The plaintiff sued C.T. plc and its directors in respect of misrepresentations in the prospectus, in that it represented the system as fully developed, whereas in fact it was not. He alleged that the misrepresentations had caused him loss.

HELD that directors did not owe a duty of care to shareholders or anyone else who relied on the prospectus in making a purchase on a public market, as the prospectus was addressed to prospective shareholders for the purpose of inviting subscriptions for shares from the company by way of a rights issue. Accordingly, in respect of the market purchases, there was not a sufficiently proximate relationship to give rise to a duty of care on the part of the directors. Those claims which related to purchase of shares on the market would be struck out.

MERVYN DAVIES, J. In the *Caparo* case [*Caparo Industries plc* v. *Dickman*] Lord Jauncey said [1990] 1 All ER 568 at 607, [1990] 2 WLR 358):

> "If the statutory accounts are prepared and distributed for certain limited purposes, can there nevertheless be imposed on auditors an additional common law duty to individual shareholders who choose to use them for another purpose without the prior knowledge of the auditors? The answer must be no. Use for that other purpose would no longer be use for the 'very transaction' which Denning L.J. in *Candler* v. *Crane, Christmas & Co.* [1951] 1 All ER 426 at 435, [1951] 2 KB 164 at 183 regarded as determinative of the scope of any duty of care. Only where the auditor was aware that the individual shareholder was likely to rely on the accounts for a particular purpose such as his present or future investment in or lending to the company would a duty of care arise. Such a situation does not obtain in the present case."

Those words show that a duty of care is not fastened on to a situation when a statement has been made for a particular purpose and the statement is used for another purpose. . . . In the present case we have statements in the prospectus made by the directors. It is said that the Al-Nakib company (acting by Mr Al-Nakib) in reliance on the prospectus entered into transactions 2, 3, and 4. So does a duty of care exist as between the directors and the Al-Nakib company? I would suppose that a duty of care would not be regarded as arising because Mr Al-Nakib made use of the prospectus for a purpose otherwise than that for which it was issued. The prospectus was given to Comtech shareholders to enable them to consider whether or not to take up an offer of 1 Mnemos share for every 5 Comtech shares at a price of 65p per share. In these circumstances there appears not to arise "the special relationship" that is referred to in the *Scott Group* case [1978] 1 NZLR 553 [*Scott Group Ltd* v. *McFarlane*] : so that the facts pleaded do not suffice to ground any duty of care as respects transactions 2, 3, and 4. On that footing my conclusion would be the same (as respects the company and Mrs Al-Nakib) in respect of transactions 5 and 6. The interim reports (whether read alone or conjoined with the prospectus) were issued for the purpose of informing the shareholders of Mnemos of the activities of the company. Mr Al-Nakib used the reports for the purpose of making up his mind whether or not to buy in the market.

. . . I am confirmed in my view that the defendants did not owe to the plaintiffs a duty of care in respect of transactions 2 to 6; in that a prospectus (and the interim reports) having been addressed to the first plaintiff for a particular purpose (i.e. considering the rights issue) it was used by the plaintiffs for another purpose (i.e. buying shares in the market).

NOTE

The case does not determine whether or not a duty of care was established in respect of the purchase of shares in the rights issue following the inaccurate prospectus. It would, however, be likely that a duty would lie in that event, if the facts were established.

For a report of *Caparo Industries plc* v. *Dickman* [1990] see Chapter 10 page 199 below.

Precision Dippings Ltd. v. Precision Dippings Marketing Ltd. and others

[1986] 1 Ch 447; [1985] BCLC 385

Court of Appeal

The plaintiff company brought an action against its parent company and the directors of both companies to recover a dividend payment on the ground that it was paid in contravention of section 39 of the Companies Act 1980 (now section 263 of the Companies Act 1985) as not having been made out of distributable profits, and hence *ultra vires*. The facts were that the auditors had qualified their report on the annual accounts, but no statement as to the materiality of the qualification was made as required by section 43(3)(c) of the Companies Act 1980. The plaintiff company went into liquidation. A statement was later issued by the auditors to the effect that the qualifications were not material for the purposes of determining whether the dividend contravened sections 39 and 43 of the Companies Act 1980. Summary judgment was entered by the registrar against all three defendants, but on appeal, the judge gave all the defendants unconditional leave to defend.

HELD, on appeal from the plaintiff from so much of the judge's order as related to the first defendant, that the statement required by section 43(3)(c) of the Companies Act 1980 had to be available before a distribution was made and, therefore, the payment of the dividend was an *ultra vires* act, and as the first defendant received the money with notice of the facts and did not give valuable consideration, it held it as constructive trustee for the plaintiff company.

Re Cleveland Trust plc

[1991] BCLC 424

Chancery Division

Cleveland Trust plc had a wholly owned subsidiary, G. Ltd., which in turn had a wholly owned subsidiary, M. Ltd. M. Ltd. realised a capital profit on the sale of assets, and declared a dividend based on these profits, which was ultimately passed on to Cleveland Trust plc. The memorandum of association of M. Ltd. empowered it to realise its assets, but prohibited the use of any resulting capital surplus for payment of dividends. Following the receipt of the dividend, Cleveland Trust plc made a bonus issue of fully paid shares to be capitalised out of its profit and loss account. Cleveland Trust plc petitioned the court under section 359 of the Companies Act 1985 for rectification of the register on the ground that the issue of the bonus shares was invalid and should be cancelled, because the company had no available funds out of which the bonus shares could be paid up.

HELD *per* Scott, J., that M. Ltd. lacked the capacity to pay a dividend out of capital surpluses, and therefore G. Ltd. were liable as constructive trustees to return the part of the dividend to M. Ltd. which was represented by these capital surpluses. The directors and auditors of G. Ltd., who were also directors and auditors of M. Ltd., should have realised that the payment of the dividend was *ultra vires*. To include the dividend in the accounts of G. Ltd. meant that the dividend had not been properly authorised under section 270 of the Companies Act 1985. As the directors of G. Ltd. were also directors of Cleveland Trust plc, they knew or ought to have known that the dividend was not properly declared and accordingly Cleveland Trust plc held the dividend on a constructive trust for G. Ltd. Since both Cleveland Trust plc and its shareholders were mistaken in thinking that the capital profit of M. Ltd. could be used to fund the bonus shares, the bonus issue could be declared void on the grounds of common mistake and the share register rectified.

NOTE
In Scots law the same result would arise by applying the common law
of error (common error).

6. Shares

Summary

1. Sources of the law

The law relating to shares is found largely in the Companies Act 1985.
The case law is concerned with implementation of rights provided by
statute or by the memorandum and articles of association.

2. Statutory provisions

The Companies Act 1985 contains rules relating to allotment of shares
(sections 80–116), rules relating to the transfer and registration of
shares (sections 182–97), and rules on disclosure of interests in shares
(sections 198–220). It is not appropriate to a casebook such as this to
explain these statutory rules in detail.

3. Constitutional rules

Many of the procedural rules relating to shares, such as the rules
relating to share certificates, calls on shares, liens on shares and
transfer of shares, are found in the articles of association. See, for
example, Table A regulations 2–35.

4. Cases on implementation of rights provided by the memorandum and articles of association, and other case law on shares

A definition of a share is provided in *Borland's Trustee* v. *Steel Bros.
& Co. Ltd.* [1901].
    A common provision of the articles of association of a private
company, particularly of a family company, is a clause of pre-emption,

by which existing members must be given first refusal when shares are to be sold by members. Members cannot disregard these rights. See *Tett* v. *Phoenix Property and Investment Co. Ltd.* [1986].

Often directors are given wide discretion by the articles of association to refuse to register transfers of shares to persons of whom they do not approve. In such a case, it is hard to challenge such a refusal, the only challenge possible being on the basis that the directors have not acted *bona fide* in the interests of the company as a whole. See *Re Smith & Fawcett Ltd.* [1942].

The rules laid down in the articles have to be strictly adhered to, otherwise they can be challenged. In *Parkstone Ltd.* v. *Gulf Guarantee Bank plc* [1990], an unsuccessful challenge was made in relation to forfeiture of shares, based on a provision in the articles of association relating to the giving of notice.

5. The register of members

A register of members must be maintained by the company under section 232 of the Companies Act 1985. This shows the names and addresses of members, and the date on which each person became and ceased to be a member, plus details of the shareholdings of each member in a company limited by shares. The register is open to public inspection on payment of a small fee, and can be inspected free of charge by members. If entries in the register are incorrect the register can be corrected by order of the court on petition to court for the rectification of the register if the company refuses to make a justified correction. See *Re Fagin's Bookshop plc* [1992].

Borland's Trustee v. Steel Brothers & Co. Ltd.

[1901] 1 Ch 279

Chancery Division

The plaintiff, Borland's trustee in bankruptcy, sought a declaration that the defendant company were not entitled to require the transfer of certain shares held by the bankrupt at any price whatever, and that the articles which purported to contain such power were void. He also sought an injunction restraining the company from calling for or enforcing the transfer of the ordinary shares of the bankrupt at any price, or at any price less than the fair and actual value of the shares. The articles provided that, on bankruptcy, notice could be served calling for the transfer of shares at 'par value' as specially defined for the purposes of the article. The 'par value' of the shares was calculated to be £8,650, whereas the market value of the shares was claimed by the plaintiff to be £34,000.

HELD that articles of association which compel a shareholder to transfer shares to particular persons at particular prices are not void as being repugnant to absolute ownership, or as tending to perpetuity, neither did such a provision breach bankruptcy law; and that a share is to be regarded as the interest of a shareholder in the company, measured for the purpose of liability and dividend by a sum of money, but consisting of a series of mutual agreements entered into by all the shareholders with one another in terms of section 16 of the Companies Act 1862 (now section 14 of the Companies Act 1985).

FARWELL, J. It is said that the provisions of these articles compel a man at any time during the continuance of this company to sell his shares to particular persons at a particular price to be ascertained in the manner prescribed in the articles. Two arguments have been founded on that. It is said, first of all, that such provisions are repugnant to absolute ownership. It is said, further, that they tend to perpetuity. They are likened to the case of a settlor or testator who settles or gives a sum of money subject to executory limitations which are to arise in the future, interpreting the articles as if they provided that if at any time hereafter, during centuries to come, the company should desire the shares of a particular person, not being a manager or assistant, he must sell them. To my mind this is applying to company law a principle which is wholly inapplicable thereto. It is the first time that any such suggestion has been made, and it rests, I think, on a misconception of what a share in a company really is. A share, according to the plaintiff's argument, is a sum of money which is dealt with in a particular manner by what are called, for the purpose of argument, executory limitations. To my mind it is nothing of the sort. A share is the interest of a shareholder in the company measured by a sum of money, for the purpose of liability in the first place, and of interest in the second, but also consisting of a series of mutual covenants entered into by all the shareholders *inter se* in accordance with s. 16 of the Companies Act, 1862. The contract contained in the articles of association is one of the original incidents of the share. A share is not a sum of money settled in the way suggested, but is an interest measured by a sum of money and made up of various rights contained in the contract, including the right to a sum of money of a more or less amount.

Tett v. Phoenix Property and Investment Co. Ltd. and others
[1986] BCLC 149; (1986) 2 BCC 99, 140
Court of Appeal

The executors of a shareholder of the Phoenix Property and Investment Co. Ltd. sold his holding of ninety shares to the plaintiff for £20 per share, and executed a transfer in his favour. The company had articles of association containing a right of pre-emption in favour of existing members of the company and their spouses, parents and children. The company refused to register the transfer, because the rights of pre-emption had been ignored. The company then sent a circular to its members advising them of their right to offer for the shares, and advising them that shares had recently changed hands at £5 per share, but not mentioning the sale to the plaintiff at £20 per share. The plaintiff sued for an order for the entry of his name on the register of members as the holder of the ninety shares. The trial judge, Vinelott, J., held that as an offer to the other members and their families had in the end been made, and none of them had taken up the offer, the rights of pre-emption had been honoured, and the directors could proceed to use their discretion to register the shares in the name of the plaintiff. The defendants (who were the company itself, its chairman, secretary, and a director and shareholder) appealed to the Court of Appeal.

HELD that the appeal should be allowed: (1) the effect of the right of pre-emption was to cut down the right to transfer the shares to a non-member without the provision of reasonable notice to members and their relations; (2) the condition in the articles had not been satisfied, and the transfer to the plaintiff was accordingly in breach of the articles; and (3) the directors had no power to register the transfer, which had, to their knowledge, been made in breach of the articles.

SLADE, L.J. As the argument in this court has developed, the principal outstanding questions can, I think, now be conveniently summarised under three heads:

(A) Did Article 5(E) and 5(F) on their true construction impose a valid and enforceable condition which had to be satisfied if the executors were to have the right to transfer the 90 shares to a non-member of the company, such as the plaintiff, and if so what condition? (''Question (A)''.)

(B) If the answer to the first part of Question (A) is Yes, had that condition been complied with on the facts, either by the time when the transfer of 26 February 1982 was executed or at least by 18 May 1982 when the proceedings were begun? (''Question (B)''.)

(C) If the answer to the first part of Question (A) is Yes and the answer to Question (B) is No, are there any other grounds upon which the plaintiff can still claim to be entitled to registration in respect of the 90 shares? (''Question (C)''.)

. . . My answer to Question (A) is thus as follows. Articles 5(E) and 5(F), on their true construction, do impose a valid and enforceable condition which first had to be satisfied if the executors were to have the right to transfer the 90 shares to an outsider. This condition was that the executors should have first taken reasonable steps to give all the other members and their specified relatives a reasonable opportunity to make an offer to purchase the shares at a fair value to be determined by the auditors in default of agreement and that no such offer should have been made. . . . I am satisfied that the executors before executing the transfer of their shares, did not take reasonable steps to give even *the other members of the company* a reasonable opportunity to make such an offer.

As to Question (B)
. . . In my opinion it is therefore clear that the relevant condition had not been satisfied when the transfer of the 90 shares was executed, that the transfer was in breach of the articles and that the condition still had not been satisfied by the time when the proceedings were instituted.

As to Question (C)
. . . The directors would have had no power to register a transfer such as this which had to their knowledge been made in breach of Article 5. I am not able to agree with the learned judge's views that this question of registration fell to be dealt with by the directors as a matter of the exercise of their discretion under Article 5(D). The question of discretion did not in my opinion arise.

Conclusion
For the reasons given . . . my conclusion is that the plaintiff is not entitled to any of the relief which he claims, essentially because the restrictive provisions of Article 5 have never been complied with. I would accordingly allow this appeal.

Re Smith & Fawcett Ltd.

[1942] Ch 304; [1942] 1 All ER 542
Court of Appeal
The articles of association of the company, which was a private company, provided an absolute and uncontrolled discretion to the directors to refuse to register any transfer of shares. The appellant sought to have 4,001 shares registered in his name as the executor of his father. The directors refused to register the shares but instead offered to register 2,001 of the shares in the name of the appellant, provided he sold the remaining 2,000 shares to one of the directors at a price proposed by the directors. The appellant raised an action on the High Court seeking an order compelling the directors to register the transfers in full. The High Court held that the directors were acting properly within the ambit of their discretion. The appellant appealed to the Court of Appeal.

HELD that, within the meaning of the article, the only limit on the exercise of the directors' discretion was that it be exercised *bona fide* for the benefit of the company and, accordingly, in the absence of proof of *mala fides*, the refusal to register the transfer was valid; the appeal was accordingly dismissed.

LORD GREENE, M.R. In the present case the article is as follows:

> The directors may at any time in their absolute and uncontrolled discretion refuse to register any transfer of shares.

As I have said, it is beyond question that that is a fiduciary power, and the directors must exercise it *bona fide* in what they consider to be the interests of the company. The language of the article does not point to any particular matter as being the only matter to which the directors are to pay attention in deciding whether or not they will allow the transfer to be registered. The article does not, for instance, say, as is to be found in some articles, that they may refuse to register any transfer of shares to a person not already a member of the company, nor does it say that they may refuse to register any transfer of shares to a transferee of whom they do not approve. In cases where articles are framed with some such limitation on the discretionary power of refusal as I have mentioned in the two examples which I have given, it follows on plain principle that, if they go outside the matters which the articles say are to be the only matters to which they are to have regard, the directors will have exceeded their powers.

. . . The question therefore is, simply whether, on the true construction of the particular article, the directors are limited by anything except their *bona fide* view as to the interests of the company. In the present case the article is drafted in the widest possible terms, and I decline to write into that clear language any limitation other than a limitation, which is implicit by law, that a fiduciary power of this kind must be exercised *bona fide* in the interests of the company. Subject to that qualification, an article in this form appears to me to give the directors what it says, namely, an absolute and uncontrolled discretion.

. . . On the evidence I am satisfied, as the judge was satisfied, that there is no ground shown here for saying that the directors' refusal has been due to anything but a *bona fide* consideration of the interests of the company as the directors see them. That being so, and that being on the true construction of the article the only matter to which the directors have to pay regard, I am of opinion that the judge was perfectly right in the conclusion to which he came and that this appeal fails and must be dismissed with costs.

Parkstone Ltd. v. Gulf Guarantee Bank plc

[1990] BCLC 850

Chancery Division

Parkstone, a Gibraltarian-registered company, became the registered holder of 500,000 partly paid shares in Gulf Guarantee Bank plc (the Bank). It had acquired the shares from Breezevale, another company in the same group. K., the chairman of Breezevale, agreed to buy back the shares from Breezevale, and Breezevale alleged that K. had agreed to assume liability for payment of the remaining instalments due in respect of the shares. After giving K. an opportunity to pay the outstanding instalments, the Bank sent notice to Parkstone as the registered holder of the shares that unless payment of the calls was received, the shares would be forfeited. The notice was sent to Parkstone's Gibraltar address despite the fact that Parkstone had informed the Bank of an address in London for the service of notices. Parkstone claimed, therefore, that the notice was invalid. The articles of association of the Bank incorporated regulation 131 of Table A in schedule 1 to the Companies Act 1948 (now regulation 112 of Table A), which allowed the company to choose whether to give notice to a member personally, by sending it by post to him, by sending it by post to his registered address or, in the case of a member with no registered address within the United Kingdom, by sending it by post to an unregistered address within the United Kingdom supplied by the member. Parkstone sought interlocutory injunctions to restrain Gulf Guarantee Bank plc until trial from proceeding with the forfeiture.

HELD (1) that Parkstone had failed to establish that it had any real chance of being able to succeed at trial in claiming that the Bank was not entitled to proceed with the forfeiture and, accordingly, the interlocutory injunction restraining the forfeiture of shares until after trial was not granted; and (2) that regulation 131 of Table A in schedule 1 to the Companies Act 1948 allowed the Bank the choice between the methods of service of notice named in the regulation and, accordingly, service at the Gibraltar address was valid and, therefore, the interlocutory injunction restraining Gulf Guarantee Bank plc from relying on the notice failed.

WARNER, J. The contention of counsel for Parkstone was that under regulation 131 it was not permissible for the company to serve a notice on a member whose registered address was outside the United Kingdom by sending it to him by post to that address. If he had supplied an address within the United Kingdom for the giving of notice to him, the notice might be sent to him by post to that address. Otherwise it must be sent to him personally, in the case of a corporate member by leaving it at its registered office. Counsel suggested that the underlying reason for that might be mistrust of foreign postal services. He relied on two authorities which he submitted showed that "in the ordinary course of post" meant "in the ordinary course of United Kingdom post", namely *Re Union Hill Silver Co. Ltd.* (1870) 22 LT 400 [1861–73] All ER Rep 214 and *Re Warden & Hotchkiss Ltd.* [1945] 1 All ER 507, [1945] Ch 270.

. . . On a straightforward reading of the first sentence of regulation 131 it affords the company a choice of methods by which it may give notice to a member. In the case of any member it may give the notice to him either "personally" or "by sending it by post to him" or "by sending it by post . . . to his registered address". I suppose that the second of those methods may be used where, for instance, the company knows that the member's true address differs from his registered address. In the case of a member who has no registered address within the United Kingdom but who has supplied to the company an address within the United Kingdom for the giving of notice to him there is available to the company the additional method of sending the notice by post to the latter address.

. . . The argument of counsel for Parkstone involves saying that in the case of a member whose registered address is not within the United Kingdom the second and third methods are eliminated, leaving only the first and fourth available. I find that difficult to reconcile with the grammar of the sentence. I find it even more difficult to reconcile with common sense. The 1948 Table A contains a number of provisions which may necessitate the company serving a notice on a member. Apart from regulation 33 relating to forfeiture of shares, there are regulation 12, which relates to the exercise by the company of a lien on shares, regulation 15, which relates to calls on shares, and the proviso to regulation 32, which relates to the registration of the shares of a deceased or bankrupt member. That the authors of regulation 131 were aware of the difference between the notices that they might be required to give under provisions of that kind and notices summoning meetings is shown by the second sentence of regulation 131. Counsel for Parkstone accepted, indeed asserted, that his construction of regulation 131 meant that, in the case of a member with a registered address outside the United Kingdom who had not supplied the company with an address within the United Kingdom for the giving of notice to him, the only course open to the company would be to give him the notice personally. It seems to me highly improbable that such a result could have been intended by the authors of the regulation. Indeed it might mean that in the case of a corporate member notice could not be given to it at all, because it is at least doubtful whether a corporation can be given notice personally in the absence of express provisions prescribing how that should be done: see *per* Wynn-Parry J. in *Stylo Shoes Ltd.* v. *Prices Tailors Ltd.* [1959] 3 All ER 901 at 904, [1960] Ch 396 at 403.

Counsel for Parkstone submitted that the rejection of his construction might lead to anomalies too. Suppose, he said, that a member with a registered address in a distant land outside the United Kingdom had supplied to the company an address within the United Kingdom for the giving of notice to him but that the company none the less chose to post notice of a meeting to him at his registered address. By virtue of the second sentence of regulation 131 he would be deemed to have received the notice 24 hours after its posting, though he might not receive it until much later. I accept that this is so, but it seems to me a lesser anomaly than that to which counsel's construction would give rise.

. . . I conclude that Gulf's notice dated 16 February 1990 was effectively served on Parkstone.

Re Fagin's Bookshop plc
[1992] BCLC 118
Chancery Division

Two applicants sought rectification of the register under section 359 of the Companies Act 1985 by deletion of the entry showing Banque Leu as the holder of 500,000 shares, and substituting a new entry showing Banque Leu as the holder of 333,320 shares and opening another folio showing another company as the holder of 166,680 shares. Banque Leu claimed that it could only be sued in Luxembourg where it was domiciled.

HELD, according to the Convention on Jurisdiction and Judgments in Civil and Commercial Matters the court had jurisdiction. Further, for a court to grant an order for rectification under section 359 of the Companies Act 1985, it was not necessary to prove any wrong committed by the company, but was sufficient to show that the register of members is incorrect because an entry has been omitted or made in error; as it was proved that there was an error or omission on the register of members the court ordered the register to be rectified as craved.

7. Insider dealing

Summary

1. Sources of the law

The law in this area is contained partly in the Company Securities (Insider Dealing) Act 1985 (criminal law) and the Financial Services Act 1986 (investigations into insider dealing) and partly in case law (criminal law of fraud and cases on contract and tort (*delict)). Changes are expected to be made to the Company Securities (Insider Dealing) Act 1985 in the United Kingdom following the EC Directive co- ordinating regulations on insider dealing (Council Directive of 13 November 1989 co-ordinating regulations on insider dealing 89/592/EEC) and the Council of Europe Convention on Insider Trading (20 April 1989). The directive would widen the scope of the prohibition on insider dealing to include futures contracts, options and financial futures traded on a regulated public market. The directive is scheduled to be implemented into United Kingdom law in 1992.

2. The Company Securities (Insider Dealing) Act 1985

This legislation was introduced in the Companies Act 1980. Since then it has been revised and consolidated as the Company Securities (Insider Dealing) Act 1985, which has in turn been added to by the Financial Services Act 1986 (sections 173–8), the Criminal Justice Act 1988 (section 48) and the Companies Act 1989 (section 209).

The Company Securities (Insider Dealing) Act 1985 is a criminal statute which makes particular dealings by certain parties a criminal offence. The dealings in question are those in securities (shares or debentures) on a recognised stock exchange. The parties are as follows:

(1) individuals who have been knowingly connected with the company during the past six months, who hold confidential

price-sensitive information by reason of their connection with the company, which it would be reasonable to expect such a person not to reveal except for the proper performance of his duties;

(2) individuals contemplating or who have contemplated making a takeover offer for a company, if they know that information regarding whether the offer is contemplated or no longer contemplated is unpublished price-sensitive information;

(3) public servants (crown servants and employees of government agencies, the stock exchange, and clearing houses) who hold unpublished price-sensitive information, which it would be reasonable to expect such public servants not to reveal except for the proper performance of their duties, and which they know to be unpublished price-sensitive information;

(4) tippees, who are persons who knowingly obtain information from persons connected with the company, or from public servants, and who know or have reasonable cause to believe that the information was held by the connected person or by the public servant by virtue of his position, and who know or have reasonable cause to believe that because of the position of the connected person or the public servant, it would be reasonable to expect that person not to reveal the information except for the proper performance of his duties.

It is also an offence for a person who would himself be prohibited by the Act from dealing, to counsel or procure another person to deal in his place, or to communicate information to another person if he knows or has reasonable cause to believe that that person or some other person will make use of the information for the purpose of dealing, or of counselling or procuring another person to deal on a recognised stock exchange in such securities.

The Act demands proof of *mens rea*. Proof of *mens rea* involves proving the subjective element of human intention, and is hard to establish. The standard of proof in criminal matters is beyond reasonable doubt. See *Attorney General's Reference (No. 1 of 1988)* [1989].

There are statutory exceptions to liability, chief among which is the defence that the trading was done for some reason other than making a profit or avoiding a loss, for example, a sale of shares brought about by the need to realise assets to meet creditors' claims. See *R.* v *Cross* [1991].

Cases of insider dealing can be tried either on indictment or by solemn procedure. On indictment, the penalty can be either an unlimited fine and/or imprisonment for up to seven years.

This Act does not affect the validity of contracts.

The Financial Services Act 1986 section 177–8 permits the Secretary of State for Trade and Industry to investigate insider dealing by appointing inspectors, who have power to require production of documents and attendance of persons. Failure to co-operate can result in fines or imprisonment, or in the case of persons authorised to carry on an investment business, restrictions on their powers to carry on such a business.

Since the introduction of statutory criminal liability for insider dealing, there have been few convictions, and very rarely have jail sentences been used.

3. Common law

Some types of insider dealing may constitute fraud at common law. Moreover, for an employee, or a director as a fiduciary, to provide a tip based on inside information would be a breach of duties of confidentiality, for which he would be liable to the company in damages, and may be liable to dismissal. For a director or employee himself to deal based on confidential price-sensitive information would constitute a breach of the duty to keep the company's interest separate from his own, and not to make a secret profit.

In many companies, senior employees and directors are bound by the terms of a written contract to seek permission before buying or selling the company's securities, and may be contractually prevented at certain times of year, such as the period before the announcement of half-yearly trading results, from dealing at all. Breach of these provisions may render the director or employee liable in damages or to dismissal. The Stock Exchange Rules for Admission of Securities to Listing contains a model code for securities transactions by directors of listed companies, which places restrictions on directors' freedom to deal in the securities of their own company to prevent insider dealing.

Attorney General's Reference (No. 1 of 1988)

[1989] AC 971; [1990] BCLC 172
House of Lords

The appellant had contemplated making a take-over offer for a publicly quoted company. He was informed by an employee of the company's merchant bankers that the company had agreed to another take-over offer, but that the information had not yet been made public, and was confidential price-sensitive information. The appellant proceeded to purchase 6,000 shares in the company, and made a substantial profit on the sale of shares in the take-over. The appellant was charged with offences under the Company Securities (Insider Dealing) Act 1985 (as a tippee). The jury acquitted the appellant on the ground that the Company Securities (Insider Dealing) Act 1985 required that the accused must have 'obtained' the information, and that the word 'obtained' involved an active element of having acquired the information by purpose and effort that was missing in this case, where the information had been unsolicited. The Attorney General referred the question to the Court of Appeal for an opinion on the meaning of the word 'obtained' in section 1(3) of the Company Securities (Insider Dealing) Act 1985. The Court of Appeal considered that the word 'obtained' could encompass the acquisition of information without any positive action. On the appellant's application the Court of Appeal referred the point to the House of Lords.

HELD that the word 'obtained' as used in sections 1(3) and 4(a) of the Act included the acquisition of the information without any positive effort, and a party could be guilty of the offence of insider dealing if he dealt in securities contrary to the Act, following the receipt of confidential price-sensitive information which was volunteered to him; Parliament must have intended the word 'obtained' in the Company Securities (Insider Dealing) Act 1985 to convey or include its secondary meaning of 'acquire' or 'get'. *Per* Lord Keith, Lord Ackner, Lord Oliver, and Lord Lowry: for a person to be guilty of 'knowingly' obtaining confidential information within the meaning of section 1(3)(a) and 2(1)(a) of the Act, a person must know from whom he obtains it.

LORD LOWRY. The answer depends on the meaning in context of the word "obtained". The first meaning in the *Oxford English Dictionary* is:

"To come into the possession or enjoyment of (something) by one's own effort, or by request; to procure or gain, as a result of purpose and effort: hence, generally, to acquire, get."

The primary meaning of "obtain", which stems from the Latin, is consistent, and consistent only, with the appellant's case; but the words following the colon and commencing "hence generally" clearly denote a *general* meaning *derived* from the primary meaning: the words "acquire" and "get" unaccompanied by the adverb or adverbial phrase, are wide enough to cover both the primary meaning and the secondary meaning of coming into possession of a thing without effort on one's own part.

The appellant relies on the principle that any ambiguity in a penal statute should be resolved in favour of the defence (see *Tuck & Sons* v. *Priester* (1887) 19 QBD 629 at 368 *per* Lord Esher MR) and says that the statute is, at best from the Crown's point of view, ambiguous.

. . . The next step, therefore, is to decide whether Parliament must have intended the word "obtained" to convey and include its secondary or general meaning. If so, the offence is made out; if, however, one cannot be satisfied of that, then the ambiguity remains and the *Tuck & Sons* v. *Priester* principle compels your Lordships to adopt the primary or narrow meaning.

The following points assist the Crown.

(1) The offence is dealing on a stock exchange in securities of a company in defined circumstances. It can be committed by a primary insider or by a secondary insider who has knowingly obtained information (directly or indirectly) from a primary insider. Whether the secondary insider solicited the information or merely received it does not increase or diminish the undesirability of his making use of it or the ultimate effect on the other party to his dealing.

(2) It is permissible to look at circumstances preceding the legislation in order to see what was considered to be the mischief in need of a remedy. . . . I draw attention to paragraph 22 of the White Paper entitled *The Conduct of Company Directors* (Cmnd 7037 (1977)):

> "Insider dealing is understood broadly to cover situations where a person buys or sells securities when he, but not the other party to the transaction, is in possession of confidential information which affects the value to be placed on those

securities. Furthermore the confidential information in question will generally be in his possession because of some connection which he has with the company whose securities are to be dealt in (e.g. he may be a director, employee or professional adviser of the company) or because someone in such a position has provided him, directly or indirectly, with the information. Public confidence in directors and others closely associated with companies requires that such people should not use insider information to further their own interests. Furthermore, if they were to do so, they would frequently be in breach of their obligations to the companies, and could be held to be taking an unfair advantage of the people with whom they were dealing.''

This tends to show that the mischief consists of dealing in securities while in possession of the confidential information.

(3) A primary insider is forbidden to use any information of the specified description. One may properly ask why a secondary insider should be prohibited *only* from using part of the information which may come to his hands, namely that which he has procured by his own efforts: the procurement is not the guilty act . . .

(4) The object of the legislation must be partially defeated if the narrow meaning of ''obtained'' is adopted.

(5) That meaning would create a need to make fine distinctions, which will not arise if the wider meaning prevails . . .

At first I thought that the word ''knowingly'' might further support the Crown's interpretation, but I accept as correct the explanation of counsel for the appellant that its use in sections 1(3)(a) and 2(1)(a) denotes that, to be guilty, the user of the confidential information has to know from whom he has obtained it.

Against these points the appellant advanced arguments which it is necessary to take account of before reaching a conclusion. They were as follows.

(1) ''Obtain'' is used in its primary sense in the statutory provisions which were considered in cases like *Fisher* v. *Raven* [1963] 2 All ER 389, [1964] AC 210 and *R.* v. *Hayat* (1976) 63 Cr App R 181 and also in section 15 of the Theft Act 1968. . . . More potent, though less specific, is counsel's observation that, whenever a

criminal statute uses the word "obtain", it uses that word in the primary sense. The reason for this, however, is not hard to understand.

(2) Relying on what he called a family relationship between the 1985 Act and the Insolvency Act 1986, counsel pointed to the word "obtains" used in its primary meaning in section 360 of the 1986 Act which, as sec. 155 of the Bankruptcy Act 1914, was considered in *Fisher* v. *Raven* [1963] 2 All ER 389, [1964] AC 210. But the word "obtains" and "obtained" are used in different contexts with a difference, I would suggest, in meaning which the "relationship" is powerless to annul.

(3) By reference to Lord Diplock's test in *Black-Clawson's* case [1975] 1 All ER 810 at 836, [1975] AC 591 at 638 of "what the words in the statute would be reasonably understood to mean by those whose conduct it regulates", it was suggested that someone in the position of a secondary insider would (particularly if he consulted a dictionary) feel safe in using confidential information which he had acquired unsolicited from a forbidden source. With respect, I feel that it could as easily be asserted that someone in that position would feel far from safe, particularly if his dictionary contained the words "hence, generally, to acquire, get".

(4) It was further submitted that words ought to be given their natural and ordinary meaning . . . In this case the choice is between the primary meaning and the secondary but correct and acceptable meaning.

(5) The appellants' next argument was based on paragraph 14 of his printed case:

> "Even if the Attorney General is right to suggest that the word 'obtained' is capable of meaning no more than 'has', the rules of construction still require the word to be given its natural and ordinary meaning where it appears in section 1 of the Act."

This point relies on the words used in the reference "who has, from another, information". But the question of law for your Lordships would still have been the same if the reference had said "who has received from another information". It is the Act, and not the reference, which has to be construed.

(6) Finally, by reference to the change of wording from "information which . . . he holds" in sections 1(1) and (2) to "information which he knowingly obtained" in section 1(3), it has been submitted that, unless the word "obtained" connotes effort on the part of the individual concerned, it adds nothing to the requirement of having or holding information which applies in the case of the earlier subsections. I cannot accept this reasoning; the addition of the relative clause ("which he knowingly obtained" etc.) in section 1(3) is due to the need to describe the forbidden *source* from which a secondary insider must have obtained the information. The *grammatical* construction of section 1(3)(a) is equally consistent with both meanings of the word "obtained". Therefore this argument does not help the appellant.

Having carefully weighed the points on either side, and not forgetting that we are dealing with a penal statute, I am, in the words of Lord Reid in *DPP* v. *Ottewell* [1968] 3 All ER 153 at 157, [1970] AC 642 at 649, satisfied that the wider meaning is the meaning which Parliament must have intended the word "obtained" to have in this Act and that, accordingly, there is no room for the kind of ambiguity on which the appellant has attempted to rely.

Therefore I would answer the questions posed by the reference in the same way as the Court of Appeal.

R. v. Cross

[1991] BCLC 125

Court of Appeal, Criminal Division

Cross appealed against conviction and sentence, following a conviction on a charge of insider dealing contrary to the Company Securities (Insider Dealing) Act 1985. He had been fined £7,000. The facts were that Cross had been the managing director of a company, Wordplex, and a participant in the company's share option scheme. He had also taken part in discussions at board meetings on a rights issue and a placing of shares, and during these discussions the subscription price and the effect on the share price of the company were discussed. The chairman had stated at the board meetings that these were price-sensitive matters. Cross left Wordplex, and requested that one-third of the options which had vested in him be allotted to him.

The company secretary advised Cross's solicitor in writing of the law on insider dealing in relation to those shares. On the same day as the secretary wrote that letter, Cross sold his shares. Cross alleged that it was a term of the share option scheme that the shares had to be sold within a limited period, otherwise he understood that the right to exercise the options would be lost. Once the proposals for the rights issue and placing were made public, the share price dropped below the level at which Cross had sold his shares. The company thereafter rejected the proposals and the company was taken over, causing the price to rise again. Cross also alleged that he had been shut out of discussions and did not know very much about the proposals. In any event, he alleged that any price-sensitive information which he did have was not all adverse. Cross also sought to rely on the statutory defence in section 3(1) that the dealing was not done with a view of making a profit or avoiding a loss, because he alleged that the dealing had taken place because he had thought he had to deal within thirty days.

HELD (1) that where the defence under section 3(1) is pleaded, the burden of proof is on the accused to establish that he falls within the defence; and (2) the trial judge had misdirected the jury. The appeal was accordingly allowed and the conviction quashed.

McCOWAN, L.J. Section 3(1) in so far as it is relevant, reads:

"Sections 1 and 2 do not prohibit an individual by reason of his having any information from:

(a) doing any particular thing otherwise than with a view to the making of a profit or the avoidance of a loss (whether for himself or another person) by the use of that information;

(b) entering into a transaction in the course of the exercise in good faith of his functions as liquidator, receiver or trustee in bankruptcy; or

(c) doing any particular thing if the information:
(i) was obtained by him in the course of a business of a jobber in which he was engaged or employed, and
(ii) was of a description which it would be reasonable to expect him to obtain in the ordinary course of that business, and he does that thing in good faith in the course of that business."

The prosecution plainly have to prove all the matters in section 1(1) and not least (c) therein. On the face of it there is an offence established if the prosecution prove those matters, and the burden then shifts to the defence to prove, on the balance of probabilities, any defence provided by section 3(1). Moreover, this would seem appropriate since the matters referred to in section 3(1) are likely to be peculiarly within the defendant's own knowledge. There is no authority upon the point, but Mr Langdale (counsel for the defendant) has conceded that all the existing commentary is against him. However, Mr Langdale relies on the opening words of section 1(1), namely, "Subject to section 3" and the opening words of section 3(1), namely, "Sections 1 and 2 do not prohibit an individual by reason of his having any information . . ."

We see the force of that, but on the other hand we can see no reason why, if the intention was that the prosecution would have to disprove the matters in section 3(1)(a) in order to establish their case, section 1(1) could not have contained a paragraph (d) reading "he used that information with a view to the making of a profit or the avoidance of a loss". Mr Langdale accepts that it could have been done that way and even that it should and would have been done that way were it not for poor drafting.

What then of paragraphs (b) and (c) of section 3(1)? Must the prosecution refer in the indictment to the matters in (b) and (c) and call evidence as part of their case to disprove them? Mr Langdale does not go that far. He submits that a proper construction of section 3(1) is that (b) and (c) are defences but (a) is not. It would indeed be very strange drafting if (b) and (c) are defences to be established by the defence but (a) is not, and yet they are lumped together in section 3(1).

However, Mr Langdale says that (a) is in a category of its own because it reflects the mischief at which the legislation is aimed. To discover that mischief he relies on the decision of the House of Lords in *Attorney General's Reference (No. 1 of 1988)* (1989) 88 Cr App R 191, [1989] AC 971 as establishing that it is permissible to look at the relevant White Paper which preceded the Act in order to discover the mischief at which the Act was aimed. In this case the White Paper is The Conduct of Company Directors presented to Parliament in November 1977. Mr Langdale relies on two passages in it which he says show that the mischief at which the Act is aimed is, in fact, to be found in paragraph (a) of section 3 (1).

The first of those passages is in paragraph 22 and reads:

"Public confidence in directors and others closely associated with companies requires that such people should not use inside information to further their own interests."

The second passage is in paragraph 23 and reads:

"The Government intends to establish as soon as possible that insider dealing is an offence and to create penalties which will be sufficient in most cases to deter those who are tempted to use inside information for their own personal gain."

If, however, we are to be influenced by this perusal, coupled with the argument that, most unfortunately, the draftsman of the Act got it wrong, we do not see how we can be expected to shut our eyes to paragraph 25 of the White Paper which reads:

"The Government's principal proposal is that it shall be a criminal offence for an insider to deal on the market in quoted securities in certain circumstances where he has inside information. We intend, however, that this offence should not be one of absolute liability. The prosecution will need to show that the insider knew or had reasonable grounds to believe that the information was not generally known and was price sensitive and that he dealt nevertheless. Also, it will be possible for a person to offer as a defence that this purpose in dealing was not to make a profit or avoid a loss by the use of his inside information."

From this it is apparent that the draftsman of the Act, far from getting it wrong, did exactly as he was instructed. We cannot accept Mr Langdale's argument on the interpretation of the Act. In our judgment the contents of section 3(1)(a) are a matter of defence to be established by a defendant.

8. The directors

Summary

1. Sources of the law

The law on directors and directors' duties is partly statutory—the
Companies Act 1985 and the Company Directors Disqualification Act
1986—and partly contained in case law.

2. The role of the director

Directors are the managers of the company. Unless statute or the
constitution of the company demands that particular decisions must be
made by the members, generally powers are in the hands of the
directors. Certain powers are by statute always given to the members,
including the power to remove the directors by ordinary resolution on
special notice under sections 303 and 304 of the Companies Act 1985,
and the power to alter the articles of association by special resolution
under section 9 of the Companies Act 1985.

Directors act collectively. They normally act by board resolutions,
which are generally simple majority resolutions, although the board
may give a director or a committee of directors express authority to
make particular decisions or contracts if the articles allow: see Table A
regulation 72.

Directors are officers of the company. Directors may also be
employees of the company if they work for it in some capacity other
than as director, e.g. as production manager, management accountant,
or sales manager: see *Anderson* v. *James Sutherland (Peterhead) Ltd.*
1941. As employees they will be entitled to wages or a salary, whereas
as directors they may be entitled to a fee, but only if it is provided for
in the articles of association. Generally, the articles of association
require remuneration to be approved by the general meeting: see Table
A regulation 82; and *In re Duomatic Ltd.* [1969]. Directors who are
also employees are known as executive directors, whereas those who

are not, are non-executive directors.

Managing directors may be appointed by the board of directors provided the articles of association allow: see Table A regulation 72; and *Southern Foundries (1926) Ltd.* v. *Shirlaw* [1940]. A managing director holds delegated power from the directors to manage the company. Unlike a director acting alone, a managing director has apparent authority to make contracts alone in the name of the company: see *Freeman & Lockyer* v. *Buckhurst Park Properties (Mangal) Ltd.* [1964]; and **Allison* v. *Scotia Motor and Engineering Co. Ltd.* 1906.

3. Appointment, removal and disqualification of directors

The first directors are appointed by the promoters and may be named in the articles of association. Notwithstanding the above, the persons named in the statement of first directors and secretary which is sent to Companies House are deemed to have been appointed the first directors and secretary: section 13 of the Companies Act 1985. The articles may provide for the whole board to stand down at the first annual general meeting when they will all be eligible for re-election. Thereafter, the articles may provide for one-third of the directors to retire each year by rotation. Often the articles will allow a casual vacancy to be filled by the board itself, on the basis that the appointee stands down at the next annual general meeting and can offer himself for re-election: see Table A regulations 73–80.

Whatever the articles may provide to the contrary, a director can always be removed from office by ordinary resolution on special notice: sections 303 and 304 of the Companies Act 1985. However, it is possible for the articles of association to provide weighted voting in the case of the removal of a director, and this can in effect render a director irremovable: see *Bushell* v. *Faith* [1970].

Directors may be disqualified from office under statute and under the articles of association. The Company Directors Disqualification Act 1986 provides various grounds on which a court can disqualify a director from office for up to fifteen years. The grounds include being an unfit person to take part in the management of a company, which is established by evidence that the company is insolvent, and that the director's conduct in relation to that or other companies, makes him unfit to be a director of a company: see *Re T & D Services (Timber Preservation & Damp Proofing Contractors) Ltd.* [1990]; and *Re Sevenoaks Stationers (Retail) Ltd.* [1990]. The 1986 Act provides for a public register of disqualification orders. The Companies Act 1985 also contains a disqualification on age grounds for directors of public companies: under section 293, a director aged over seventy cannot be appointed unless the articles specifically permit, or there has been an ordinary resolution stating his age, passed on special notice. The articles of association may also contain disqualifications.

4. Directors' duties

These are governed partly by statute, partly by the memorandum and articles of association of the company, and partly by case law. The principal statutory restrictions are imposed by sections 311–47 of the Companies Act 1985, which place obligations of fair dealing on directors, including restrictions on the making of loans to directors, and sections 213 and 214 of the Insolvency Act 1986. The articles of association may impose duties on directors: for example, Table A regulation 85 permits self-dealing by a director, but obliges him to disclose his interest to the board, and regulation 94 disqualifies a director with a self-interest from voting. The common law as modified by the statutory provisions mentioned above imposes the following fiduciary duties on directors:

* to act *bona fide* in the interests of the company as a whole: see *Lee* v. *Chou Wen Hsien* [1985]; and **Dawson International plc* v. *Coats Patons plc* 1989.

* to use power for a proper purpose: *Howard Smith Ltd.* v. *Ampol Petroleum Ltd.* [1974]; and *Rolled Steel Products (Holdings) Ltd.* v. *British Steel Corporation* [1986].

* as custodian of company assets, not to misapply them: *Cook* v. *Deeks* [1916].

* not to permit a conflict of interest to arise: **Aberdeen Railway Co.* v. *Blaikie Bros.* (1854); *Guinness plc* v. *Saunders and another* [1990]; *Movitex Ltd.* v. *Bulfield* (1986); and *Lee Panavision Ltd.* v. *Lee Lighting Ltd.* [1992].

* not to make a secret profit: *Regal (Hastings) Ltd.* v. *Gulliver* [1942].

There is also a duty on directors to take reasonable care in carrying out their duties: for the extent of this duty see *In re City Equitable Fire Insurance Co. Ltd.* [1925]; *Dorchester Finance Co. Ltd* v. *Stebbing* [1989]; and *Norman and another* v. *Theodore Goddard (a firm) and others* [1991]. These fiduciary duties and duties of care are owed to the company collectively and not to individual shareholders. Section 309 Companies Act 1985 also imposes a fiduciary duty on the directors to have regard to the interests of the employees.

5. Legal consequences of breach of duty and relief of liability therefor

If directors act in breach of their statutory, constitutional or common law fiduciary duties, any resulting contract may be voidable: see *Rolled Steel Products (Holdings) Ltd.* v. *British Steel Corporation* [1986]. The directors will also be personally liable to account for any secret profit, and may be sued for damages in respect of any resulting harm to the company. However, it may be that the directors will be relieved of potential liability by ratification by the members by resolution in general meeting: see *Hogg* v. *Cramphorn Ltd.* [1967]. In addition, under section 727 of the Companies Act 1985, directors can be relieved from liability by a court if it appears that they have acted honestly and reasonably and ought in the circumstances to be excused: see *Multinational Gas and Petrochemical Co.* v. *Multinational Gas and Petrochemical Services Ltd.* [1983]; and *In re Duomatic Ltd.* [1969]. Provisions in the articles of association or in a separate contract exempting directors from liability for breach of duty are void, with the exception that companies are now allowed to hold insurance against liability for breach of duty, and are allowed to indemnify directors against liability in defending legal proceedings in which they are given judgment or are acquitted, or where a court relieves them of liability: section 310 of the Companies Act 1985.

Directors' breach of fiduciary duty may also be excused by ratification (adoption) by the company in general meeting. Transactions which are *ultra vires* the memorandum of association may now be ratified by special resolution: section 35 of the Companies Act 1985. Transactions which are *intra vires* the memorandum or articles may generally be ratified unless they are in breach of the law (see *Aveling Barford Ltd.* v. *Perion Ltd.* [1989]), or the directors are acting in bad faith, or are committing a fraud on the minority (see *Cook* v. *Deeks* [1916]).

★ **Anderson v. James Sutherland (Peterhead) Ltd. and others**
1941 SC 203
Court of Session

The articles of association of a company allowed the directors to appoint a managing director, and granted them power of removal. Another provision of the articles stated that if an employee of the company were dismissed for misconduct, the directors could resolve that such a person should cease to be eligible to hold shares in the company, and that any shares he held must be offered to other members. The managing director was convicted of assault on one of the directors after firing his revolver at the director and injuring him at a board meeting. The directors then passed a resolution that the pursuer be dismissed from the post of managing director. They then sought to apply the rule of the articles to strip the ex-managing director of his shareholding. The pursuer disputed the right of the company to do this, on the grounds that he had been appointed managing director and, within the meaning of the articles, could not be removed, on the basis that the provision for removal in the articles related to removal of a director and not a managing director. The pursuer raised an action contesting the validity of the resolution to remove him from his managing directorship, and contending that the resolution depriving him of his shareholding was *ultra vires* in that the provision related to employees, and did not apply to a managing director, who was not employed by the company. In the Outer House, Lord Stevenson agreed that a managing director is not employed by the company, and granted decree in favour of the pursuer. The defenders appealed to the Inner House of the Court of Session.

HELD that in the absence of an indication to the contrary from other articles of association, the managing director was employed by the company.

LORD PRESIDENT (NORMAND). The functions of a director and manager are not identical . . . In my opinion, therefore, a managing director has two functions and two capacities. *Qua* managing director he is a party to a contract with the company, and this contract is a contract of employment; more specifically I am of opinion that it is a contract of service and not a contract for services. There is nothing anomalous in this; indeed, it is a commonplace of law that the same individual may have two or more capacities, each including special rights and duties in relation to the same thing or matter or in relation to the same persons.

. . . I turn now to the articles. In construing them I think it is important to bear in mind that slight indications of intention have been held sufficient to show that a managing director is not intended to be included among ''employees'' as used in the articles. I begin with the expression ''employed by the company in any capacity''. That expression seems to me to indicate a plain intention that ''employee'' should be given a wide rather than a restricted meaning. Counsel for the respondent, desiring to limit ''employee'' to workmen and other subordinate employees, was unable to give any value to the words ''in any capacity''. I think they should neither be ignored nor read in any other than their natural sense. So read they seem to me, not only apt, but deliberately intended, to include a managing director.

In re Duomatic Ltd.

[1969] 2 Ch 365; [1969] 1 All ER 161; [1969] 2 WLR 114

Chancery Division

An action was brought by the liquidator of Duomatic Ltd. for recovery of salaries paid to two of the directors Elvins (E.) and Hanly (H.), (on the grounds that the salaries had not been approved by the company in general meeting), and for repayment of compensation of £4,000 paid to H. for loss of office. Initially the entire voting share capital was held by the three directors of Duomatic Ltd. In addition, there were non-voting preference shares, which were held by a Dutch company. Subsequently, 25,000 additional ordinary shares were issued. Two of the directors became critical of the way H. performed his duties. Although he could have been voted off the board, the remaining directors instead paid him £4,000 to leave the company, because he threatened to sue the company for wrongful dismissal. Thereafter he ceased to hold shares, and various other shareholders later joined the company. The company had articles of association which required directors' remuneration to be decided by the company in general meeting. None of the directors had written service contracts. Instead, they drew sums according to their personal needs which were entered as 'directors' salaries' in the accounts, without the payments being approved by the shareholders.

HELD that where all the shareholders with a right to attend and vote at a meeting had agreed to some matter which could have been decided at a general meeting, the assent was as binding as if it had been decided at a general meeting. Accordingly, the remuneration payments to the directors were valid, except for one payment to E. which had not been agreed by the parties. Because the preference shareholders had no vote, it did not matter that they were not aware of the payments. *In re Express Engineering Works Ltd.* [1920] 1 Ch 446 CA was applied. In relation to the compensation payment for loss of office paid to H., it was held that since section 191 of the Companies Act 1948 (now section 312 of the Companies Act 1985) required disclosure to and approval by the members of the company, and since disclosure had not been made to the preference shareholders, the payment was *ultra vires*, and E. and H. were liable for misappropriation of company funds; since legal advice had not been sought by E. he did not qualify to be excused liability under section 448 of the Companies Act 1948 (now section 727 Companies Act 1985), and therefore E. and H. were jointly and severally liable to repay the £4,000 to the liquidator with interest.

BUCKLEY, J. . . . I proceed upon the basis that where it can be shown that all shareholders who have a right to attend and vote at a general meeting of the company assent to some matter which a general meeting of the company could carry into effect, that assent is as binding as a resolution in general meeting would be. The preference shareholder, having shares which conferred upon him no right to receive notice of or to attend and vote at a general meeting of the company, could be in no worse a position if the matter were dealt with informally by agreement between all the shareholders having voting rights than he would be if the shareholders met together in a duly constituted general meeting.

Accordingly, the evidence that I have heard leads to the conclusion that the drawings by Mr Elvins and Mr Hanly during the accounting year ending April 30 1963, which are covered by the item of directors' salaries £15,661 1s. 8d. in the profit and loss account cannot now be disturbed.

The position for the year ending on April 30, 1964, is different: the draft accounts were at no time finally agreed, and Mr McCulloch [counsel for Mr Elvins] does not dispute that unless Mr Elvins can be excused under section 448 of the Act of 1948, he is liable to repay to the liquidator the sum of £9,000 which is shown in the profit and loss account for that year as being his salary. In that respect he relies on the power conferred on the court by section 448 to excuse a director where he has acted honestly and reasonably and in circumstances in which he ought to be excused.

. . . The conclusion I reach, therefore, with regard to the drawings after April 30, 1964, is that Mr Elvins is liable to repay to the liquidator only such excess as there may be over what he would have been entitled to draw on the basis of the £60-a-week arrangement. That, I take it, would be the amount which he could draw, calculated at £60 a week, less the appropriate sum for income tax having regard to his PAYE liability.

With regard to the compensation for loss of office, the £4,000 paid to Mr Hanly, the requirements of section 191 of the Companies Act 1948, were not complied with. That section provides:

> "It shall not be lawful for a company to make to any director of the company any payment by way of compensation for loss of office, or as consideration for or in connection with his retirement from office, without particulars with respect to the proposed payment (including the amount thereof) being disclosed to members of the company and the proposal being approved by the company."

That section must, I think, require disclosure to all members of the company, and it must require disclosure while the payment is still a proposed payment, that is to say, before the payment is made; and it further requires that the proposal be approved by the company, which must, I think, mean by the company in general meeting.

In the present case it is clear that no particulars of this payment of £4,000 were, before the date that the payment was made, given to all the members of the company, for no such disclosure was at any time made to the preference shareholder. There would, I think, be good reason for making such disclosure to him, notwithstanding that he would have no right to attend at any general meeting convened for the purpose of approving the payment, because although he was not, by virtue of his preference shareholding, entitled to receive notice of general meetings or attend and vote at them, he might nevertheless wish to make his views known to those who would attend and vote at the general meeting, and therefore notice to him of the proposal to make the payment might well be a matter of some importance to him and of some ultimate consequence in the affairs of the company. It follows that the payment was an *ultra vires* payment, for it was a payment which the section says it was not lawful for the company to make. The directors responsible for making it are liable in respect of it on the grounds of misapplication of the company's funds unless they ought to be excused under section 448. The section enables the court to grant relief where three circumstances are shown to exist. First of all the position must be such that the person to be excused is shown to have acted honestly; secondly, he must he shown to have acted reasonably; and thirdly, it must be shown that, having regard to all the circumstances of the case, he ought fairly to be excused.

. . . In my judgment a director of a company dealing with a matter of this kind who does not seek any legal advice at all but elects to deal with the matter himself without a proper exploration of the considerations which contribute, or ought to contribute, to a decision as to what should be done on the company's behalf, cannot be said to act reasonably. In my judgment Mr Elvins did not act reasonably in this respect. He failed to take those steps which, as a director of the company, he should have taken before making the bargain which he made with Mr Hanly. It may be that, after considering legal advice, and any other advice that he might have sought, he still would have thought it desirable to pay Mr Hanly something to get rid of him with as little friction as possible, but it does not follow that the sum which he would have paid him would have been £4,000. The question which I have to ask myself is whether, in acting in the way in which he did, Mr Elvins acted reasonably. I do not think that he was acting in the way in which a man of affairs dealing with his own affairs with reasonable care and circumspection could reasonably be expected to act in such a case, for I think that any such imaginary character would take pains to find out all the relevant circumstances, many of which in this case depended upon some knowledge of the law, and ought to have encouraged Mr Elvins to seek the assistance of a legal adviser. Moreover, it was Mr Elvins' failure to seek legal advice that resulted in this payment being made in contravention of section 191 of the Act and constituted it an *ultra vires* payment which the company could not lawfully make. In these circumstances I do not think that the provisions of section 448 avail Mr Elvins in respect of this sum.

Southern Foundries (1926) Ltd v. Shirlaw

[1940] AC 701; [1940] 2 All ER 445
House of Lords
One of the directors of Southern Foundries (the respondent), was appointed managing director for ten years. A term of the articles of

association provided that a managing director could, subject to the provisions of the contract, be removed in the same way as a director, and that if he ceased to be a director he would simultaneously cease to be managing director. All the shares in Southern Foundries were acquired by Federated Foundries Ltd. New articles of association were adopted by Southern Foundries following the takeover. The new articles of association empowered Federated Foundries to remove any director of Southern Foundries by a written instrument subscribed by two directors and the secretary. The articles also stated that if the managing director ceased to hold the office of director, he would cease also to hold the office of managing director. After the acquisition of Southern Foundries by Federated Foundries, negotiations took place with the respondent to attempt to vary the terms of his appointment, but these were unsuccessful. The respondent was removed from office as director by written instrument as provided in the articles of association, and Southern Foundries thereupon treated him as having ceased to hold office as managing director also. The respondent commenced legal proceedings for damages against Southern Foundries for wrongful repudiation of the contract, and against Federated Foundries for wrongfully procuring the breach of contract. The trial judge decided in favour of the respondent, and awarded £12,000 damages. The award was upheld by the Court of Appeal. Southern Foundries appealed to the House of Lords.

HELD (Viscount Maugham and Lord Romer dissenting) that there was an implied term in the contract that the respondent should not be removed from his directorship for ten years and, therefore, damages should be awarded.

LORD ATKIN. The office of director involves contractual arrangements between the director and the company. If the company removes the director it puts an end to the contract: and indeed the contract relations cannot be determined unless by events stipulated for in the contract, by operation of law, or by the will of the two parties. The altered article 8 which gives power to the Federated Foundries Ltd., to remove from office any director of the company is, when analysed, a power to the Federated to terminate a contract between the Southern and its director. It is an act which binds the Southern as against its promisee; and if a wrong to the respondent be done by the Southern it surely must be a wrong to the respondent if done by the Federated who derive their power to do the act from the Southern only.

. . . I do not think that it could be said that the Southern committed any breach by adopting the new articles. But when the Federated acted upon the power conferred upon them in the new articles they bound the Southern if they acted in such a way that action by the Southern on the same articles would be a breach. It is not a question of agency but of acting under powers conferred by contract to interfere with a contract between the party granting the power and a third person. For these reasons I am of opinion that this appeal should be dismissed with costs.

LORD WRIGHT.   . . . No one, individual or company, can be compelled against his or her will, to employ a man, though, if the contract is broken, damages will have to be paid. When the respondent was appointed managing director for ten years, the contract necessarily meant that the appellant company would not without good cause remove him from his directorship during that period, because if they did they would *ipso facto* terminate his employment. There is no question of implying a term that the appellant company would not remove the respondent from his directorship. He could not serve for the agreed term of ten years unless the appellant company continued him in his office.

LORD PORTER.   . . . But though it is true that ultimately the Southern company could not prevent the Federated company from removing the respondent from his directorship, the act of removal is not, I think, solely the act of the Federated company. Rather, it is the combined act of both, an act impossible to the latter but for the act of the former and not resulting in a breach of contract until the power of dismissal given by the former was acted on by the latter. To say that the Southern company could have helped themselves if they removed the respondent from his directorship but could not do so where they authorised the removal by another would seem to me to treat what is at best a technicality as if it were the substance of the case. It is the Southern company's act which has resulted in the respondent's removal and none the less so though his dismissal required two acts and not one for its accomplishment.

I would confirm the judgment of the Court of Appeal.

Freeman & Lockyer v. Buckhurst Park Properties (Mangal) Ltd. and another

[1964] 2 QB 480; [1964] 1 All ER 630; [1964] 2 WLR 618

Court of Appeal

Kapoor and Hoon formed the defendant company for the purpose of purchasing and reselling a large estate. Kapoor was the chief instigator of the venture. Kapoor and Hoon and a nominee of each were appointed the directors of the company. The articles of association contained power to appoint a managing director, but none was ever appointed. Kapoor instructed a firm of architects to apply for planning permission for developments to the estate. He instructed them to make the application in his own name as owner rather than in the name of the company. The work was carried out but the defendant company refused to pay on the ground that the debt was not a company debt but was due personally by Kapoor since he had no authority as agent to make the contract with the architects. The architects raised an action against the defendant company and Kapoor. The county court judge held that despite Kapoor's lack of express authority, he had nevertheless been held out to the architects as having authority and, therefore, the defendant company was liable to meet the account. The defendant company appealed to the Court of Appeal.

HELD that although Kapoor had no actual authority, he did have ostensible authority, because he had been allowed to act as if he were a managing director to the knowledge of the rest of the board, and the act of engaging a firm of architects to do some work in connection with the company's estate was within the normal ambit of the authority of a managing director. Therefore the plaintiffs did not have to be on their enquiry as to the extent of Kapoor's authority. The appeal was dismissed.

WILLMER, L.J. . . . The plaintiffs contended (1) that on the true inference from all the facts Kapoor had actual authority to engage the plaintiffs on behalf of the defendant company; alternatively, (2) that Kapoor was held out by the defendant company as having ostensible authority, so that the latter is estopped from denying responsibility for his acts. . . . The judge found that Kapoor, although never appointed as managing director, had throughout been acting as such in employing agents and taking other steps to find a purchaser, and that this was well known to the board. In the light of this finding he gave judgment in favour of the plaintiffs . . . I take this to be a finding, not that Kapoor had actual authority to employ the plaintiffs, but that in so doing he was acting within the scope of his ostensible authority.

In this court the plaintiffs have adhered to their contention that Kapoor had actual authority to employ the plaintiffs. But I do not think that this view can be supported. Actual authority might, of course, be either express—for example, if Kapoor were specifically authorised to engage the plaintiffs—or it might be implied—for example, if Kapoor had been appointed to some office which carried with it authority to make such a contract on behalf of the defendant company. There is certainly no resolution of the board specifically authorising Kapoor to engage the plaintiffs. The articles of association, however, incorporate regulations 102 and 107 of Table A, Part I. By the former, directors may delegate any of their powers to a committee of one. By the latter, they may appoint one of their body to the office of managing director. But there was never any resolution of the board whereby the directors here purported to exercise either of these powers. Nor can I find any trace of any resolution in writing signed by all the directors such as would be validated by regulation 106 to the same extent as a resolution passed at a board meeting. In all the mass of documents which have been produced I can find no record in writing of Kapoor ever being appointed to the office which would carry with it authority to engage the plaintiffs. In these circumstances I think it is hopeless to contend that Kapoor was ever clothed with actual authority to do what he did.

The real question to be determined is whether the judge was right in finding that Kapoor has ostensible authority to engage the plaintiffs. This is partly a question of fact and partly one of law. So far as the facts are concerned, Mr Holdsworth on behalf of the defendant company has attacked the judge's finding that Kapoor acted throughout as managing director to the knowledge of the board. He has argued that there is no evidence to support this finding. I find myself unable to accept this submission. In my judgment there was abundant evidence; indeed, when the realities of the case are examined, I think it is the only inference that could properly be drawn.

. . . In the present case, the plaintiffs do not have to rely on the articles of association of the defendant company in order to establish their claim. . . . The plaintiffs here rely on the fact that Kapoor, to the knowledge of the defendant company's board, was acting throughout as managing director, and was therefore held out by the board as such. The plaintiffs accordingly do not have to enquire whether he was properly appointed. It is sufficient for them that under the articles there was in fact power to appoint him as such.

DIPLOCK, L.J. It is necessary at the outset to distinguish between an "actual" authority of an agent on the one hand, and an "apparent" or "ostensible" authority on the other. Actual authority and apparent authority are quite independent of one another. Generally they co-exist and coincide, but either may exist without the other and their respective scopes may be different. As I shall endeavour to show, it is upon the apparent authority of the agent that the contractor normally relies in the ordinary course of business when entering into contracts.

An "actual" authority is a legal relationship between principal and agent created by a consensual agreement to which they alone are parties. Its scope is to be ascertained by applying ordinary principles of construction of contracts, including any proper implications from the express words used, the usages of the trade, or the course of business between the parties. To this agreement the contractor is a stranger; he may be totally ignorant of the existence of any authority on the part of the agent. Nevertheless, if the agent does enter into a contract pursuant to the "actual" authority, it does create contractual rights and liabilities between the principal and the contractor. It may be that the rule relating to "undisclosed principals", which is peculiar to English law, can be rationalised as avoiding circuity of action, for the principal could in equity compel the agent to lend his name in an action to enforce the contract against the contractor, and would at common law be liable to indemnify the agent in respect of the performance of the obligations assumed by the agent under the contract.

An "apparent" or "ostensible" authority, on the other hand, is a legal relationship between the principal and the contractor created by a representation, made by the principal to the contractor, intended to be and in fact acted upon by the contractor, that the agent has authority to enter on behalf of the principal into a contract of a kind within the scope of the "apparent" authority, so as to render the principal liable to perform any obligations imposed upon him by such a contract. To this relationship so created the agent is a stranger. He need not be (although he generally is) aware of the existence of the representation but he must not purport to make the agreement as a principal himself. The representation, when acted upon by the contractor by entering into a contract with the agent, operates as an estoppel, preventing the principal from asserting that he is not bound by the contract. It is irrelevant whether the agent had actual authority to enter into the contract.

In ordinary business dealings the contractor at the time of entering into the contract can in the nature of things hardly ever rely on the "actual" authority of the agent. His information as to the authority must be derived either from the principal or from the agent or from both, for they alone know what the agent's actual authority is. All that the contractor can know is what they tell him, which may or may not be true. In the ultimate analysis he relies either upon the representations of the principal, that is, apparent authority, or upon the representation of the agent, that is, warranty of authority.

The representation which creates "apparent" authority may take a variety of forms of which the commonest is representation by conduct, that is, by permitting the agent to act in some way in the conduct of the principal's business with other persons. By so doing the principal represents to anyone who becomes aware that the agent is so acting that the agent has authority to enter on behalf of the principal into contracts with other persons of the kind which an agent so acting in the conduct of his principal's business has usually "actual" authority to enter into.

. . . If the foregoing analysis of the relevant law is correct, it can be summarised by stating four conditions which must be fulfilled to entitle a contractor to enforce against a company a contract entered into on behalf of a company by an agent who had no actual authority to do so. It must be shown:

(1) that a representation that the agent had authority to enter on behalf of the company into a contract of the kind sought to be enforced was made to the contractor;

(2) that such representation was made by a person or persons who had "actual" authority to manage the business of the company either generally or in respect of those matters to which the contract relates;

(3) that he (the contractor) was induced by such representations to enter into the contract, that is, that he in fact relied upon it;

(4) that under the memorandum or articles of association the company was not deprived of the capacity either to enter into a contract of the kind sought to be enforced or to delegate authority to enter into a contract of that kind to the agent.

. . . In the present case the findings of fact by the county court judge are sufficient to satisfy the four conditions, and thus to establish that Kapoor had "apparent" authority to enter into contracts on behalf of the company for their services in connection with the sale of the company's property, including the obtaining of development permission with respect to its use. The judge found that the board knew that Kapoor had throughout been acting as managing director in employing agents and taking other steps to find a purchaser. They permitted him to do so, and by such conduct represented that he had authority to enter into contracts of a kind which a managing director or an executive director responsible for finding a purchaser would in the normal course be authorised to enter into on behalf of the company. Condition (1) was thus fulfilled. The articles of association conferred full powers of management on the board. Condition (2) was thus fulfilled. The plaintiffs, finding Kapoor acting in relation to the company's property as he was authorised by the board to act, were induced to believe that he was authorised by the company to enter into contracts on behalf of the company for their services in connection with the sale of the company's property, including the obtaining of development permission with respect to its use. Condition (3) was thus fulfilled. The articles of association, which contained powers for the board to delegate any of the functions of management to a managing director or to a single director, did not deprive the company of capacity to delegate authority to Kapoor, a director, to enter into contracts of that kind on behalf of the company. Condition (4) was thus fulfilled.

I think the judgment was right, and would dismiss the appeal.

★ Allison v. Scotia Motor and Engineering Co. Ltd.

1906 SLT (OH) 9

Court of Session

This was an action for damages for wrongful dismissal. Prior to the incorporation of the company, the pursuer had been approached by Wark (who became managing director following the incorporation of the company). The pursuer agreed to become works manager, subject to the contract being put into writing on the company's coming into existence. The pursuer claimed that the appointment was for five years. He began work on 29 May and the company was incorporated on 14 July. Wark wrote to the pursuer on 7 July engaging him as works manager, and signed as managing director. A further letter was sent out on 9 October after incorporation confirming the terms. Wark was not formally appointed managing director until 25 October. The company's business did not prosper, and the directors instructed Wark to dismiss the pursuer. This was admitted by the company to be wrongful dismissal. The company disputed that the contract had been agreed to run for five years, and contended that Wark was not managing director at the time of the appointment and therefore the appointment was invalid. The articles of association empowered the directors to appoint and, at their discretion, remove or suspend the company's servants. Article 94 empowered the directors to entrust to a managing director any of the directors' powers except the power to borrow and the power to make calls.

HELD that Wark did have authority to appoint the pursuer and damages were accordingly awarded.

LORD MACKENZIE. Wark was described as the managing director in the prospectus, and though it may be true that the pursuer cannot plead that he contracted on the basis of the prospectus, yet Wark's description in it is evidence of the fact that he was to hold the position of managing director when the company was formed. I think it is proved that the directors recognised Wark as, *de facto*, the managing director from the first. In that capacity he engaged not only the pursuer for a term of years, but also other employees viz: Shillinglaw, who was engaged for three years as an engineer, and Mohr, who was engaged also for three years, as traveller . . . The directors who gave evidence were aware that the pursuer had been engaged by Wark as works manager. The pursuer says that the directors came about the works from June onwards; that he was introduced to them as works manager, and that they talked to him about the business. There was no express delegation by minute of the Board of any of their powers to Wark, as managing director, under Article 94. In my opinion the question of whether there had been express delegation or not does not affect the rights of the pursuer. What Wark did in appointing him was not *ultra vires* under the articles of association. Wark might have been invested by the Board with power to enter into such an agreement with the pursuer. I do not think it matters whether the pursuer knew or not that there was such a provision in the articles of association as that contained in Article 94. In my opinion the defenders are bound by this engagement which was entered into with the pursuer on 9th October. The previous appointment on 7th July would not bind the company before its incorporation, unless it was adopted, and there is no evidence of that. In appointing the pursuer as works manager, Wark took it upon himself, with the knowledge of the directors, to act for the company.

NOTE

This case, like that of *Freeman & Lockyer* v. *Buckhurst Park Properties (Mangal) Ltd. and another* [1964], is based upon the principle of holding out in agency: Wark, although not a managing director at the time when he purported to appoint the pursuer as works manager, did so with the tacit approval of the board of directors. Therefore they lost the power to challenge the contract through their own conduct. It is not concerned with liability on pre-incorporation contracts, the contract being made post incorporation, through the medium of the managing director.

Bushell v. Faith

[1970] AC 1099; [1970] 1 All ER 53; [1970] 2 WLR 272
House of Lords

The entire share capital of a private company was held by a brother and two sisters who each held 100 £1 shares. The plaintiff and the defendant (sister and brother) acted as directors. The articles of association provided at article 9 that in the event of the removal of a director, any shares held by that director should carry three votes per share. The two sisters were dissatisfied with their brother's conduct as a director, and requisitioned an extraordinary general meeting to pass an ordinary resolution to remove their brother from office as a director (nowadays the relevant provisions are contained in sections 303 and 304 Companies Act 1985). On a poll they both voted in favour of the resolution and their brother voted against it. The parties disagreed as to the vote: the plaintiff, Mrs Bushell, contended that the resolution had been carried by 200 votes to 100, while the defendant contended that he should be entitled to the benefit of article 9, and claimed that the vote had been lost by the sisters by 300 votes to 200. The plaintiff claimed a declaration that the resolution had been validly passed and an injunction restraining the defendant from continuing to act as a director of the company. The High Court found in favour of the plaintiff, and awarded the injunction. The defendant appealed to the Court of Appeal which allowed the appeal. The plaintiff appealed to the House of Lords.

HELD by majority (Lord Morris of Borth-y-Gest dissenting), that article 9 was valid, despite an apparent conflict with the wording of the section (at that time section 184(1) of the Companies Act 1948, now section 303 of the Companies Act 1985), which permitted an ordinary resolution to be used by a company for removal of a director 'notwithstanding anything in its articles'. The reasoning was that Parliament by this provision had not attempted to fetter a company's right to attach whatever rights to shares that it wished, but was only seeking to provide that an ordinary resolution would be sufficient to remove a director.

LORD MORRIS OF BORTH-Y-GEST (dissenting). My Lords, it is provided by section 184(1) that a company may by ordinary resolution remove a director before the expiration of his period of office. The company may do so notwithstanding anything to the contrary in its articles. So, if an article provided that a director was irremovable, he could nevertheless be removed if an ordinary resolution to that effect was passed. So also, if an article provided that a director could only be removed by a resolution greater than a simple majority, he would nevertheless be removed if a resolution was passed by a simple majority.

Some shares may, however, carry greater voting power than others. On a resolution to remove a director shares will therefore carry the voting power they possess. But this does not, in my view, warrant a device such as article 9 introduces. Its unconcealed effect is to make a director irremovable. If any question is posed whether the shares of the respondent possess any added voting weight the answer must be that they possess none whatsoever beyond, if valid, an *ad hoc* weight for the special purpose of circumventing section 184. If article 9 were writ large it would set out that a director is not to be removed against his will and that in order to achieve this and to thwart the express provision of section 184, the voting power of any director threatened with removal is to be deemed to be greater than it actually is. The learned judge thought that to sanction this would be to make a mockery of the law. I think so also.

I would allow the appeal.

LORD UPJOHN. My Lords, when construing an Act of Parliament it is a canon of construction that its provisions must be construed in the light of the mischief which the Act was designed to meet. In this case the mischief was well known; it was a common practice, especially in the case of private companies, to provide in the articles that a director should be irremovable or only removable by extraordinary resolution; in the former case the articles would have to be altered by special resolution before the director could be removed and of course in either case a three-quarters majority would be required. In many cases this would be impossible, so the Act provided that notwithstanding anything in the articles an ordinary resolution would suffice to remove a director. That was the mischief which the section set out to remedy; to make a director removable by virtue of an ordinary resolution instead of an extraordinary resolution or making it necessary to alter the articles.

. . . Parliament has never sought to fetter the right of the company to issue a share with such rights or restrictions as it may think fit. There is no fetter which compels the company to make the voting rights or restrictions of general application and it seems to me clear that such rights or restrictions can be attached to special circumstances and to particular types of resolution. This makes no mockery of section 184; all that Parliament was seeking to do thereby was to make an ordinary resolution sufficient to remove a director. Had Parliament desired to go further and enact that every share entitled to vote should be deprived of its special rights under the articles it should have said so in plain terms by making the vote on a poll, one vote one share. Then, what about shares which had no voting rights under the articles? Should not Parliament give them a vote when considering this completely artificial form of ordinary resolution? Suppose there had been some preference shares in the name of Mr Faith's wife, which under the articles had in the circumstances no vote; why in justice should her voice be excluded from consideration in this artificial vote?

I only raise this purely hypothetical case to show the great difficulty of trying to do justice by legislation in a matter which has always been left to the corporators themselves to decide.

I agree entirely with the judgment of the Court of Appeal, and would dismiss the appeal.

NOTE

The case shows that the device of attaching weighted votes to shares can have the effect of making directors of certain companies irremovable. Probably the legislators of section 184(1) of the Companies Act 1948 (now section 303 of the Companies Act 1985) never foresaw the possibility of using weighted votes to defeat an ordinary resolution on the removal of a director.

It is interesting to contrast the judgment of Lord Morris of Borth-y-Gest with that of the other judges in this case, as their conclusions are entirely different.

Re T & D Services (Timber Preservation & Damp Proofing Contractors) Ltd.
(1990) BCC 592

Chancery Division

The Official Receiver sought an order under section 6 of the Company Directors Disqualification Act 1986 disqualifying the respondent on the grounds of being an unfit person to take part in the management of a company. The respondent was a director of four companies which had become insolvent. The liquidator had previously sued the respondent in respect of an alleged sale of a property by the company to him at an undervalue, and of a payment made to the respondent by the company in preference to other creditors at a time when he should have known that the company was insolvent. The Official Receiver also alleged failure to keep proper books of account. In relation to the other three companies the Official Receiver alleged deficiencies of many thousands of pounds and failure to keep proper books of account and to file accounts at Companies House. The director had been made bankrupt in 1976, obtaining his discharge in 1979. He had previously been convicted for making false VAT returns, and for procuring the execution of a security by deception.

HELD, disqualifying the respondent for ten years, that there was evidence of serious want of probity in the respondent's conduct justifying disqualification. All of the companies had been financed by withholding money due to the Crown, and the director's duty to ensure that proper books of account were kept and returns promptly made to Companies House were ignored.

VINELOTT, J. This is a serious case—the most serious that has yet come before me. The respondent manipulated the affairs of T & D for his own benefit and to the detriment of creditors and induced the local authority to advance public moneys to a company which was not entitled to receive them and which he knew would not be in a position to repay them. All these companies (and in particular T & D) were financed by the retention of moneys due to the Crown, much of which was allowed to build up over a long period of time. The affairs of all these companies were conducted without regard to a director's duty to see that proper books of account are kept and that returns are promptly made to the Companies Registry. . . . I need hardly say that I am reluctant to take any step that might imperil the livelihood of innocent employees. However, even if I thought that a disqualification order would have this result it would still be my duty to make the order: in my judgment, it is impossible on the evidence that I have seen to avoid the conclusion that the respondent has shown himself unfit to be concerned in the management of a company and a disqualification order for two years is therefore mandatory.

. . . I shall defer the operation of the order for two weeks to give him the opportunity of deciding whether the company could continue to trade under new management with or without his assistance in dealing with Dutch and German suppliers. . . . Subject to that the disqualification will be for a period of ten years from today.

Re Sevenoaks Stationers (Retail) Ltd.

[1991] BCLC 325

Court of Appeal

Mr Cruddas, (C.), had been a director of five companies which had gone into insolvent liquidation. The accounts of the companies had not been properly audited and, in the case of one of the companies, the accounting records were inadequate. Crown debts were owed by the companies. There were other allegations of impropriety on the part of C. C. was disqualified for seven years and appealed against the order.

HELD, allowing the appeal and reducing the period of disqualification to five years, (1) in determining the length of a disqualification order under section 6 of the Company Directors Disqualification Act 1986 the top bracket of ten to fifteen years should be reserved for serious cases; the middle bracket of six to ten years should be used for cases that did not deserve the maximum sentence, and the minimum bracket of two to five years should be used for the least serious cases; (2) it was of paramount importance that a director facing disqualification should know the charges that he had to meet; (3) non-payment of Crown debts could not be treated as automatic grounds for disqualification; (4) as the judge had considered matters which he should not have considered, the court would review the sentence and reduce it to five years.

DILLON, L.J. I would for my part endorse the division of the potential 15-year disqualification period into three brackets, which was put forward by Mr Keenan for the Official Receiver to Harman J in the present case and has been put forward by Mr Charles for the Official Receiver in other cases *viz*: (i) The top bracket of disqualification for periods over ten years should be reserved for particularly serious cases. These may include cases where a director who has already had one period of disqualification imposed on him falls to be disqualified yet again. (ii) The minimum bracket of two to five years' disqualification should be applied where, though disqualification is mandatory, the case is, relatively, not very serious. (iii) The middle bracket of disqualification for from six to ten years should apply for serious cases which do not merit the top bracket.

. . . Mr Charles submits for the Official Receiver that even if in making out his case for disqualification the Official Receiver can only rely on the allegations made in his report and/or affidavit, yet when the court comes to fix the length of the period of disqualification, the court can take into account any other shortcomings in the director's conduct as a director of the companies in question. In other words the director can be sentenced not only on the charges on which he has been convicted, but also on charges which were never made against him, if they happen to be made out in the evidence given. I emphatically disagree. It is inconsistent with the whole conception of giving notice of the charges the director has to meet, and would in many cases stultify r.3(3) which I have quoted, if in fixing a period of disqualification other matters could be alleged of which no notice had been given. Matters of mitigation can of course be taken into account in favour of the director in fixing the period of disqualification; but otherwise the period should be fixed by reference only to the matters properly alleged against him which have been found to be established and to make him unfit to be concerned in the management of a company.

. . . This is not a case in which it was alleged that Mr Cruddas had, in the colloquial phrase, ''ripped off'' the public and pocketed the proceeds. On the contrary, as the judge found, he had lost a lot of his own money which he had put into Rochester and Retail.

. . . Mr Cruddas made a deliberate decision to pay only those creditors who pressed for payment. The obvious result was that the two companies traded, when in fact insolvent and known to be in difficulties at the expense of those creditors who, like the Crown, happened not to be pressing for payment. Such conduct on the part of a director can well, in my judgment, be relied on as a ground for saying that he is unfit to be concerned in the management of a company.

. . . Taking that view of the Crown debts in Rochester and Retail and adding to it: (i) that there were never any audited accounts in any of the five companies, (ii) the inadequacy of the accounting records of Retail, (iii) the loan by Retail to Rochester, (iv) the payment of debts of Hoo Paper by Hoo Waste Paper, (v) the guarantee given by Sevenoaks Stationers for liabilities of Hoo Paper, (vi) the continued trading while insolvent and known to be in difficulties of Rochester and Retail, and (vii) the extent of the deficiency in each company after a relatively short period of trading, I have no doubt at all that it is amply proved that Mr Cruddas is unfit to be concerned in the management of a company. His trouble is not dishonesty, but incompetence or negligence in a very marked degree and that is enough to render him unfit.

. . . As it is, the judge took into account matters which he was not entitled to take into account, and in particular the supposed failure to keep proper accounting records for the four companies in addition to Retail. Failure to keep proper accounting records is such a serous matter in the case of a director in the position of Mr Cruddas that the period of disqualification imposed on him must be reduced. In all the circumstances, I would reduce it to five years, and would allow this appeal to that extent.

Lee v. Chou Wen Hsien and others

[1985] BCLC 45; [1984] 1 WLR 1202
Privy Council

The articles of association of Ocean-Land Development Ltd., one of the defendants in the case, provided that a director must vacate office if required in writing to resign by all his co-directors. Two days before a board meeting was due to be held at the request of the plaintiff (to discuss the sale of some of the company's holdings which the plaintiff suspected had been made to a company owned by two of his co-directors without full disclosure and approval), the plaintiff was served with such a notice. The plaintiff raised proceedings for a declaration that the notice of removal was ineffective and void and that he remained a director of the company. The trial judge dismissed the action, and the appeal was dismissed by the Court of Appeal of Hong Kong.

The case was appealed to the Privy Council.

HELD that the appeal should be dismissed. The Privy Council considered that although the power of expulsion in the articles of association was a fiduciary power, and had to be exercised *bona fide* in the interests of the company as a whole and for a proper purpose, the expulsion provision in the articles of association was so drafted that an expulsion would nevertheless be effective if the proper procedure had been followed. In this case, therefore, the plaintiff had been properly removed from his directorship. It was also stated that a director who had been expelled from office could not maintain an action against the company to have himself restored to office because the case could not be brought under any of the heads of exception to the rule in *Foss* v. *Harbottle* (1843) 2 Hare 461.

LORD BRIGHTMAN. Their Lordships are in agreement with the majority of the Court of Appeal that the power given by article 73 to directors to expel one of their number from the board is fiduciary, in the sense that each director concurring in the expulsion must act in accordance with what he believes to be in the best interests of the company, and that he cannot properly concur for ulterior reasons of his own. It does not, however, follow that a notice will be void and of no effect, and that the director sought to be expelled will remain a director of the board, because one or more of the requesting directors acted from an ulterior motive. Their Lordships have not been referred to any reported case directly in point. . . . To hold that bad faith on the part of any one director vitiates the notice to resign and leaves in office the director whose resignation is sought, would introduce into the management of the company a source of uncertainty which their Lordships consider is unlikely to have been intended by the signatories to the articles and by others becoming shareholders in the company. In order to give business sense to the article, it is necessary to construe the article strictly in accordance with its terms without any qualification, and to treat the office of director as vacated if the specified event occurs. If this were not the case, and the expelled director challenged the *bona fides* of all or any of his co-directors, the management of the company's business might be at a standstill pending the resolution of the dispute by one means or another, in consequence of the doubt whether the expelled director ought or ought not properly to be treated as a member of the board. Their Lordships therefore take the view that the appellant's claim, as spelt out in the endorsement on the writ, in argument before the Court of Appeal, and in his printed case, inevitably fails at this point.

It is not strictly necessary to deal with the appellant's third submission, to the effect that if article 73(d) confers a fiduciary power and a request made in breach of that duty is of no effect, the wrongly expelled director is nevertheless entitled to maintain an action in his own name to restore himself to office and is not bound to sue, if at all, in a derivative action on behalf of the company to repair a wrong done to the company. Without developing the matter at length, their Lordships agree with the Court of Appeal that, of the two hypotheses stated, the ordinary principles of *Foss* v. *Harbottle* (1843) 2 Hare 461 would preclude such an action.

★ Dawson International plc v. Coats Patons plc and others

1989 SCLR 452; (1989) 5 BCC 405
Court of Session

This was a damages action for breach of contract. The pursuers claimed that there was an agreement between the boards of the two companies according to which the board of the defender company would recommend to shareholders the acceptance of a bid from the pursuer company offering an exchange of shares. The pursuer alleged that in breach of that agreement the board of the defender company encouraged and co-operated with a rival, successful bidder. The defender company contended that the fiduciary duty of the directors to act in the best interests of the company as a whole was overriding, and would justify their subsequently doing something they may have agreed not to do.

HELD that a proof before answer should be allowed (further proof of the facts) to establish whether the board of the defender company had given encouragement and co-operation to the rival bid, and whether the actions of the directors were or were not honestly performed in fulfilment of their fiduciary duty to act *bona fide* in the best interests of the company as a whole.

LORD PRESIDENT EMSLIE. An agreement such as that allegedly entered into by the board of Coats Patons is always subject to the qualification imported by the general law that the directors in question may, if circumstances alter materially, decide, in fulfilment of their continuing duty to the company and its shareholders, not to implement it.

. . . Both parties accept, correctly in my opinion, that the alleged agreement was subject to the qualification derived from the law which defined directors' overriding duties to their company and their shareholders. They are at one as to what that qualification was. . . . All that remains is the question whether Dawson's averments of breach of their agreement are sufficiently relevant and specific to entitle them to proof before answer. In my opinion they are. . . . If Dawson succeed in establishing that the agreement on which they rely included an obligation by the board of Coats Patons not to encourage, or co-operate with, an approach by a rival bidder, the answer to the allegation of breach will be discovered by finding out what actually happened in the communings between Vantona Viyella and Coats Patons to see whether there was anything done by the directors of Coats Patons which could properly be described as amounting to encouragement or co-operation and, if so, whether the actings of those directors were or were not honestly performed in fulfilment of their overriding duty to promote the best interests of their company and their shareholders.

Rolled Steel Products (Holdings) Ltd. v. British Steel Corporation and others

[1986] 1 Ch 246; [1985] 3 All ER 52; [1985] 2 WLR 908

Court of Appeal

Rolled Steel Products (Holdings) Ltd. (Rolled Steel Products) owed money to S. Ltd., a company in which one of the directors of Rolled Steel Products was also a director. S. Ltd. was itself indebted to Colvilles Ltd., (C. Ltd.), a subsidiary of British Steel Corporation, a debt which was guaranteed personally by S., the director. C. Ltd. doubted the ability of S. Ltd. and S. to repay the loan and, therefore, proposed to Rolled Steel Products that C. Ltd. would lend it the money to repay S. Ltd.; S. Ltd. would then be able to repay part of its debt to C. Ltd., and Rolled Steel Products would grant a guarantee and debenture covering the balance. The articles of association of Rolled Steel Products contained a provision permitting it to give guarantees or become security for such persons, firms or companies 'as may seem expedient'. A board resolution was passed by Rolled Steel Products to approve the proposals. However, S. did not declare an interest as he was required to do by the articles of association, and proceeded to vote on the resolution. If his vote had not been counted, the meeting would have been inquorate. Following the resolution, a guarantee and a debenture were granted to C. Ltd. From what followed, it was evident that C. Ltd. was aware that the transaction was not in the interests of Rolled Steel Products. All of the shareholders of Rolled Steel Products were also aware of the irregularity of the transaction. Subsequently S. Ltd. failed to repay the loan, and a receiver was appointed. The sums secured were paid by Rolled Steel Products to the defendants as successors to C. Ltd.

Rolled Steel Products subsequently raised an action against the British Steel Corporation and the receiver, claiming that the guarantee and the debenture, and also the appointment of the receiver, were void; their argument was that the resolution was invalid for lack of the requisite quorum, and because of lack of power to grant the guarantee and security in the constitution. The trial judge, Vinelott, J., held that the rule of indoor management as decided in the *Royal British Bank* v. *Turquand* (1856) 6 E & B 327 applied to validate the resolution despite the lack of quorum. However, the judge held that the guarantee, and to the extent of the sum guaranteed, the debenture, were executed to the knowledge of C. Ltd. for a purpose other than those authorised by the memorandum of association and therefore they should be set aside as *ultra vires*, and the money repaid to Rolled Steel Products. The case was appealed to the Court of Appeal, and a cross-appeal was made by the plaintiff.

HELD, by LAWTON, SLADE, and BROWNE-WILKINSON, L.J.J., that the appeal should be dismissed and the cross-appeal allowed on the following grounds: (1) the defence based on the rule of indoor management was made very late in the proceedings, namely at the time of judgment and, therefore, it could not succeed, as it had not been properly established; (2) although the power in the memorandum of association to give guarantees and grant security were mere powers rather than objects, the *company* did have the contractual capacity to make the guarantee and grant the security and, therefore, they were not *ultra vires*; however, granting the guarantee was beyond the power of the *directors* as being for a purpose not authorised by the memorandum of association, and as British Steel Corporation knew of the lack of authority, they could acquire no rights under the guarantee, and to the extent covered by the guarantee, the debenture also; (3) the directors were acting in breach of fiduciary duty in purporting to authorise and in executing the guarantee and debenture, and as the defendants and the receiver had notice of the breach of duty they were accountable as constructive trustees; and (4) the plaintiff was entitled to a declaration that the guarantee and debenture were not deeds of the plaintiff, and that the appointment of the receiver was void, and accordingly Rolled Steel Products was entitled to repayment of the interest paid to British Steel Corporation as part of the guarantee.

SLADE, L.J. The legal personality of a company incorporated under the Companies Acts exists only for the purpose of its incorporation, as defined in the objects clause, which have to be set out in its memorandum of association as required by section 2(1)(c) of the Companies Act 1948. It does not, however, follow that any act is beyond its capacity unless expressly authorised by its objects clause. Any such company is treated as having implied powers to do any act which is reasonably incidental to the attainment or pursuit of any of its express objects, unless such act is expressly prohibited by the memorandum. See *In re Horsley & Weight Ltd.* [1982] Ch 442, 448 *per* Buckley L.J. Strictly, therefore, it is not essential for the memorandum to insert any reference at all to mere powers as distinct from objects . . .

[The judge considered a series of authorities and went on to say:]

(1) The basic rule is that a company incorporated under the Companies Acts only has the capacity to do those acts which fall within its objects as set out in its memorandum of association or are reasonably incidental to the attainment or pursuit of those objects. Ultimately, therefore, the question whether a particular transaction is within or outside its capacity must depend on the true construction of the memorandum.

(2) Nevertheless, if a particular act (such as each of the transactions of 22 January 1969 in the present case) is of a category which, on the true construction of the company's memorandum, is *capable* of being performed as reasonably incidental to the attainment or pursuit of its objects, it will not be rendered *ultra vires* the company merely because in a particular instance its directors, in performing the act in its name, are in truth doing so for purposes other than those set out in its memorandum. Subject to any express restrictions on the relevant power which may be contained in the memorandum, the state of mind or knowledge of the persons managing the company's affairs or of the persons dealing with it is irrelevant in considering questions of corporate capacity.

(3) While due regard must be paid to any express conditions attached to or limitations on powers contained in a company's memorandum (e.g., a power to borrow only up to a specified amount), the court will not ordinarily construe a statement in a memorandum that a particular power is exerciseable "for the purposes of the company" as a condition limiting the company's corporate capacity to exercise the power; it will regard it as simply imposing a limit on the authority of the directors; see the *David Payne* case [1904] 2 Ch 608.

(4) At least in default of the unanimous consent of all the shareholders (as to which see below), the directors of a company will not have *actual* authority from the company to exercise any express or implied power other than for the purposes of the company as set out in its memorandum of association.

(5) A company holds out its directors as having *ostensible* authority to bind the company to any transaction which falls within the powers expressly or impliedly conferred on it by its memorandum of association. Unless he is put on notice to the contrary, a person dealing in good faith with a company which is carrying on an *intra vires* business is entitled to assume that its directors are properly exercising such powers for the purposes of the company as set out in its memorandum. Correspondingly, such a person in such circumstances can hold the company to any transaction of this nature.

(6) If, however, a person dealing with a company is on notice that the directors are exercising the relevant power for purposes other than the purposes of the company, he cannot rely on the ostensible authority of the directors and, on ordinary principles of agency, cannot hold the company to the transaction.

In the present case I construe the words "as may seem expedient" in clause 3(k) of the plaintiff's memorandum not as limiting the corporate capacity of the plaintiff but as simply imposing a limit on the authority of its directors. To adapt the wording of Harman L.J. in the *Introductions Ltd.* case [1970] Ch 199 following the *David Payne* decision [1904] 2 Ch 608, the guarantee and *pro tanto* the debenture were not executed for a legitimate purpose of the plaintiff; Colvilles and British Steel Corporation knew it and, therefore, cannot rely on the guarantee and *pro tanto* the debenture. All this results from the ordinary law of agency, not from the corporate powers of the plaintiff. The relevant transactions in the present case, in my opinion, were not beyond its corporate capacity. . . .

. . . To sum up, my conclusions on the *ultra vires* point are these. The relevant transactions of 22 January 1969 were not beyond the corporate capacity of the plaintiff and thus were not *ultra vires* in the proper sense of that phrase. However, the entering into the guarantee and to the extent of the sum guaranteed, the debenture was beyond the authority of the directors, because they were entered into in furtherance of purposes not authorised by the plaintiff's memorandum. Despite this lack of authority, they might have been capable of conferring rights on Colvilles if Colvilles had not known of this lack of authority. Colvilles, however, did have such knowledge and so acquired no rights under these transactions. Even if the no due authorisation point discussed earlier in this judgment were not open to the plaintiff, because Mr Shenkman *had* duly declared his interest at the relevant board meeting, the plaintiff could disclaim these transactions, which its directors had carried out on its behalf, as being unauthorised, inasmuch as they were carried out for improper purposes. The practical relevance of the no due authorisation point discussed in an earlier section of this judgment is that it enables the plaintiff also to disclaim the borrowing of the £401,448 and the *whole* (as opposed to part only) of the security given by the debenture (as having been in each case entered into by the directors without its authority) and also to attack the validity of the receiver's appointment.

BROWNE-WILKINSON, L.J. In the case of a limited company, if a transaction falls within the objects of the company (and is therefore within its capacity) it is effective to vest rights in a third party even if the transaction was carried out in excess or abuse of the powers of the company. If the members of the company learn of what is proposed in time, they will be able to restrain such transaction: if they only discover the facts later, their remedy lies against those who have wrongly caused the company to act in excess or abuse of the company's powers. If a third party has received the company's property with notice of the excess or abuse of powers, such third party will be personally liable as a constructive trustee and the company will be able to recover the property: see *Belmont Finance Corporation Ltd v. Williams Furniture (No. 2)* [1980] 1 All ER 393. . . .

. . . The critical distinction is, therefore, between acts done in excess of the capacity of the company on the one hand and acts done in excess or abuse of the powers of the company on the other. If the transaction is beyond the capacity of the company it is in any event a nullity and wholly void: whether or not the third party had notice of the invalidity, property transferred or money paid under such a transaction will be recoverable from the third party. If, on the other hand, the transaction (although in excess or abuse of powers) is within the capacity of the company, the position of the third party depends upon whether or not he had notice that the transaction was in excess or abuse of the powers of the company. As between the shareholders and the directors, for most purposes it makes no practical difference whether the transaction is beyond the capacity of the company or merely in excess or abuse of its power: in either event the shareholders will be able to restrain the carrying out of the transaction or hold liable those who have carried it out.

. . . I summarise my conclusions as follows: (1) to be *ultra vires* a transaction has to be outside the capacity of the company, not merely in excess or abuse of the powers of the company. (2) The question whether a transaction is outside the capacity of the company depends solely upon whether, on the true construction of its memorandum of association, the transaction is capable of falling within the objects of the company as opposed to being a proper exercise of the powers of the company. (3) Notwithstanding the fact that the provision authorising the company to enter into the particular transaction is found in the objects clause and there is a provision requiring each paragraph to be construed as a separate object, such provision may be merely a power, and not an object, if either it is incapable of existing as a separate object or it can only be construed as a power ancillary to the other objects in the strict sense. (4) If a transaction falls within the objects, and therefore the capacity, of the company, it is not *ultra vires* the company and accordingly it is not absolutely void. (5) If a company enters into a transaction which is *intra vires* (as being within its capacity) but in excess or abuse of its powers, such transactions will be set aside at the instance of the shareholders. (6) A third party who has notice— actual or constructive—that a transaction, although *intra vires* the company, was entered into in excess or abuse of the powers of the company cannot enforce such transaction against the company and will be accountable as constructive trustee for any money or property of the company received by the third party. (7) The fact that a power is expressly or impliedly limited so as to be exerciseable only ''for the purposes of the company's business'' (or other words to that effect) does not put a third party on inquiry as to whether the power is being so exercised i.e., such provision does not give him constructive notice of excess or abuse of such power.

Applying those principles to the present case, in my judgment, no question of *ultra vires* arises. For the reasons given both by the judge and by Slade L.J. the provision of clause 3(k) of the memorandum of association of the plaintiff do not constitute a separate object but can only be construed as a power. The plaintiff had the capacity to enter into the transactions involving the giving of guarantees and could properly have done so if they had been expedient in the interest of the plaintiff's business. If British Steel Corporation had known no more than that the plaintiff was purporting to give the guarantee as being expedient for the plaintiff's business, the transaction would have been unimpeachable as against British Steel Corporation.

But, as the judge and Slade L.J. have demonstrated, British Steel Corporation had actual knowledge of facts which showed that the giving of the guarantee and the debenture was an abuse of powers by the directors of the plaintiff since the transaction was not even considered to be for the benefit of the plaintiff. The borrowing by the plaintiff from Colvilles of the £401,448 was formally invalid since such borrowing was not approved by a quorate board meeting of the plaintiff and the defence based on the rule in *Turquand*'s case 6 E. & B. 327 was neither pleaded nor established. British Steel Corporation had constructive knowledge of this formal invalidity. Accordingly, British Steel Corporation and the receiver are accountable as constructive trustees for all the moneys of the plaintiff received by them with such notice.

NOTE

This case is important because it demonstrates the difference between a transaction which is *ultra vires* the company and one which is beyond the powers of the directors. Previously many cases were decided on the basis that a contract could be *ultra vires* and void if it was beyond the powers of the directors as opposed to being beyond the powers of the company. The law has, however, changed since then: firstly, the case was decided before the enactment of section 9 of the European Communities Act 1972 (the forerunner to sections 35 and 35A and 35B of the Companies Act 1985), and so the statutory outsider protection afforded by section 9 does not apply to this case; secondly, the *ultra vires* doctrine has been largely abolished by the Companies Act 1989, with the effect that *ultra vires* obligations can now be ratified by the members (by special resolution), and constructive notice no longer applies (sections 35 and 711A Companies Act 1985). However, the importance of the case in relation to the exercise of powers by directors remains undiminished.

Howard Smith Ltd. v. Ampol Petroleum Ltd. and others

[1974] AC 821; [1974] 1 All ER 1126; [1974] 2 WLR 689
Privy Council

Ampol Petroleum Ltd. (Ampol) and another company, Bulkships Ltd. (Bulkships), together held 55 per cent of the issued share capital of a third company, R.W. Miller (Holdings) Ltd. (Miller), and made an offer for the whole of the remainder. The directors of Miller considered that the offer was too low, and decided to recommend that it be rejected. Howard Smith Ltd. announced an intention to make a higher bid for the shares. Ampol and Bulkships then announced that they would act together to reject any offer for their shares. The directors of Miller then made an allotment of shares to Howard Smith Ltd. which was sufficient to enable them to secure a majority shareholding, and hence to make a takeover bid. There was evidence that Miller was in need of further capital. It was also proved that the directors of Miller honestly believed that they were acting in the interests of the company as a whole in supporting the bid from Howard Smith Ltd. Ampol challenged the validity of the share issue and sought an order for rectification of the register by the removal of Howard Smith Ltd. as a member of Miller in respect of the fresh allotment of shares. In the Supreme Court of New South Wales the trial judge held that the share issue had been made for an improper purpose and should be set aside, despite the fact that the directors had not been influenced by personal gain. An appeal was made to the Judicial Committee of the Privy Council.

HELD, dismissing the appeal, that, despite the fact that the directors had acted honestly, the use in this way by the directors of their power of allotment was unconstitutional and a breach of the fiduciary duty to use their power for a proper purpose and, as Howard Smith had notice that the allotment was being made for an improper purpose, the share issue was therefore voidable. They found that the primary purpose of the allotment was to destroy the existing majority vote and create a different one, rather than the need to provide fresh capital.

LORD WILBERFORCE. In order to assist him in deciding upon the alternative motivations contended for, the judge considered first, at some length, the objective question whether Miller was in fact in need of capital. This approach was criticised before their Lordships: it was argued that what mattered was not the actual financial condition of Miller, but what the majority directors *bona fide* considered that condition to be. Their Lordships accept that such a matter as the raising of finance is one of management within the responsibility of the directors: they accept that it would be wrong for the court to substitute its opinion for that of the management, or indeed to question the correctness of the management's decision, on such a question, if *bona fide* arrived at. There is no appeal on merits from management decisions to courts of law: nor will courts of law assume to act as a kind of supervisory board over decisions within the powers of management honestly arrived at.

But accepting all of this, when a dispute arises whether directors of a company made a particular decision for one purpose or for another, or whether, there being more than one purpose, one or another purpose was the substantial or primary purpose, the court, in their Lordships' opinion, is entitled to look at the situation objectively in order to estimate how critical or pressing, or substantial or, *per contra*, insubstantial an alleged requirement may have been.

. . . The issue was clearly *intra vires* the directors. But, *intra vires* though the issue may have been, the directors' power under this article is a fiduciary power: and it remains the case that an exercise of such power though formally valid, may be attacked on the ground that it was not exercised for the purpose for which it was granted. It is at this point that the contentions of the parties diverge. The extreme argument on one side is that, for validity, what is required is *bona fide* exercise of the power in the interests of the company; that once it is found that the directors were not motivated by self-interest—i.e. by a desire to retain their control of the company or their positions on the board—the matter is concluded in their favour and that the court will not enquire into the validity of their reasons for making the issue. All decided cases, it was submitted, where an exercise of such a power as this has been found invalid, are cases where the directors are found to have acted through self-interest of this kind.

On the other side, the main argument is that the purpose for which the power is conferred is to enable capital to be raised for the company, and that once it is found that the issue was not made for that purpose, invalidity follows.

In their Lordships' opinion, neither of the extreme positions can be maintained. It can be accepted, as one would only expect, that the majority of cases in which issues of shares are challenged in the courts are cases in which the vitiating element is the self-interest of the directors, or at least the purpose of the directors to preserve their own control of management . . .

Further it is correct to say that where the self-interest of the directors is involved, they will not be permitted to assert that their action was *bona fide* thought to be, or was, in the interest of the company; pleas to this effect have invariably been rejected (e.g. *Fraser* v. *Whalley* (1864) 2 Hem & M 10 and *Hogg* v. *Cramphorn Ltd.* [1967] Ch 254)—just as trustees who buy trust property are not permitted to assert that they paid a good price.

But it does not follow from this, as the appellants assert, that the absence of any element of self-interest is enough to make an issue valid. Self-interest is only one, though no doubt the commonest, instance of improper motive.

NOTE

Nowadays, since the enactment of what is now section 80 of the Companies Act 1985, the directors are much more strictly controlled in their exercise of the power of allotment by the requirement that allotments have to be approved in advance by the members. The provision was first enacted in the Companies Act 1980.

Cook v. Deeks and others

[1916] AC 554; [1916–17] All ER 285

Privy Council

An action was brought by a director and member of the Toronto Construction Co. on behalf of himself and the other shareholders against the other three directors of the company. The grounds of the action were that the three directors had used the company connection to obtain a construction contract for themselves, which should properly have been awarded to the company. The three directors were also majority shareholders and had passed a resolution in general meeting declaring that the company had no interest in the contract. The action was first raised in the High Court Division of the Supreme Court of Ontario, where it was dismissed. It was appealed to the appellate division which affirmed the decision of the court of first instance. A further appeal was made to the Privy Council.

HELD that the benefit of the contract belonged in equity to the company and, further, that the directors were in breach of duty to the company when they as members passed the resolution to dissociate the company from the contract; the previous judgments of the Supreme Court should be set aside.

LORD BUCKMASTER, L.C. It is quite right to point out the importance of avoiding the establishment of rules as to directors' duties which would impose upon them burdens so heavy and responsibilities so great that men of good position would hesitate to accept the office. But, on the other hand, men who assume the complete control of a company's business must remember that they are not at liberty to sacrifice the interests which they are bound to protect, and, while ostensibly acting for the company, divert in their own favour business which should properly belong to the company they represent.

Their Lordships think that, in the circumstances, the defendants T.R. Hinds and G.S. and G.M. Deeks were guilty of a distinct breach of duty in the course they took to secure the contract, and that they cannot retain the benefit of such contract for themselves, but must be regarded as holding it on behalf of the company.

There remains the more difficult consideration of whether this position can be made regular by resolutions of the company controlled by the votes of the three defendants. The Supreme Court have given this matter the most careful consideration, but their Lordships are unable to agree with the conclusion which they reached.

In their Lordships' opinion the Supreme Court has insufficiently recognized the distinction between two classes of case and has applied the principles applicable to the case of a director selling to his company property which was in equity as well as at law his own, and which he could dispose of as he thought fit, to the case of a director dealing with property, which, though his own at law, in equity belonged to his company.

. . . If, as their Lordships find on the facts, the contract in question was entered into under such circumstances that the directors could not retain the benefit of it for themselves, then it belonged in equity to the company and ought to have been dealt with as an asset of the company. Even supposing it be not *ultra vires* of a company to make a present to its directors, it appears quite certain that directors holding a majority of votes would not be permitted to make a present to themselves. This would be to allow a majority to oppress the minority.

NOTE

If this case arose today, sections 459–61 of the Companies Act 1985 could be used by the plaintiff to seek a remedy on the ground of unfairly prejudicial conduct. See Chapter 13, page 236.

★ Aberdeen Railway Co. v. Blaikie Bros.

(1854) 1 MacQ. 461

House of Lords

Blaikie Bros., a partnership, contracted to supply Aberdeen Railway Co. with iron chairs at £8 10s. per ton. Blaikie, the managing partner of Blaikie Bros., also happened to be the chairman of the board of directors of the railway company. After completion of part of the contract by Blaikie Bros., the railway company refused to accept delivery of the remainder of the goods and refused to pay the account. Blaikie Bros. brought an action against Aberdeen Railway for implement of contract. The railway company contended that due to the conflict of interest of Blaikie the contract was voidable. The Court of Session decided for the pursuers, and the case was appealed to the House of Lords.

HELD, reversing the decision of the Court of Session, that the contract was voidable owing to the conflict of interest.

LORD CRANWORTH, L.C. The directors are a body to whom is delegated the duty of managing the general affairs of the company.

A corporate body can only act by agents, and it is of course the duty of those agents so to act as best to promote the interests of the corporation whose affairs they are conducting. Such agents have duties to discharge of a fiduciary nature towards their principal. And it is a rule of universal application, that no one, having such duties to discharge, shall be allowed to enter into engagements in which he has, or can have, a personal interest conflicting or which may possibly conflict, with the interests of those whom he is bound to protect.

So strictly is the principle adhered to, that no question is allowed to be raised as to the fairness or unfairness of a contract so entered into.

. . . It was Mr Blaikie's duty to give to his co-directors and through them to the company, the full benefit of all the knowledge and skill which he could bring to bear on the subject. He was bound to assist them in getting the articles contracted for at the cheapest possible rate. As far as related to the advice he should give them, he put his interest in conflict with his duty, and whether he was a sole director or only one of many, can make no difference in principle.

Guinness plc v. Saunders and another

[1990] 1 All ER 652; [1990] 2 WLR 324
House of Lords

Following the takeover by Guinness plc of Distillers Co. plc, Ward, one of the directors of Guinness, submitted an invoice to Guinness plc for £5.2m for services rendered in connection with the bid. The appellant claimed that the fee had been agreed to reflect 0.2 per cent of the value of the bid if successful. During the bid, a sub-committee of the board of directors consisting of Ward, Saunders (the chairman of the company) and one other director was established to oversee the bid, and the sub-committee approved and made the payment. However, the articles of association of Guinness did not empower a sub-committee of the board of directors to authorise special remuneration. Guinness sought repayment of the £5.2m.

HELD by LORD KEITH OF KINKELL, LORD BRANDON OF OAKBROOK, LORD TEMPLEMAN, LORD GRIFFITHS, and LORD GOFF OF CHIEVELEY, that the appeal would be dismissed on the following grounds: (1) the sub-committee of directors lacked power in the articles of association to bind the company as to remuneration to be paid to a director, as did the chief executive, and the contract was accordingly void; (2) in the absence of proof of a binding contract, the appellant could not claim a right to be paid a reasonable amount *quantum meruit*; (3) the appellant had allowed a conflict of interest to arise by agreeing to carry out services for a fee which was geared to the value of the takeover bid, which was a breach of fiduciary duty; (4) the appellant sought remuneration as a member of the committee of the board and not for professional services which the articles allowed; and (5) since the House of Lords did not accept that there was a right to remuneration, the contract was void and, as the money was held by the defendant as constructive trustee, the House refused a request for relief from liability under section 727 of the Companies Act 1985.

NOTE

The trial judge had earlier held that Ward held the money as constructive trustee for the company, on the ground of lack of proper disclosure of personal interest in breach of both common law fiduciary duty and section 317 of the Companies Act 1985. The Court of Appeal dismissed his appeal on similar grounds. By contrast, the reasoning of the House of Lords is based not on breach of the statutory disclosure requirement in section 317, but on lack of authority on the part of the committee of the board of directors to approve the payment in the first place.

Movitex Ltd v. Bulfield and others

(1986) 2 BCC 99, 403

Chancery Division

The facts of this case were complex: the liquidator of Movitex Ltd. sought a declaration that property conveyed to another company be handed back to Movitex Ltd., and that a mortgage and further legal charge granted over the company's leasehold interest in that property be set aside on the ground that two out of the three directors had a personal interest in the transferee company, which had also benefited from the mortgage and legal charge. The articles of association excluded the prohibition on self-dealing by directors provided a director declared the nature of his interest at the meeting of the board of directors at which the question of entering into the contract in which he had an interest first arose, and provided he did not vote on the approval of the contract. There was an exception in the articles to the prohibition on voting: a director could vote on a contract in which he had an interest, if that interest was that the contract was with another company of which he was a director or other officer, member or creditor. The plaintiff contended that the two directors had breached the articles and had not obtained the authorisation of the board, in that disclosure of their personal interest had not been made to the third director, and that the mortgage and legal charge had not been authorised by the full board.

HELD that sufficient disclosure had been made to the third director for the court to refuse to grant an order for re-conveyance of the property to the company. The reasoning was that the vote to approve the contract was not invalidated by the conflict of interest of the two directors because of the exemption in the articles which could apply to cases where the directors were *both* members and directors of the other company and because it was established that the third director was aware of all necessary information about the property. The court also made clear that if a director placed himself in a position in which his duty to the company conflicted with his personal interest then, unless he could rely on a provision in the articles entitling him to do so, the court would set aside the transaction as voidable without enquiry as to whether there had been any breach of duty to the company.

HELD on the evidence that the mortgage was executed by authority of the board but that the further charge was not. The further legal charge therefore fell.

VINELOTT, J. I do not think it strictly accurate to say that a director of a company owes a fiduciary duty to the company not to put himself into a position where his duty to the company may conflict with his personal interest or with his duty to another. The true rule is that if a director puts himself in such a position then (unless he can rely on a provision entitling him to do so in the articles) the transaction will be set aside *ex debito justitiae* and without enquiring into the fairness of the transaction.

Lee Panavision Ltd. v. Lee Lighting Ltd.
[1992] BCLC 22
Court of Appeal
The plaintiffs acquired an option to purchase the defendants at any time up to December 1990. They also entered into a management agreement according to which the plaintiffs ran the defendant's business and nominated its directors. After the option had expired the management agreement was terminable on notice. It was clear that the option was not going to be exercised, and that once it expired the nominated directors would be removed from office. The plaintiffs wished to continue to manage the defendants to ensure that they paid back a loan note in favour of a company associated with the plaintiffs. Just before the expiry of the option, the directors of the defendants

voted in favour of entering a second management agreement and, thereafter, the plaintiffs issued an indemnity to the directors of the defendants against any claim arising with the second agreement. After the management agreement expired, the directors of the defendants were removed from office, and the defendants announced that they were not bound by the second agreement. The plaintiffs sought an injunction restraining the defendants from terminating the agreement. The defendants alleged that the directors had failed to disclose at a board meeting that they were interested in the agreement as required by the company's articles of association. Harman, J. held that the indemnity was voidable at the instance of the defendants because of the failure of the directors to disclose an interest, and that the second agreement had not been entered into in the interests of the defendants. The plaintiffs appealed to the Court of Appeal.

HELD affirming the judgment of Harman, J., that it was unconstitutional for the directors to enter the second management agreement knowing that the shareholders intended to appoint new directors, since the agreement would deprive those directors of all managerial powers.

Per curiam. The court would hesitate to hold that there had been a breach of section 317 of the Companies Act 1985 where a matter had not been disclosed which was common to all members of the board and known to all.

DILLON, L.J. The function of the directors is to manage, but the appointment of the directors who are to do the managing is constitutionally a function of the shareholders in general meeting. Therefore it must have been unconstitutional for the directors, knowing from Memery Crystal's letters that the shareholders were proposing as soon as they could to exercise their constitutional right to appoint new directors, to take all managerial powers away from any new directors who might be appointed by committing Lee Lighting to the second management agreement and giving exclusive managerial power to Panavision over the possibly crucial period until the end of April 1992. . . . I do not doubt that Mr Sibley and the directors honestly believed that the directors had power to do what was done but in my view the directors did not have that power.

. . . If the judge was entitled to make the findings of non-disclosure and non-declaration of interests that he did, the position is that each of the directors has failed to disclose formally at the board meeting an interest common to all the directors, and, *ex hypothesi*, already known to all the directors. I would hesitate to hold that such apparently technical non-declaration of an interest in breach of section 317 has the inevitable result, as to which the court has no discretion, that the second management agreement is fundamentally flawed and must be set aside if Lee Lighting chooses to ask sufficiently promptly that it be set aside.

Regal (Hastings) Ltd. v. Gulliver and others

[1967] 2 AC 134; [1942] 1 All E R 378

House of Lords

Regal (Hastings) Ltd. owned a cinema in Hastings. A subsidiary company was formed for the purpose of acquiring two other cinemas, in order that the three cinemas could be sold together as a going concern. The subsidiary company needed more capital than the parent company (Regal) could provide, and therefore the directors of Regal and the company solicitor subscribed for shares. The shares which were to be allotted to the chairman were in fact allotted to and paid for by two companies and one private individual, who bought as individuals and not as his nominees. The arrangement for the share purchases was made at two simultaneous board meetings of Regal and of the subsidiary company, but was not disclosed to the shareholders of either company. Eventually, instead of a sale of the subsidiary company as a going concern, the shares of both Regal and the subsidiary company were sold, and the directors made a profit on the sale. The company, under a new board of directors, raised an action against the former directors and its former solicitor for damages in respect of the secret profit made on the sale of the shares. It was proved that all the directors had acted from the best of motives. In the court of first instance, judgment was given for the defendants, and the Court of Appeal dismissed the appeal. The case was appealed to the House of Lords.

HELD that the directors, other than the chairman, were in breach of their fiduciary duty to Regal and therefore were liable to repay to the company the profit they had made on the shares. Since the chairman did not acquire a beneficial interest in the shares, he was not accountable to the company for the profit made by those who did make the profit, as they were not in a fiduciary relationship to the company. Furthermore, the solicitor was not accountable to the company for the profit because he too was not subject to a fiduciary relationship towards the company.

VISCOUNT SANKEY. In my view, the respondents were in a fiduciary position and their liability to account does not depend on proof of *mala fides*. The general rule of equity is that no one who has duties of a fiduciary nature to perform is allowed to enter into engagements in which he has or can have a personal interest conflicting with the interests of those whom he is bound to protect.

LORD RUSSELL OF KILLOWEN. . . . The rule of equity which insists on those, who by use of a fiduciary position make a profit, being liable to account for that profit, in no way depends on fraud, or absence of *bona fides*; or upon such questions or considerations as whether the profit would or should otherwise have gone to the plaintiff, or whether the profiteer was under a duty to obtain the source of the profit for the plaintiff, or whether he took a risk or acted as he did for the benefit of the plaintiff, or whether the plaintiff has in fact been damaged or benefited by his action. The liability arises from the mere fact of a profit having, in the stated circumstances, been made. The profiteer, however honest and well-intentioned, cannot escape the risk of being called upon to account. . . . In the result, I am of the opinion that the directors standing in a fiduciary relationship to Regal in regard to the exercise of their powers as directors, and having obtained these shares by reason and only by reason of the fact that they were directors of Regal and in the course of the execution of that office, are accountable for the profits which they have made out of them. . . . The suggestion that the directors were applying simply as members of the public is a travesty of the facts. They could, had they wished, have protected themselves by a resolution (either antecedent or subsequent) of the Regal shareholders in general meeting. In default of such approval, the liability to account must remain.

LORD MACMILLAN. The plaintiff company has to establish two things: (i) that what the directors did was so related to the affairs of the company that it can properly be said to have been done in the course of their management and in utilisation of their opportunities and special knowledge as directors; and (ii) that what they did resulted in a profit to themselves.

NOTE

In this case, the reason why the directors were held accountable for the profit was because it was a *secret* profit. Had it been disclosed to and approved by the shareholders of Regal they would not have been accountable. As the case shows, the prohibition on directors making a secret profit applies even when directors are acting *bona fide* in the interests of the company as a whole.

In re City Equitable Fire Insurance Co. Ltd.

[1925] 1 Ch 407; [1924] All ER 485
Court of Appeal

In the liquidation of the City Equitable Fire Insurance Co. Ltd. it was discovered that there was a shortfall in the funds, partly due to depreciation, but largely due to the actions of the managing director, Mr Bevan, which included a deliberate fraud for which he had been convicted and sentenced. The company had articles of association which provided at article 150 that none of the directors, auditors, secretary or other officers should be answerable for the acts, receipts, neglects or defaults of the others or other of them, or for any bankers or other persons with whom any moneys or effects belonging to the company might be lodged or deposited for safe custody, or for deficiency of any security, or for any other loss, misfortune or damage which might happen in the execution of their offices or trusts, unless these should happen as a result of their own wilful neglect or default. The Official Receiver as liquidator sought to make the directors liable for negligence in respect of losses caused by investments and loans, including a loan to the managing director and another to the company's brokers and by payment of dividends out of capital. With the exception of the managing director, it was established that the other directors had acted honestly throughout. The Official Receiver also sought to make the auditor liable for negligence in carrying out the audit of the accounts for the three preceding years.

HELD by ROMER, J. that the directors other than the managing director were not liable for negligence because article 150 exonerated them from liability. The Official Receiver was, however, held entitled to claim relief against the managing director, Bevan. The case laid down a standard for the directors' duty of skill and care. In relation to the auditors, they were liable for breach of duty in not personally inspecting securities in the hands of stockbrokers, but there had been no breach of duty in wrongly describing certain items in the accounts after receiving false information, or in failing to spot purchases by the stockbrokers of treasury bills on behalf of the company, which never came into the possession of the company. The decision on the auditors was appealed to the Court of Appeal, which upheld the whole decision of Romer, J.

ROMER, J. [After detailing the losses of the City Equitable Fire Insurance Co. Ltd.] . . . Nearly the whole of these enormous losses were brought about through Bevan's instrumentality, and a large part of them by his deliberate fraud. For that fraud he has been tried, and convicted, and is now suffering the just penalty. But the question not unnaturally arises as to whether, during the period covered by Bevan's nefarious activities, the other directors and the auditors of the company were properly discharging the duties that they owed to the company's shareholders. The Official Receiver, as the liquidator of the company, alleges that they were not. He has accordingly included them, or such of them as are still living, as respondents to the summons which he issued against Bevan under section 215 of the Companies Act; and whilst admitting, and rightly admitting, that they have acted honestly throughout, he claims that they have been guilty of such negligence as to render themselves liable to the company in damages. Whether they are, or are not so liable, is the question that I have to determine . . .

It has sometimes been said that directors are trustees. If this means no more than that directors in the performance of their duties stand in a fiduciary relationship to the company, the statement is true enough. But if the statement is meant to be an indication by way of analogy of what those duties are, it appears to me wholly misleading. I can see but little resemblance between the duties of a director and the duties of a trustee of a will or a marriage settlement. It is indeed impossible to describe the duty of directors in general terms, whether by way of analogy or otherwise. The position of a director of a company carrying on a small retail business is very different from that of a director of a railway company. The duties of a bank director may differ widely from those of an insurance director, and the duties of a director of one insurance company may differ from those of a director of another. In one company, for instance, matters may normally be attended to by the manager or other members of the staff that in another company are attended to by the directors themselves. The larger the business carried on by the company the more numerous, and the more important, the matters that must of necessity be left to the managers, the accountants and the rest of the staff. . . .

In order, therefore, to acertain the duties that a person appointed to the board of an established company undertakes to perform, it is necessary to consider not only the nature of the company's business, but also the manner in which the work of the company is in fact distributed between the directors and the other officials of the company, provided always that this distribution is a reasonable one in the circumstances, and is not inconsistent with any express provisions of the articles of association. In discharging the duties of his position thus ascertained a director must, of course, act honestly; but he must also exercise some degree of both skill and diligence . . .

There are, in addition, one or two other general propositions that seem to be warranted by the reported cases: (1) A director need not exhibit in the performance of his duties a greater degree of skill than may reasonably be expected from a person of his knowledge and experience. A director of a life insurance company, for instance, does not guarantee that he has the skill of an actuary or of a physician. In the words of Lindley M.R.: "If the directors act within their powers, if they act with such care as is reasonably to be expected from them, having regard to their knowledge and experience, and if they act honestly for the benefit of the company they represent, they discharge both their equitable as well as their legal duty to the company": see *Lagunas Nitrate Co.* v. *Lagunas Syndicate* [1899] 2 Ch 392 at 435. It is perhaps only another way of stating the same proposition to say that the directors are not liable for mere errors of judgement. (2) A director is not bound to give continuous attention to the affairs of his company. His duties are of an intermittent nature to be performed at periodic board meetings, and at meetings of any committee of the board upon which he happens to be placed. He is not, however, bound to attend all such meetings, though he ought to attend whenever, in the circumstances, he is reasonably able to do so. (3) In respect of all duties that, having regard to the exigencies of business, and the articles of association, may properly be left to some other official, a director is, in the absence of grounds for suspicion, justified in trusting that official to perform such duties honestly. . . .

I must now turn to the facts of the case for the purpose of ascertaining first, whether in any of the matters charged against them the respondents have been guilty of negligence, and secondly, whether any such negligence was wilful, negligence and default meaning for all practical purposes one and the same thing. That Bevan was guilty not merely of wilful negligence but also of fraud will appear quite clearly. The real question that I have to decide is with reference to his co-directors. . . . Cases have not been unknown in which a director has lent his name to a company for what may be called window dressing purposes, and has treated himself as having thereby given ample consideration for his remuneration and as being absolved from any further effort towards promoting the welfare of the company. . . . But I am satisfied from the evidence adduced before me that each one of the respondent directors was willing and anxious to give of his best to the company and at all times took as active a part in the work of the board as circumstances would reasonably permit.

Dorchester Finance Co. Ltd. and another v. Stebbing and others

[1989] BCLC 498
Chancery Division
The executive director and the two non-executive directors of Dorchester Finance Co. Ltd. all had considerable accounting experience. The two non-executive directors left the day-to-day running of the company to Stebbing, the executive director. As the two non-executive directors did not often attend the company's office, they made a practice of signing blank cheques for Stebbing to use. Dorchester Finance Co. Ltd. sued all three directors alleging negligence and claiming damages.

HELD that all three directors had been negligent and were liable to compensate the company. Their claim for statutory relief from liability was rejected. The judge laid down the following standards of skill and care for company directors: a director in carrying out his duties: (1) was required to show such skill as may reasonably be expected from a person with his knowledge and experience; (2) must take such care as an ordinary man might be expected to take in his own affairs; and (3) must exercise any power vested in him in good faith in the interests of the company. The judge also held that no distinction was to be made between the standards applying to executive and non-executive directors.

NOTE

Although the case was not reported until 1989, it took place in 1977.

Norman and another v. Theodore Goddard (a firm) and others

[1991] BCLC 1028

Chancery Division

The principal asset of a trust consisted of all the issued shares of a property company, LB Investments Ltd. The trustees were a partner in Theodore Goddard and a company controlled by Theodore Goddard's Jersey office. Another partner, B., administered the trust. Quirk (Q.), a chartered surveyor with no knowledge of company law or offshore financial matters, was made a director of LB Investments Ltd. B. suggested to Q. that cash held by LB Investments Ltd. should be invested offshore in Gibbon Ltd. (Gibbon) and assured Q. that the investment would be safe as it was controlled by Theodore Goddard. Money was accordingly invested in Gibbon. Gibbon was in fact a company controlled by B., who stole the money transferred to it by LB Investments Ltd. The trust sued Theodore Goddard for the replacement of the stolen money. Theodore Goddard sought a contribution from Q. under the Civil Liability (Contribution) Act 1978 on the basis that he had breached his duty of care as a director of LB Investments Ltd. and 'was liable in respect of the same damage'.

HELD that section 214(4) of the Insolvency Act 1986 (wrongful trading) lays down the test of a director's duty of care. A director was entitled to trust persons in positions of responsibility unless there was a reason to distrust them. Q. acted reasonably in accepting the information from B. and acting on it without further enquiry as B. was a senior partner in an eminent firm of city solicitors. On the facts there was nothing which should have prompted Q. to stop sending cash to Gibbon or to try to recover the money already deposited. Therefore the claim for a contribution failed.

Hogg v. Cramphorn Ltd. and others

[1967] 1 Ch 254

Chancery Division

The directors of a company set up an employees' share scheme operating through the medium of a trust for employees, and gave the trustees ten votes per share. The trustees were also granted an interest-free loan to enable them to fund the share purchase. The objective of the scheme was to frustrate a takeover bid by conferring special voting rights upon the trust. Although the articles gave the directors discretion in the issue of share capital, they were not empowered to attach more than one vote to every share. An action was brought by a shareholder representing all but three of the shareholders against the company and the trustees of the employee shareholding trust, challenging the constitutionality of the special voting rights, and also contending that the allotment by the directors of the shares and the making of the interest-free loans to the trustees was in breach of their fiduciary duty to use their power for a proper purpose.

HELD by BUCKLEY, J., (1) that the directors had no power under the terms of the company's articles to attach the special voting rights to the shares; (2) the plaintiff had no title to sue to have the allotment set aside (although the trustees might be competent to do so), but was justified in suing in relation to the loans to the trust; (3) the power of allotment was a fiduciary power, and if exercised for an improper motive was liable to be set aside, despite the fact that the issue might have been made in the belief on the part of the directors that it was *bona fide* for the benefit of the company as a whole; and (4) the loan to the trustees, the execution of the trust deed and the allotment of the shares were all part of a scheme aimed at securing control for the directors and were all *ultra vires*. However, the judge granted the company an opportunity to allow the share issue and associated documentation to be ratified, on condition that the votes belonging to the trust's shares were not counted. A general meeting then took place which ratified the establishment of the trust, and approved the allotment to it of the shares on the basis of one vote per share rather than ten votes per share as before, and the advance of the loan from the company to the trust.

BUCKLEY, J. A majority of shareholders in general meeting is entitled to pursue what course it chooses within the company's powers, however wrong-headed it may appear to others, provided the majority do not unfairly oppress other members of the company. These considerations lead me to the conclusion that the issue of the 5,707 shares, with the special voting rights which the directors purported to attach to them, could not be justified by the view that the directors genuinely believed it would benefit the company if they could command a majority of the votes in general meetings. The fact that, as I have held, the directors were mistaken in thinking they could attach to these shares more than one vote each is irrelevant. The power to issue shares was a fiduciary power and if, as I think, it was exercised for an improper motive, the issue of these shares is liable to be set aside.

. . . Before setting the allotment and issue of the 5,707 shares aside, therefore, I propose to allow the company an opportunity to decide in general meeting whether it approves or disapproves of the issue of these shares to the trustees. Mr Goulding will undertake on behalf of the trustees not to vote at such meeting in respect of the 5,707 shares.

. . . If the company in general meeting elects to ratify what the board has done, there will be no objection to the trustees continuing to hold the shares they have bought upon the trusts of the trust deed. Otherwise the loans to the trustees must be treated as having been made by the directors in excess of their powers, and since the trustees cannot rely on the doctrine of *Royal British Bank* v. *Turquand* (1843) 2 Hare 461, the moneys would fall to be treated as having always remained the property of the company held by the trustees upon a resulting trust for the company.

Multinational Gas and Petrochemical Co. v. Multinational Gas and Petrochemical Services Ltd. and others

[1983] 1 Ch 258; [1983] 2 All ER 563; [1983] 3 WLR 492
Court of Appeal

Three oil companies jointly formed the plaintiff company with the objective of purchasing, transporting and storing gas and liquefied gas. The plaintiff was a Liberian registered company, which had an English subsidiary, S. (the defendant in the action), which acted as its agent in the United Kingdom. The three oil companies were the shareholders of the plaintiff company, and they also appointed the directors. The plaintiff company had no place of business in the United Kingdom and all meetings, therefore, took place abroad. After trading profitably for some time, a fall in the market led to the liquidation of both the plaintiff company and S. The plaintiff company sought leave from the Companies Court to bring an action against S. for breach of its agency agreement, against the oil companies for breach of duty of care in exercising powers of management and direction, and against the plaintiff company's own directors for negligence. Much of the case was concerned with whether service of writs could be made out of the jurisdiction. Leave was granted by the court, but overturned on appeal.

HELD, *inter alia*, that although the plaintiff had a separate legal existence from its shareholders, it existed for their benefit, and provided they acted *intra vires*, they could manage its affairs as they chose while it remained solvent, and that the shareholders, who owed no duties to third parties or to future creditors, by approving the directors' acts had made them the acts of the plaintiff company, and it could not now complain of the lack of commercial judgment of the directors in decision-making.

LAWTON, L.J. The submission in relation to the defendants was as follows. No allegation had been made that the plaintiff's directors had acted *ultra vires* or in bad faith. What was alleged was that when making the decisions which were alleged to have caused the plaintiff loss and giving instructions to Services to put them into effect they had acted in accordance with the directions and at the behest of the three oil companies. These oil companies were the only shareholders. All the acts complained of became the plaintiff's acts. The plaintiff, although it had a separate existence from its oil company shareholders, existed for the benefit of those shareholders, who, provided they acted *intra vires* and in good faith, could manage the plaintiff's affairs as they wished. If they wanted to take business risks through the plaintiff which no prudent businessman would take they could lawfully do so. Just as an individual can act like a fool provided he keeps within the law so could the plaintiff, but in its case it was for the shareholders to decide whether the plaintiff should act foolishly. As shareholders they owed no duty to those with whom the plaintiff did business. It was for such persons to assess the hazards of doing business with them. It follows, so it was submitted, that the plaintiff as a matter of law, cannot now complain about what it did at its shareholders' behest.

This submission was based upon the assumption, for which there was evidence, that Liberian company law was the same as English company law and upon a long line of cases starting with *Salomon* v. *Salomon & Co. Ltd.* [1897] AC 22 and ending with the decision of this court in *In re Horsley & Weight Ltd.* [1982] Ch 442. In my judgment these cases establish the following relevant principles of law: first, the plaintiff was at law a different legal person from the subscribing oil company shareholders and was not their agent: see the *Salomon* case [1897] AC 22, *per* Lord Macnaghten at p. 51. Secondly, that the oil companies as shareholders were not liable to anyone except to the extent and the manner provided by the Companies Act 1948: see the same case at the same page. Thirdly, that when the oil companies acting together required the plaintiff's directors to make decisions or to approve what had already been done, what they did or approved became the plaintiff's acts and were binding on it: see by way of examples *Attorney-General for Canada* v. *Standard Trust Co. of New York* [1911] AC 498; *In re Express Engineering Works Ltd.* [1920] 1 Ch 466 and *In re Horsley & Weight Ltd.* [1982] Ch 442. When approving whatever their nominee directors had done, the oil companies were not, as the plaintiff submitted, relinquishing any causes of action which the plaintiff might have had against its directors. When the oil companies, as shareholders, approved what the plaintiff's directors had done there was no cause of action because at that time there was no damage. What the oil companies were doing was adopting the directors' acts and as shareholders, in agreement with each other, making those acts the plaintiff's acts.

It follows, it seems to me, that the plaintiff cannot now complain about what in law were its own acts. Further I can see no grounds for adjudging that the oil companies, as shareholders were under any duty of care to the plaintiff . . . I would dismiss the appeal.

DILLON, L.J. The heart of the matter is therefore that certain commercial decisions which were not *ultra vires* the plaintiff were made honestly, not merely by the directors but by all the shareholders of the plaintiff at a time when the plaintiff was solvent. I do not see how there can be any complaint of that.

An individual trader who is solvent is free to make stupid, but honest commercial decisions in the conduct of his business. He owes no duty of care to future creditors. The same applies to a partnership of individuals.

A company, it seems to me, likewise owes no duty of care to future creditors. The directors indeed stand in a fiduciary relationship to the company, as they are appointed to manage the affairs of the company and they owe fiduciary duties to the company though not to its creditors, present or future, or to individual shareholders. The duties owed by a director include a duty of care, as was recognised by Romer J. in *In re City Equitable Fire Insurance Co. Ltd.* [1925] Ch 407, 426-429, though as he pointed out the nature and extent of the duty may depend on the nature of the business of the company and on the particular knowledge and experience of the individual director.

The shareholders, however, owe no such duty to the company. Indeed, so long as the company is solvent the shareholders are in substance the company . . .

. . . The well known passage in the speech of Lord Davey in *Salomon* v. *Salomon & Co. Ltd.* [1987] AC 22,57 that the company is bound in a matter *intra vires* by the unanimous agreement of its members is, in my judgment, apt to cover the present case whether or not Lord Davey had circumstances such as the present case in mind.

If the company is bound by what was done when it was a going concern, then the liquidator is in no better position. He cannot sue the members because they owed no duty to the company as a separate entity and he cannot sue the directors because the decisions which he seeks to impugn were made by, and with the full assent of, the members.

Aveling Barford Ltd. v. Perion Ltd. and others

[1989] BCLC 626
Chancery Division
The plaintiff company (which by the time of judgment was in liquidation) was not in a position to make a distribution to shareholders because of an accumulated deficit on its profit and loss account. It sold property valued at £650,000 to the first defendant company, Perion Ltd., a company controlled by Lee (L.), who also controlled the plaintiff company, for £350,000. The purchase by the defendant company was to be financed in part by a mortgage, and the mortgage company valued the property at £1,150,000. It appeared that the plaintiff and the defendant had also agreed that £400,000 would be paid by the defendant to the plaintiff if they sold the property within a year, and the sale price exceeded £800,000. The property was sold

within the year, for £1,526,000. The plaintiff brought an action against the defendant seeking the return of the proceeds of sale, and obtained judgment in default. The defendant sought to have the judgment set aside.

HELD that as L. knew that the property was worth £650,000, it was a breach of fiduciary duty to sell the property for £350,000, and as the first defendant was aware of the facts, the transaction was voidable and the first defendant was accountable as constructive trustee. The sale was a means of allowing L. to obtain an unauthorised return of capital and hence was *ultra vires* and not ratifiable. The motion to set aside the judgment was dismissed.

HOFFMAN, J. Aveling Barford is a well-known Grantham company, now in liquidation, whose most famous product was steam-rollers. In late 1986 its entire issued share capital was directly or indirectly owned or controlled by a Singapore businessman called Dr Lee Kin Tat. The company was in financial difficulties and had exhausted its credit facilities with its bankers, Standard Chartered Bank.

. . . The general rule is that any act which falls within the express or implied powers of a company conferred by its memorandum of association, whether or not a breach of duty on the part of the directors, will be binding on the company if it is approved or subsequently ratified by the shareholders: see *Rolled Steel Products (Holdings) Ltd.* v. *British Steel Corporation* [1984] BCLC 466 at 507, [1985] All ER 52 at 85 [1985] Ch 246 at 296. But this rule is subject to exceptions created by the general law and one such exception is that a company cannot without the leave of the court or the adoption of a special procedure return its capital to its shareholders. It follows that a transaction which amounts to an unauthorised return of capital is *ultra vires* and cannot be validated by shareholder ratification or approval. Whether or not the transaction is a distribution to shareholders does not depend exclusively on what the parties choose to call it. The court looks at the substance rather than the outward appearance. . . . It seems to me in this case that looking at the matter objectively, the sale to Perion was not a genuine exercise of the company's power under its memorandum to sell its assets. It was a sale at a gross undervalue for the purpose of enabling a profit to be realised by an entity controlled and put forward by its sole beneficial shareholder. . . . The company had at no time distributable reserves and the sale was therefore *ultra vires* and incapable of validation by the approval or ratification of the shareholder. The fact that the distribution was to Perion rather than to

Dr Lee or his other entities which actually held the shares in Aveling Barford is in my judgment irrelevant.

. . . It follows that in my judgment even on the view of the facts most favourable to Perion, it has no arguable defence and the motion to set aside the judgment must be dismissed.

9. The secretary

Summary

1. Sources of the law

The law relating to the company secretary is contained partly in the Companies Act 1985 (sections 283–90), and partly in case law. Much of the secretary's authority and the procedures to be used by the secretary derive from the articles of association, e.g. Table A regulations 99 and 101.

2. The role of the company secretary

Every company must have a secretary and if a private company has only one director, that director cannot also act as the company secretary: section 283 of the Companies Act 1985. A company can have joint secretaries.

The first secretary is chosen by the promoters and named in form 10 submitted to Companies House at incorporation. Thereafter, depending on what the constitution provides, the secretary is generally chosen by the directors and is removable by them: see Table A regulation 99. The secretary's position is thus one of delegated authority from the board of directors.

The tasks of the secretary are generally of an administrative nature. They include:

* Dealing with the procedure associated with general meetings and board meetings, such as sending out notices, arranging a poll, counting votes and taking minutes.

* Keeping the statutory registers, such as the register of members, register of directors and secretaries, and register of charges.

* Sending returns of information to Companies House. These include the annual return, returns of allotments, and a copy of the annual audited accounts.

* Keeping custody of the common seal (if the company has one), and affixing it to official documents and deeds. Whether or not the seal is used, generally the secretary is one of the authorised signatories of the company on official contracts and deeds: see section 36, 36A and 36B of the Companies Act 1985. Also, Table A regulation 101 provides that unless the directors otherwise determine, such documents should be signed either by two directors or one director and the secretary.

The company secretary may be given other duties by the directors (express authority). However, he may have a considerable amount of ostensible or apparent authority to make contracts as an agent of the company, even where not expressly authorised by the directors to do so. Such contracts would bind the company, even if the directors had not granted authority, and do not approve of the contract. This arises where the secretary makes contracts which are within what would be perceived by the other party to the contract to be the normal ambit of the authority of the secretary of a company of that size and type. The scope of a secretary's ostensible authority may depend on the type of work he carries out within the company. He may, for example, also be the company's management accountant or a solicitor. However, any such contracts must lie within the administrative function of the secretary. For example, it has been held that a company secretary had authority to hire cars in the company name: see *Panorama Developments (Guildford) Ltd* v. *Fidelis Furnishing Fabrics Ltd.* [1971]. The secretary would probably be able to hire office staff for his own department, and to purchase office equipment costing a reasonable amount, without being authorised by the directors. The ostensible authority would not extend to the making of a trading contract, or summoning a general meeting without authority from the directors. The attitude of the judges to the ostensible authority of the secretary has grown over time in response to the changing duties of the company secretary: see *Barnett Hoares & Co.* v. *The South London Tramways Co.* [1887].

3. Qualifications

Since the enactment of the Companies Act 1980, the secretary of a public company is required to have professional qualifications. The current rules are found in section 286 Companies Act 1985. They do not apply to secretaries of private companies.

Barnett, Hoares & Co. v. The South London Tramways Co.

[1887] 18 QB 815
Court of Appeal
The defendants, a tramway company, employed contractors to carry out construction work. Under the contract the defendants had the right to retain money until after completion of the construction work. The contractors applied to the plaintiffs, a bank, for an advance upon the security of the retention money. In answer to enquiries made by the plaintiffs, the defendant's secretary erroneously informed them that there would be a certain amount of retention money payable after completion of the works, when in fact a much smaller amount was actually due, as most of the money had already been paid over. The contractors defaulted on repayment of the loan, and the plaintiffs applied to the defendants for payment of the retention money. Except for the sum of £675 which they held for the contractors, the defendants denied liability. It appeared that the statements of the secretary had been made in error. There was no evidence that the secretary had had express authority to make the representations, or as to the nature and scope of his duties. In the court of first instance the judge held that the secretary had no authority to make the representations, with the result that the company was not estopped from denying what the secretary had stated. Accordingly, the defendants were not liable beyond the balance due by them to the contractors. The plaintiffs appealed to the Court of Appeal.

HELD by LORD ESHER, M.R., FRY, and LOPES, L.JJ., that representations of the type made were not within the ostensible authority of a company secretary, and therefore the defendants were not estopped from denying the truth of the representations. The appeal was therefore dismissed.

LORD ESHER, M.R. The question in this case is whether, upon the mere fact that the person making these representations was the secretary of the company, and, in the absence of evidence of any express authority or of any course of business from which authority might be inferred, we ought to hold that the secretary was a person upon whose statements the plaintiffs were entitled to rely as having authority thereby to bind the defendants. I am content to give my judgment in the same terms as I employed in *Newlands* v. *National*

Employers' Accident Association 54 L.J. (QBD) 428. A secretary is a mere servant; his position is to do what he is told, and no person can assume that he has any authority to represent anything at all; nor can anyone assume that statements made by him are necessarily to be accepted as trustworthy without further inquiry, any more than in the case of a merchant it can be assumed that one who is only a clerk has authority to make representations to induce persons to enter into contracts. For these reasons I think the appeal must be dismissed.

Panorama Developments (Guildford) Ltd. v. Fidelis Furnishing Fabrics Ltd.

[1971] 2 QB 711; [1971] 3 All ER 16; [1971] 3 WLR 440
Court of Appeal

Bayne, the secretary of Fidelis Furnishing Fabrics Ltd., hired cars from the plaintiffs, who operated a car-hire business. The cars included Jaguars and Rolls-Royces, which the secretary told the plaintiffs were needed to meet important clients at the airport. He signed himself 'Company Secretary' when placing the order for the cars. He provided references for the company, which were taken up and proved satisfactory. The hiring agreements named Bayne as the hirer, and were signed by Bayne who was described on the agreements as ''Company Secretary''. In fact the arrangement was a fraud and the cars were used by the secretary himself for private purposes. The hire charge was not paid, and the plaintiffs sued the defendants. The defendants denied liability on the ground that they had not contracted to hire the cars because the secretary had no ostensible authority to make the contract on behalf of the company. In the court of first instance the judge decided in favour of the plaintiffs. The defendants appealed to the Court of Appeal.

HELD by LORD DENNING, M.R., SALMON and MEGAW L.JJ., dismissing the appeal, that the hire agreement did not replace the original correspondence between the parties and that, taking all the facts into account, the secretary did have ostensible authority to enter into contracts for the hire of cars. Dicta of Lord Esher M.R. in *Barnett Hoares & Co.* v. *South London Tramways Co.* (1887) QBD 815 held no longer applicable.

LORD DENNING, M.R. Times have changed. A company secretary is a much more important person nowadays than he was in 1887. He is an officer of the company with extensive duties and responsibilities. This appears not only in the modern Companies Acts, but also by the role which he plays in the day-to-day business of companies. He is no longer a mere clerk. He regularly makes representations on behalf of the company and enters into contracts on its behalf which come within the day-to-day running of the company's business. So much so that he may be regarded as held out as having authority to do such things on behalf of the company. He is certainly entitled to sign contracts concerned with the administrative side of a company's affairs, such as employing staff, and ordering cars, and so forth. All such matters now come within the ostensible authority of a company's secretary.

Accordingly, I agree with the judge that Mr R.L. Bayne, as company secretary, had ostensible authority to enter into contracts for the hire of these cars and, therefore, the company must pay for them. Mr Bayne was a fraud. But it was the company which put him in the position in which he, as company secretary, was able to commit the fraud. So the defendants are liable. I would dismiss the appeal, accordingly.

SALMON, L.J. Whatever the position of a company's secretary may have been in 1887, I am quite satisfied that it has altered a great deal from what it was then. At the end of the last century a company secretary still occupied a very humble position—very little higher, if any, than that of a minor clerk. Today, not only has the status of the company secretary been much enhanced, but that state of affairs has been recognised by the statutes to which Lord Denning M.R. has referred. I think there can be no doubt that the secretary is the chief administrative officer of the company. As regards matters concerned with administration, in my judgment, the secretary has ostensible authority to sign contracts on behalf of the company. If a company is ordering cars so that its servants may go and meet foreign customers at airports, nothing, to my mind, is more natural than that the company should hire those cars through its secretary. The hiring is part of his administrative functions. Whether the secretary would have the authority to sign a contract relating to the commercial management of the company, for example, a contract for the sale and purchase of goods in which the company deals, does not arise for decision in the present case and I do not propose to express any concluded opinion upon the point; but contracts such as the present fall within the ambit of administration and I entertain no doubt that the secretary has ostensible power to sign on behalf of the company.

NOTE

These two cases taken together show how the ostensible authority of the company secretary grew over the period since 1887. Probably it has grown still further since then, following the introduction of qualifications for secretaries of public companies by the Companies Act 1980 (now found in section 286 of the Companies Act 1985), thus further enhancing the position of the secretary within and outwith the company.

10. The auditors

Summary

1. Sources of the law

The law relating to the auditor is found in sections 236–7 and 384–94 of the Companies Act 1985, as amended by sections 9 and 24–54 of the Companies Act 1989, and also in case law.

The Companies Act 1989 enacts the provisions of the Eighth Directive of the European Community which is part of the European Community company law harmonisation programme: the Eighth Directive on Qualification and Independence of Auditors (OJ Vol. 27 L126).

2. The role of the auditor

The auditor is appointed by the members as a safeguard against mismanagement of the company's financial affairs by the directors.

3. Appointment and removal of the auditor

The auditor is appointed by the members. Removal of an auditor is either done by appointing another auditor at the next general meeting or by removing the auditor before the expiration of his term of office: sections 386 and 388 of the Companies Act 1985.

4. Resignation of the auditor

The auditor who resigns as a result of some occurrence within the company has special powers to explain the grounds for his resignation to the members: sections 390–392A of the Companies Act 1985.

5. Qualifications

The auditor must be a member of a recognised supervisory body which offers a professional qualification in accountancy, recognised by the Secretary of State for Trade and Industry. He must be independent of the company. Either an individual or a firm may be appointed auditor. The Secretary of State for Trade and Industry maintains a register of auditors: sections 24–54 of the Companies Act 1989.

6. Powers and duties

The auditor has the following statutory powers and duties:

(i) Examination of original books of account to ensure that proper accounting records have been kept;

(ii) Examination of annual balance sheet and profit and loss account to ensure that these agree with the accounting records;

(iii) Reporting on original books of account and annual accounts to members: sections 236–7 of the Companies Act 1985.

The auditor's report must state whether, in the auditor's opinion, the accounts have been properly prepared in accordance with the Companies Act 1985, and whether in his opinion a true and fair view is given in the accounts of the company's affairs as at the balance sheet date, and in relation to the financial year covered by the profit and loss account.

7. Legal relationship of the auditor with the company, its members and outside investors

The auditor is in a contractual relationship with the company. If mistakes are made in the audit through negligence the company can sue for damages for breach of contract. A duty of care in tort (*delict) has also been stated to be owed by the auditor to the members of the company collectively: see *Caparo Industries plc* v. *Dickman* [1990].

In relation to the audit, the auditors do not have any duty in contract or tort towards either the members individually or outside investors such as banks, (both of whom may rely on the audited accounts in considering whether to invest in the company), except where the auditors were aware that the audited accounts were to be shown to particular investors: *Caparo Industries plc* v. *Dickman* [1990]; *obiter dicta* in *Candler* v. *Crane, Christmas & Co.* [1951]; *Al Saudi Banque and others* v. *Clark Pixley (a firm)* [1989] 3 All ER 361; **Twomax Ltd* v. *Dickson McFarlane & Robinson* 1984.

Actions in tort will fail if any one of the following three elements is missing: *damnum injuria datum*, or loss caused by a legal wrong. In the case of *JEB Fasteners Ltd.* v. *Marks Bloom & Co.* [1983], the causative element was missing and the action failed. Failure to adhere to Statements of Standard Accounting Practice may provide evidence of a breach of duty of care: see *Lloyd Cheyham & Co. Ltd.* v. *Littlejohn & Co.* [1987].

Re Kingston Cotton Mill (No. 2)

[1896] 2 Ch 279

Court of Appeal

For some years before a company was wound up, the directors issued to the shareholders balance sheets signed by the auditors, on which the company's year-end stock was grossly overstated. The auditors had relied on certificates valuing the stock provided by the manager, Jackson, who was also one of the directors, which were fraudulent. Dividends were paid for some years on the strength of the audited accounts, but if the true financial position had been known, there was in fact no profit out of which to pay a dividend. The true position as to stock could have been ascertained by the auditors if they had compared the books and added to the stock figure at the beginning of the year the stock purchased during the year, and deducted the amount sold. The company went into liquidation. The liquidator raised an action against the auditors for payment of the amount of dividends improperly declared and paid. Vaughan Williams, J. had held that it was the duty of the auditors to test the accuracy of the manager's certificate by a comparison of the figures in the books, and that they were liable for the dividends which had been paid in consequence of the erroneous balance sheets. The auditors appealed to the Court of Appeal.

HELD, reversing the decision of Vaughan Williams, J., that it was not part of the auditor's duty to take stock, and that in the absence of grounds for suspicion, they were justified in relying on the certificate of the manager, who was a person of high business standing within the company. They were therefore not liable to pay to the liquidator the amount of the dividends paid out by the company to members.

LOPES, L.J. It is the duty of an auditor to bring to bear on the work he has to perform that skill, care and caution which a reasonably competent, careful and cautious auditor would use. What is reasonable skill, care and caution must depend on the particular circumstances of each case. An auditor is not bound to be a detective, or, as was said, to approach his work with suspicion or with a foregone conclusion that there is something wrong. He is a watch-dog, but not a bloodhound. He is justified in believing tried servants of the company in whom confidence is placed by the company. He is entitled to assume that they are honest, and to rely upon their representations, provided he takes reasonable care. If there is anything calculated to excite suspicion he should probe it to the bottom; but in the absence of anything of that kind he is only bound to be reasonably cautious and careful.

. . . It is not the duty of the auditor to take stock; he is not a stock expert; there are many matters in respect of which he must rely on the honesty and accuracy of others. He does not guarantee the discovery of all fraud. I think the auditors were justified in this case in relying on the honesty and accuracy of Jackson, and were not called upon to make further investigation.

NOTE

As a result of guidelines from the accounting profession relating to attendance at a stocktake, carelessness in relation to the examination of a company's stocktaking practices as evidenced in *Kingston Cotton Mill (No. 2)* [1896] might amount to professional negligence today.

Candler v. Crane, Christmas & Co.

[1951] 2 KB 164; [1951] 1 All ER 426
Court of Appeal
The plaintiff considered investing in a limited liability company but, before doing so, asked for sight of the accounts. The defendants, the company accountants, were asked by the managing director to complete them, and the clerk to the accountants was informed that the accounts were to be shown to the plaintiff, who to his knowledge was a potential investor in the company. The accounts were exhibited to the plaintiff who showed them to his own accountants and in due course did invest in the company. The accounts were negligently prepared, and gave a misleading picture of the company's affairs. The company was wound up within a year, resulting in the loss to the plaintiff of the whole value of his investment. The plaintiffs brought an action against the defendants in tort.

At first instance Lloyd-Jacob, J. held that the clerk to the accountants had not been guilty of fraud but had been extremely careless in the preparation of the accounts, but dismissed the action on the ground that the defendants owed no duty of care to the plaintiff. The plaintiffs appealed to the Court of Appeal.

HELD that in the absence of either a contractual or fiduciary relationship and in the absence of fraud, a careless misstatement was not actionable. Lord Denning dissented, holding that the accountants owed a duty of care to the plaintiffs in this case, because they knew the accounts were to be showed to them, and that they were intending investors. There would be no duty of care to strangers who relied on the accounts.

LORD DENNING. Let me now be constructive and suggest the circumstances in which I say that a duty to use care in statement does exist apart from a contract in that behalf. First, what persons are under such a duty? My answer is those persons such as accountants, surveyors, valuers and analysts, whose profession and occupation it is to examine books, accounts, and other things, and to make reports on which other people—other than their clients—rely in the ordinary course of business. Their duty is not merely a duty to use care in their reports. They have also a duty to use care in their work which results in their reports. Herein lies the difference between these professional men and other persons who have been held to be under no duty to use care in their statements, such as promoters who issue a prospectus: *Derry* v. *Peek* (1889) 14 App. Cas. 337 (now altered by statute), and trustees who answer inquiries about the trust funds: *Low* v. *Bouverie* [1891] 3 Ch 82. Those persons do not bring, and are not expected to bring, any professional knowledge or skill into the preparation of their statements: they can only be made responsible by the law affecting persons generally, such as contract, estoppel, innocent misrepresentation or fraud. But it is very different with persons who engage in a calling which requires special knowledge and skill. From very early times it has been held that they owe a duty of care to those who are closely and directly affected by their work, apart altogether from any contract or undertaking in that behalf. Thus Fitzherbert, in his new *Natura Brevium* (1534) 94D, says that: "If a smith prick my horse with a nail, I shall have my action on the case against him, without any warranty by the smith to do it well", and he supports it with an excellent reason: "for it is the duty of every artificer to exercise his art rightly and truly as he ought". This reasoning has been treated as applicable not only to shoeing smiths, surgeons and barbers, who work with hammers, knives and scissors, but also to shipbrokers and clerks in the Custom House who work with figures and make entries in books, "because their situation and employment necessarily imply a competent degree of knowledge in making such entries", *see Shiels* v. *Blackburne* (1789) IH. BI. 159, 162, per Lord Loughborough, which was not referred to by Devlin, J. in *Heskell* v. *Continental Express Ltd* [1950], All ER 1033, 1042.

The same reasoning has been applied to medical men who make reports on the sanity of others: *See Everett* v. *Griffiths* [1920] 3 KB 163, 182, 217. It is, I think, also applicable to professional accountants. They are not liable, of course, for casual remarks made in the course of conversation, nor for other statements made outside their work, or not made in their capacity as accountants. Compare *Fish* v. *Kelly* (1864) 17 CB (NS)194: but they are in my opinion, in proper cases, apart from any contract in the matter, under a duty to use reasonable care in the preparation of their accounts and in the making of their reports.

Secondly, to whom do these professional people owe this duty? I will take accountants, but the same reasoning applies to others. They owe the duty, of course, to their employer or client; and also, I think, to any third person to whom they themselves show the accounts, or to whom they know their employer is going to show the accounts, so as to induce him to invest money or take some other action on them. But I do not think the duty can be extended still further so as to include strangers of whom they have heard nothing and to whom their employer without their knowledge may choose to show their accounts. Once the accountants have handed their accounts to their employer they are not, as a rule, responsible for what he does with them without their knowledge or consent.

Thirdly, to what transactions does the duty of care extend? It extends, I think, only to those transactions for which the accountants knew their accounts were required.

JEB Fasteners Ltd. v. Marks Bloom & Co.

[1981] 3 All ER 289 affirmed [1983] 1 All ER 583

Court of Appeal

The plaintiffs, JEB Fasteners Ltd., wished to make a take-over bid for the shares in a company called BG Fasteners Ltd. The defendants were a firm of accountants who carried out the audit of the accounts of BG Fasteners Ltd. They knew that BG Fasteners Ltd. faced liquidity problems, and was seeking outside finance from the plaintiffs, among other sources. The accounts were negligently audited: the defendants had negligently accepted an inaccurate stock valuation, and as a result the accounts showed a net profit of £11.25, whereas they should have showed a loss of over £13,000. The plaintiff was shown the accounts, but carried out their own investigations, and knew that the stock valuation was overstated in the accounts. Nevertheless the plaintiffs proceeded to make a take-over bid for the share capital of BG Fasteners Ltd., largely because they wanted the services of the two directors of BG Fasteners Ltd. The take over did not result in commercial success and the plaintiffs suffered considerable loss. The plaintiffs brought an action in tort, on the ground that the defendants had made negligent misstatements in their auditor's report. Woolf, J. held that there was liability in tort, owed to the defendants as persons who relied on the accounts, but that the action failed because there was evidence that the plaintiffs would have made their bid in any event, whatever the accounts had showed, and the defendant's negligence was therefore not the cause of their loss. The plaintiffs appealed to the Court of Appeal, on the ground that it was not competent in law to hold both that the plaintiffs had relied on the accounts and that the defendant's negligence had not caused their loss.

HELD that there was no inconsistency in law in the decision of the judge in the court of first instance since a false representation might play a substantial but not decisive part in influencing decision-making, and in that sense be relied on. Therefore the appeal was dismissed, although the scheme laid down by Woolf, J. for assessing auditors' liability was criticised for being over-refined.

At first instance Woolf, J. reviewed recent developments in the law of negligent misrepresentation including *Candler* v. *Crane, Christmas & Co.* [1951], and *Hedley Byrne & Co. Ltd.* v. *Heller & Partners Ltd.* [1964] AC 465. He went on to suggest the following test for establishing whether a duty of care exists.

WOOLF, J. Without laying down any principle which is intended to be of general application, on the basis of the authorities which I have cited, the appropriate test for establishing whether a duty of care exists appears in this case to be whether the defendants knew or reasonably should have foreseen at the time the accounts were audited that a person might rely on those accounts for the purpose of deciding whether or not to take over the company and therefore could suffer loss if the accounts were inaccurate. Such an approach does place a limitation on those entitled to contend that there has been a breach of duty owed to them. First of all, they must have relied on the accounts and, second, they must have done so in circumstances where the auditors either knew that they would or ought to have known that they might.

. . . Having expressed my views as to the matters of law which are in dispute, the issues between the parties can be summarised as follows:

1. The foreseeability issue: that is, ought the defendants to have realised, when auditing BG Fasteners Ltd's accounts for the year ending 31st October 1974, that those accounts could be relied on in the circumstances in which they were allegedly relied on by the plaintiffs for the purpose of taking over BG Fasteners Ltd?

2. The reliance issue: in coming to their decision to take over BG Fasteners Ltd, did the plaintiffs rely on the accounts audited by the defendants?

3. The negligence issue: were the defendants negligent in the preparation of the accounts?

4. The causation issue: that is, did the plaintiffs suffer any loss in consequence of the alleged negligence?

5. The contributory negligence issue: that is, did the plaintiffs contribute to their alleged loss by their own negligence?

6. The quantum issue: the assessment of the plaintiffs' alleged loss.

Caparo Industries plc v. Dickman and others

[1990] 2 AC 605; [1990] 1 All ER 568; [1990] 2 WLR 358

House of Lords

Caparo Industries plc intended to make a take-over bid for the shares of Fidelity plc. It had already bought some shares prior to the bid, and received a copy of the audited accounts. The defendants were partners in the firm of Touche Ross who had carried out the audit. The accounts contained errors in that there had been an over-valuation of stock and an under-provision of after-sales credits so that whereas the accounts showed a profit of £1.3m, they should have showed a loss of £46m. Caparo alleged that had it known the true facts it never would have made a bid at all. It sued the directors for fraudulent misrepresentation and the auditors for negligence, claiming that the accounts did not show a true and fair view of the company's affairs as they stood at the relevant time. The question before the court was whether the auditors owed a duty of care to outside investors and to shareholders as individuals, as opposed to the shareholders collectively, in circumstances where the auditors had no knowledge that the plaintiffs would rely on the audited accounts.

At first instance it was held that a duty of care is owed neither to potential shareholders nor to the shareholders as individuals, but that a duty could be owed to shareholders collectively. This was reversed in the Court of Appeal, where it was held by a majority (O'Connor, L.J. dissenting) that while there was no duty of care owed by the auditors to potential shareholders, there was a duty of care owed by auditors to individual members. The case was appealed by the auditors to the House of Lords.

HELD unanimously that no duty of care is owed either to potential shareholders, or to the shareholders individually. There is, however, a duty of care in auditing the accounts which is owed to the shareholders collectively. The duty was held to be restricted and owed only to parties in a relationship of proximity to the auditors.

LORD BRIDGE OF HARWICH. The situation is entirely different where a statement is put into more or less general circulation and may foreseeably be relied on by strangers to the maker of the statement for any one of a variety of different purposes which the maker of the statement has no specific reason to anticipate. To hold the maker of the statement to be under a duty of care in respect of the accuracy of the statement to all and sundry for any purpose for which they may choose to rely on it is not only to subject him, in the classic words of Cardozo L.J. to "liability in an indeterminate amount for an indeterminate time to an indeterminate class" (*Ultramares Corporation* v. *Touche* (1931) 174 NE 441, 444) it is also to confer on the world at large a quite unwarranted entitlement to appropriate for their own purposes the benefit of the expert knowledge or professional expertise attributed to the maker of the statement.

. . . These considerations amply justify the conclusion that auditors of a public company's accounts owe no duty of care to members of the public at large who rely on the accounts in deciding to buy shares in the company. If a duty of care were owed so widely, it is difficult to see any reason why it should not equally extend to all who rely on the accounts in relation to other dealings with a company as lenders or merchants extending credit to the company. A claim that such a duty was owed by auditors to a bank lending to a company was emphatically and convincingly rejected by Millett J. in *Al Saudi Banque* v. *Clark Pixley* [1989] 3 All ER 361.

LORD OLIVER OF AYLMERTON. A defective bottle of ginger beer may injure a single consumer but the damage stops there. A single statement may be repeated endlessly with or without the permission of its author and may be relied on in a different way by many different people. Thus the postulate of a simple duty to avoid any harm that is, with hindsight, reasonably capable of being foreseen becomes untenable without the imposition of some intelligible limits to keep the law of negligence within the bounds of common sense and practicality. Those limits have been found by the requirement of what has been called a "relationship of proximity" between plaintiff and defendant and by the imposition of a further requirement that the attachment of liability for harm which has occurred be "just and reasonable".

. . . The structure of the corporate trading entity, at least in the case of public companies whose shares are dealt with on an authorised Stock Exchange, involves the concept of a more or less widely distributed holding of shares rendering the personal involvement of each individual shareholder in the day-to-day management of the company impracticable, with the result that management is necessarily separated from ownership. The management is confided to a board of directors which operates in a fiduciary capacity and is answerable to and removable by the shareholders who can act, if they act at all, only collectively and only through the medium of a general meeting. Hence the legislative provisions requiring the board of directors annually to give an account of its stewardship to a general meeting of the shareholders. This is the only occasion in each year upon which the general body of shareholders is given the opportunity to consider, to criticise and to comment upon the conduct by the board of the company's affairs, to vote upon the directors' recommendation as to dividends, to approve or disapprove the directors' remuneration and, if thought desirable, to remove and replace all or any of the directors. It is the auditor's function to ensure, so far as possible, that the financial information as to the company's affairs prepared by the directors accurately reflects the company's position in order, first, to protect the company itself from the consequences of undetected errors or, possibly, wrongdoing (by, for instance, declaring dividends out of capital) and, secondly, to provide shareholders with reliable intelligence for the purpose of enabling them to scrutinise the conduct of the company's affairs and to exercise their collective powers to reward or control or remove those to whom that conduct has been confided.

LORD JAUNCEY OF TULLICHETTLE. There is nothing in Part VII [of the Companies Act 1985] which suggests that the accounts are prepared and sent to members for any purpose other than to enable them to exercise class rights in general meeting. I therefore conclude that the purpose of annual accounts, so far as members are concerned, is to enable them to question the past management of the company, to exercise their voting rights, if so advised, and to influence future policy and management. Advice to individual shareholders in relation to present or future investment in the company is no part of the statutory purpose of the preparation and distribution of the accounts.

NOTE

A similar decision was reached by Millett, J. in *Al Saudi Banque and others* v. *Clark Pixley (a firm)* [1989] 3 All ER 361 in relation to investments by bankers who relied on negligently audited accounts, but whose reliance was unknown to the auditors.

James McNaughton Papers Group Ltd. v. Hicks Anderson & Co. (a firm)

[1991] 1 All ER 134

Court of Appeal

The plaintiff company entered into negotiations for the agreed take-over of another company called MK which was in financial difficulties. The chairman of MK asked the defendants, who were the accountants of MK, to prepare draft accounts as quickly as possible for use in the negotiations. A representative of the defendants stated that as a result of rationalisation MK was breaking even or doing marginally worse. After the take-over discrepancies were discovered in the accounts and civil proceedings were raised against the auditors on the grounds of negligence in the preparation of the draft accounts. At first instance the judge held that the defendants owed a duty of care to the plaintiffs and awarded damages. The defendants appealed to the Court of Appeal.

HELD that where a negligent statement was acted on to his loss by a person other than the person directly intended as the recipient by the maker of the statement, the relevant factors to be considered in determining whether the maker of the statement owed a duty of care to the recipient of the statement included the purpose for which the statement was made; the purpose for which the statement was communicated; the relationship between the maker, the recipient and any third party; the size of any class to which the recipient belonged; the state of knowledge of the maker; and any reliance by the recipient. Having regard to those factors, the defendants owed no duty of care to the plaintiffs in respect of the draft accounts, since the accounts were produced for MK and not for the plaintiffs, the accounts were draft accounts and the defendants could not have reasonably foreseen that the plaintiffs would treat them as final accounts, the defendants did not take part in the negotiations, and the plaintiffs were aware that MK was in a poor state and could be expected to consult their own accountants. The statement made at the meeting was a general statement and did not affect the figures in the accounts, and the defendants could not have reasonably foreseen that the plaintiffs would rely on that statement without further advice.

NEILL, L.J. From this scrutiny [of the decided cases] it seems to me clear (a) that . . . in England a restrictive approach is now adopted to any extension of the scope of the duty of care beyond the person directly intended by the maker of the statement to act on it, and (b) that in deciding whether a duty of care exists in any particular case it is necessary to take all the circumstances into account, but (c) that, notwithstanding (b), it is possible to identify certain matters which are likely to be of importance in most cases in reaching a decision as to whether or not a duty exists . . . .

(1) *The purpose for which the statement was made*
In some cases the statement will have been prepared or made by the "adviser" for the express purpose of being communicated to the "advisee" (to adopt the labels used by Lord Oliver). In such a case it may often be right to conclude that the advisee was within the scope of the duty of care. In many cases, however, the statement will have been prepared or made, or primarily prepared or made, for a different purpose and for the benefit of someone other than the advisee. In such cases it will be necessary to look carefully at the precise purpose for which the statement was communicated to the advisee.

(2) *The purpose for which the statement was communicated*
Under this heading it will be necessary to consider the purpose of and the circumstances surrounding the communication. Was the communication made for information only? Was it made for some action to be taken, and if so, what action and by whom? Who requested the communication to be made? These are some of the questions which may have to be addressed.

(3) *The relationship between the adviser, the advisee and any relevant third party*
Where the statement was made or prepared in the first instance to or for the benefit of someone other than the advisee it will be necessary to consider the relationship between the parties. Thus it may be that the advisee is likely to look to the third party and through him to the adviser for advice and guidance. Or the advisee may be wholly independent and in a position to make any necessary judgments himself.

(4) *The size of any class to which the advisee belongs*
Where there is a single advisee or he is a member of only a small class it may sometimes be simple to infer that a duty of care was owed to him. Membership of a large class, however, may make such an inference more difficult, particularly where the statement was made in the first instance for someone outside the class.

(5) *The state of knowledge of the adviser*

The precise state of knowledge of the adviser is one of the most important matters to examine. Thus it will be necessary to consider his knowledge of the purpose for which the statement was made or required in the first place and also his knowledge of the purpose for which the statement was communicated to the advisee. In this context knowledge includes not only actual knowledge but also such knowledge as would be attributed to a reasonable person in the circumstances in which the adviser was placed. On the other hand any duty of care will be limited to transactions or types of transactions of which the adviser had knowledge and will only arise where ''the adviser knows or ought to know that [the statement or advice] will be relied on by a particular person or class of persons in connection with that transaction'': see *per* Lord Oliver in the *Caparo Industries* case [1990] 1 All ER 568 at 592, [1990] 2 AC 605 at 641. It is also necessary to consider whether the adviser knew that the advisee would rely on the statement without obtaining independent advice.

(6) *Reliance by the advisee*

In cases where the existence of a duty of care is in issue it is always useful to examine the matter from the point of view of the plaintiff. As I have ventured to say elsewhere the question, ''Who is my neighbour?'' prompts the response, ''Consider first those who would consider you to be their neighbour.'' One should therefore consider whether and to what extent the advisee was entitled to rely on the statement to take the action that he did take. It is also necessary to consider whether he did in fact rely on the statement, whether he did or should have used his own judgment and whether he did or should have sought independent advice. In business transactions conducted at arms' length it may sometimes be difficult for an advisee to prove that he was entitled to act on the statement without taking any independent advice or to prove that the adviser knew, actually or inferentially, that he would act without taking such advice.

. . . In the end, however, I have come to the conclusion that, if one applies the tests which have been established in the recent authorities, the existence of a duty of care has not been made out.

. . . The following matters in particular have impressed me: (a) It is clear that in about July Mr Topsom asked Mr Pritchard to prepare the audited accounts as quickly as possible. At that stage, though the future of MK was in the melting pot, the accounts were to be produced for Mr Topsom. (b) The accounts, when produced, were merely draft accounts. In the context of this case this was an important point because the term ''draft'' showed that further work would be required before the accounts became final accounts. Accordingly Mr McNaughton was not entitled to treat them as though they were final accounts and Mr Pritchard could not be expected to foresee that Mr McNaughton would so treat them. (c) Mr Pritchard attended the meeting on 7 September and wrote the letter on that date to Mr McNaughton. There is no evidence that he took any other part in the negotiations leading to the takeover. (d) As was pointed out during the course of the hearing of the appeal, it would appear that the judge did not appreciate that the accounts showed that there was a loss for the year ended 30 June 1982 of about £48,000. MK were plainly in a poor state and Mr McNaughton can have been in no doubt about the matter. (e) This was a transaction between experienced business men. It was to be anticipated that Mr McNaughton would have access to and would consult with his own accountancy advisers. Mr Pritchard and HA were the accountants to MK. (f) Great reliance was placed by McNaughton on the answer given by Mr Pritchard to Mr McNaughton's question at the meeting on 7 September. It seems to me, however, that it was a very general answer and that it did not affect any of the specific figures in the draft accounts. Moreover, it is not possible in my view to attribute to Mr Pritchard the knowledge that Mr McNaughton would rely on this answer *without any further inquiry or advice* for the purpose of reaching a concluded agreement with Mr Topsom.

 . . . I have not found this an easy case. Having looked at length at the documents and the transcripts of the evidence, I have been driven to the conclusion that, as the law stands at present, McNaughton have not been able to establish the existence of a duty of care owed to them by Mr Pritchard or HA at any material time.

 I would allow the appeal.

NOTE

In *Morgan Crucible Co. plc* v. *Hill Samuel & Co. Ltd. and others* [1991] 1 All ER 148; [1991] BCC 82, the Court of Appeal held that a duty of care was arguably owed by *inter alia* a firm of accountants in respect of negligently prepared financial statements, financial statements in the company's defence documents, and a profits forecast which formed part of representations made to the plaintiffs prior to a take-over bid by the plaintiffs. The important difference between this case and *James McNaughton Papers Group Ltd.* v. *Hicks Anderson & Co.* [1991] is that in this case the defendants were or should have been aware that the statements would be relied on by the plaintiffs.

★ Twomax Ltd. v. Dickson McFarlane & Robinson

1984 SLT (Note) 424; 1983 SLT (OH) 98
Court of Session

The pursuers bought shares in a company called Kintyre Knitwear Ltd. having read the annual audited accounts, which showed the company to have made a profit of £20,000 in 1973 following several years of losses. Soon afterwards the company went into receivership and then into liquidation, on the grounds of insolvency. The pursuers accordingly lost the value of their entire investment. The pursuers then brought an action against the auditors, Dickson, McFarlane & Robinson, suing for the return of the sums they had invested in the shares, alleging that the accounts had been negligently prepared and that the 1973 profit was overstated in the accounts. The auditors did know that at the time of preparing the 1973 accounts the company was suffering a shortage of capital, and that unqualified auditors' reports were commonly relied on by potential investors.

HELD by Lord Stewart that an auditor did owe a duty of care to potential investors in carrying out the audit, that this had been breached, and that the pursuers were accordingly entitled to a full refund of the sums invested. The case was appealed to the Inner House of the Court of Session, and the appeal was granted, but the finding of the Lord Ordinary that the defender owed a duty of care which had been breached was not challenged.

LORD STEWART. He [Mr McFarlane] was aware that Kintyre was suffering from a shortage of capital. He was aware during the summer months of 1973 that a director, Mr Anderson, wished to dispose of his shareholding. He was aware that that shareholding was substantial, amounting to 10,000 shares. The defenders had in fact advertised in the newspaper under a box number on behalf of Mr Anderson. He knew for certain that the accounts were being made available to lenders in so far as he knew they were lodged with the company's bank. He knew that auditors' certificates, when they were "clean" certificates, were commonly relied on by shareholders, potential investors, and potential lenders. In the whole circumstances I consider that Mr McFarlane should have foreseen before he certified the 1973 accounts that these accounts might be relied on by a potential investor for the purpose of deciding whether or not to invest. . . . I therefore consider that in respect of Twomax and Mr Gordon (another pursuer) both being in the class of persons who were potential investors, Mr McFarlane owed a *prima facie* duty of care in the auditing of the 1973 accounts.

NOTE

The decision in the Scottish case of *Twomax Ltd.* v. *Dickson McFarlane & Robinson*, above, goes further than any of the English decisions in recognising a duty of care owed by auditors to potential, as opposed to actual, members. This has been expressly doubted by Lord Jauncey in *Caparo Industries plc* v. *Dickman*, on the ground that the reasoning is unsound. In the light of the fact that *Caparo* is a House of Lords decision, and Lord Jauncey is a Scottish Lord of Appeal, *Caparo* will be regarded as a highly persuasive precedent in subsequent Scottish cases, and *Twomax* is unlikely to be followed.

Lloyd Cheyham & Co. Ltd. v. Littlejohn & Co.

[1987] BCLC 303

Queen's Bench Division

Trec Rentals Ltd. (Trec) carried on the business of renting trailers. Trehaven Trust Ltd. (Trehaven) owned 39 per cent of the shares in Trec and also a debenture which was convertible into shares which would give it a 78 per cent shareholding in the company. Trec suffered a drop in rental income and Trehaven was obliged to give it financial support. Trehaven sought to sell its interest in Trec and contracted with the plaintiffs. Before entering into the agreement the plaintiffs were shown a copy of the audited accounts which had been prepared by the defendants, the auditors of Trec. Soon after the agreement was entered into, Trec was wound up. The plaintiffs raised proceedings on the grounds of negligence against the auditors in respect of their auditing of the accounts, on which the plaintiff had relied. In particular the plaintiffs alleged that the way in which the cost of replacing tyres on trailers was provided for in the accounts was inadequate in that they only took the substantial portion of the cost into account when it crystallised, whereas the plaintiffs argued that it should have been taken into account when the loss accrued, and there was no express statement in the accounts that a substantial sum would have to be paid for the replacement of the tyres.

HELD, dismissing the action, that although this was a case where the defendants owed the plaintiffs a duty of care, as they knew that the accounts were going to be relied on by the plaintiffs, on the facts there had been no breach of that duty of care because the method used by the defendants in providing for the cost of replacement of tyres was consistent with their reasonably considering that the accounts showed a true and fair view of the company's affairs.

Per curiam. While Statements of Standard Accounting Practice are not rigid rules, they are very strong evidence of what is the proper standard to be adopted and, unless there is some justification, a departure from them will be regarded as a breach of duty.

WOOLF, J. *The duty of care issue*

It is clear beyond peradventure that the defendants knew that their audited accounts were required by the plaintiffs in relation to their proposed agreement in respect of Trec. In these circumstances, subject to reserving his position if the case should go to appeal, counsel for the defendants [Mr T. Scott Baker QC] accepts that the defendants owed to the plaintiffs a duty of care in auditing the accounts of Trec. On my view of the law this is undoubtedly the position . . . .

Negligence and causation issue in relation to tyres

In a nutshell it is Mr Anderson's case that when he entered into the agreement of 28 September 1981 on behalf of the plaintiffs he was unaware that in the near future a very substantial sum was going to have to be expended by the plaintiffs in purchasing replacement tyres for the trailers, that the audited accounts should have indicated that this was the position and if they had done so he would not have entered into the agreement because the costs of replacement tyres made the whole basis on which he had entered into the agreement unworkable.

. . . The way the tyres were dealt with in the audited accounts for 31 December 1980 was the same way they had been dealt with in the previous years and reflected the proposals of Mr Palmer on the formation of the company, which proposals in this respect were accepted by the defendants. The need to replace tyres was dealt with in two ways. First of all in the trading and profit and loss account for the 13 months to 31 December 1980 there appeared the figure of £151,840 in relation to spares, maintenance and painting, which sum included approximately £24,000 in respect of replacement tyres. In the normal way the figure for the previous year also appeared and that was £62,611.

In addition in the balance sheet the figure which was given for fixed assets, as the notes make clear, included an allowance for depreciation of the trailers as a whole. This depreciation was as the note states to write off the assets concerned over their expected useful lives on a straight line basis, in the case of trailers and other plant and equipment at 10 per cent per annum.

If as was the case with the plaintiffs relatively few tyres had been replaced, the fact that a substantial sum would be required to be paid in respect of replacement tyres certainly was not expressly stated. There was no note dealing with the tyres.

. . . The reason why importance is attached to the terms of the auditors' report is because in the case of a company which is continuing to trade it is expected that in the normal way the trading income will be sufficient to cover the costs of repairs and replacements and in the case of Trec without additional financial assistance, that clearly would not be possible.

In contending that the view of the defendants is not a proper view, the plaintiffs and Mr Cade rely heavily on Statements of Standard Accounting Practice issued by the Institute and in particular Statement of Standard Accounting Practice No. 2. As to the proper treatment of such statements, the approach of both counsel was the same and I accept this approach. While they are not conclusive, so that a departure from their terms necessarily involves a breach of the duty of care, and they are not as the explanatory foreword makes clear, rigid rules, they are very strong evidence as to what is the proper standard which should be adopted and unless there is some justification, a departure from this will be regarded as constituting a breach of duty. It appears to me important that this should be the position because third parties in reading the accounts are entitled to assume that they have been drawn up in accordance with the approved practice unless there is some indication in the accounts which clearly states that this is not the case. . . .

After examining the evidence, the judge stated: I therefore come to the conclusion that the plaintiffs have failed to establish a breach of duty of care and furthermore that as far as the absence of a note was concerned, this was not causative of any loss.

. . . It follows, therefore, that the plaintiff's action fails.

11. Company meetings

Summary

1. Sources of the law and procedure of meetings

The law on company meetings is largely statutory, although there is also some case law. The principal statutory provisions are sections 366–83 of the Companies Act 1985. The courts regard many disputes over the procedure of meetings as internal matters for the company to regulate, rather than as matters for the courts to decide.

The procedure is found in the articles of association, for example, regulations 36–63, 88–98, 100 and 111–16 of Table A.

2. Types of meeting

By section 366 of the Companies Act 1985, every company must hold an annual general meeting every year, except in the case of a private company which has by elective resolution elected to dispense with the holding of annual general meetings. Extraordinary general meetings are convened as and when there are items of business to transact during the year. If members wish to have any matters discussed at an extraordinary general meeting, they can requisition one if the holders of one-tenth of the issued share capital of the company serve a written requisition on the company. The meeting has to be convened within twenty-one days, and actually held within twenty-eight days from the date of the notice convening the meeting: section 368 of the Companies Act 1985.

3. Notice

Twenty-one days' written notice must be given before an annual general meeting, and fourteen days' notice must be given for an extraordinary general meeting, unless a special resolution is to be proposed at that meeting, when twenty-one days' notice has to be given. Short notice can be given in certain circumstances. Table A contains provisions on how and where notice should be given (regulations 111–16). Regulation 39 excuses accidental omission to give notice to members. See *In re West Canadian Collieries Ltd.* [1962].

Special notice is notice to the company, not notice to members. It has to be given to the company in connection with certain resolutions, for example, an ordinary resolution to remove either a director or the auditor before the expiration of his term of office. It is given by the persons putting forward the item of business for consideration, and is given twenty-eight days before the meeting at which the resolution is due to be moved: section 379 of the Companies Act 1985.

4. Quorum

Section 370 of the Companies Act 1985 provides that the quorum for a general meeting is two members personally present, unless the articles of a company provide otherwise. Table A regulation 40 also provides for a quorum of two persons entitled to vote on business, one or both of whom can be a proxy for another member, or the representative of a corporate member. In Table A regulation 89 provides that unless a different quorum is fixed by the directors, the quorum for a board meeting is two. See *Re Sticky Fingers Restaurant Ltd.* [1992].

5. Resolutions

There are five types of resolutions used by companies to transact business at meetings. Companies can transact by means of:

* Ordinary resolutions
* Special resolutions
* Extraordinary resolutions
* Written resolutions
* Elective resolutions

Ordinary resolutions are not defined in legislation but, by implication from the definitions of the other resolutions, require a simple majority of members voting in person or, where allowed by proxy, voting at a meeting of which due notice has been given. This is the appropriate resolution to use unless statute or the articles of association of the company state otherwise. For example, the business of the annual general meeting is transacted by ordinary resolution. Directors can be removed from office by ordinary resolution.

Special resolutions are defined by section 378 of the Companies Act 1985. They require a three-quarter majority of members voting in person or where allowed by proxy at a general meeting of which twenty-one days' notice specifying the intention to propose the resolution as a special resolution has been given. Examples of business which has by statute to be transacted by special resolution are: change of name of the company, alteration of objects in the memorandum of association, and alteration of the articles of association.

Extraordinary resolutions are also defined by section 378. They also require a three-quarter majority of members voting in person or where allowed by proxy, but they do not require twenty-one days' notice. They are not very common. Examples are the resolution to wind up a company voluntarily on the ground that it is insolvent, and the resolution passed by members at a class meeting to sanction a variation of class rights.

Written resolutions were introduced by the Companies Act 1989, and are now provided for in section 381A–2A of the Companies Act 1985. Members of private companies can make decisions by unanimous written resolutions (i.e. the entire membership of the company must signify its assent) without the need for a general meeting. The auditors have the right to give an opinion that the matter to be decided upon concerns them as auditors, and that it should be decided at a general meeting. In fact for some time the courts had recognised the validity of decisions taken unanimously by companies, where no meeting had taken place: see *Cane* v. *Jones* [1980].

Elective resolutions were also introduced by the Companies Act 1989 and, again, only apply to the private company. The objective was to free such companies from procedure which may be unnecessarily formal in the case of very small companies. The rules are found at section 379A of the Companies Act 1985. These resolutions must be agreed to by all the members entitled to attend and vote at the meeting, or where allowed, voting by proxy, at a meeting of which twenty-one days' notice has been given. Elective resolutions can be passed in the following areas: a resolution to give directors permanent authority to allot shares; a resolution to dispense with the laying of accounts before the company in general meeting; a resolution to dispense with the holding of an annual general meeting; a resolution to vary the majority required to authorise short notice for a meeting; a resolution to dispense with the appointment of auditors annually. Further areas may be added by the Secretary of State by regulations. Elective resolutions can be revoked by ordinary resolution.

Copies of all special resolutions, extraordinary resolutions, elective resolutions, and of those written resolutions which would otherwise have to have been passed as special or extraordinary resolutions, must be filed at Companies House within fifteen days from the date of being passed. Copies of certain ordinary resolutions also need to be filed: section 380 of the Companies Act 1985.

6. Voting

Voting at general meetings is usually conducted by show of hands giving each member one vote, unless a poll is demanded. A poll vote gives members votes in proportion to the number of shares they hold. Section 373 of the Companies Act 1985 gives minimum rights to demand a poll: a poll can be demanded by five members with the right to vote, or by members representing not less than one-tenth of the voting rights, or by members with the right to vote, holding shares which represent one-tenth of the paid-up capital of the company. Table A regulation 46 provides better rights, allowing the chairman to demand a poll, and for two voting members to demand a poll.

Unless the articles otherwise provide, proxies can only vote on a poll and not on a show of hands. Proxies need not be members of the company, and are appointed in writing up to (but not more than) 48 hours before the meeting: section 372 of the Companies Act 1985. In a private company a proxy can speak, but in a public company a proxy can only speak if the articles allow.

7. Minutes

Minutes must be taken of all general meetings and all board meetings. Written resolutions also have to be recorded in the same way as minutes. The minutes of general meetings, but not board meetings, are available for inspection by members of the company but not by the public.

8. Board meetings

The procedure for these is set out in the articles of association: see Table A regulations 88–98.

Re Sticky Fingers Restaurant Ltd.

[1992] BCLC 84

Chancery Division

The issued share capital of one hundred shares in the company was held as to sixty-six shares by Wyman (W.) and thirty-four shares by Mitchell (M.). W. and M. were the sole directors of the company and were in dispute. M. refused to attend meetings, which meant that no valid board or general meetings could be held because a quorum could not be achieved. W. complained of financial irregularities in M.'s day-to-day handling of the company's management and sought M.'s resignation as a director. M. presented a petition under section 459 of the Companies Act 1985 seeking an order that W. purchase his shares. W. sought an order under section 371 of the Companies Act 1985 (giving the court power to convene a meeting) to convene a meeting at which the quorum could be fixed at one to enable resolutions to be considered for the appointment of two new directors.

HELD that the discretion under section 371 of the Companies Act 1985 for the court to convene a meeting should be used to bring an effective board into being, but not so as to give W. the opportunity of harming M. pending the outcome of his petition under section 459 by removing him as a director, or excluding him from participating in the company's affairs. The order would be made subject to the proviso that each of the directors appointed at the meeting would deliver a signed undertaking to M.'s solicitors to the effect that he would not exercise his right to remove M. from his directorship, or interfere in M.'s day-to-day conduct of the company's business, or effect any change in the constitution or capital of the company, and would not be allowed to act as a director until that had been done.

MERVYN DAVIES, J. I start from the basis that here there is no effective board of the company. Mr Weaver QC, for Mr Wyman, drew attention to the need for there to be an effective board pending disposal of the petition. But, he said, the relations between the two directors have broken down. They are at loggerheads. Mr Mitchell has adopted the tactic of absenting himself from meetings. Mr Weaver said the need for a board was there, despite the fact that the restaurant is managed by the manageress, with Mr Langham authorised to sign cheques required in the course of business. The need referred to was instanced in many cases, such as (a) the company accounts are in need of finalisation; (b) the company will be in default with its statutory returns; (c) there are serious difficulties to be addressed concerning the company's VAT position, referable to the company being grouped, as I understand, for VAT purposes with other restaurant companies with which Mr Mitchell is associated; (d) problems similar to those which have recently arisen (as to noise, and as to publicity) are likely to arise in the future.

. . . I turn to the consideration of the discretion conferred by section 371. It seems to me that discretion ought to be exercised so as to enable an effective board of directors to be brought into being. It cannot be right that Mr Mitchell's quorum tactics should be allowed to stop the company having its accounts, VAT difficulties, etc. dealt with. It may be many months before the section 459 petition is heard. On the other hand, it would not be right for Mr Wyman, by using section 371 for the purposes of constituting an effective board, to be given the opportunity of harming Mr Mitchell, e.g. by causing him to be dismissed as a director, or by being excluded from any participation in the affairs of the company pending the outcome of the petition proceedings.

. . . The order will provide that any director appointed pursuant to the order will be restrained from acting as such director, unless and until there is delivered to Mr Mitchell's solicitors an undertaking signed by the director to the effect that, pending the outcome of the section 459 petition proceedings, he will not (a) at any meeting vote in such a fashion as to dismiss Mr Mitchell from his directorship, or to exclude him from his rights and duties as such director, or to diminish such rights or duties in any way, and (b) interfere with Mr Mitchell's day to day conduct of the restaurant business so long as Mr Mitchell conducts such business as he has done in the past, and (c) vote to effect any alteration in the constitution or capital of the company.

Cane v. Jones and others

[1981] 1 All ER 533; [1980] 1 WLR 1451

Chancery Division

Shares in a family company, Kingsway Petrol Station Ltd., were held in the following proportions: 15,000 £1 shares by A. and B., who were brother and sister, and 15,000 £1 shares by X. and Y., the trustees of a family trust, holding the shares for C., the cousin of A. and B. C. later came to hold the shares as beneficial owner. The articles of association provided that the two fathers, P. and H. should be life directors and that the chairman should be elected by the directors and should have a casting vote at board meetings and general meetings. During the time that the shares were held in trust, A. and B., and X. and Y. had entered into an agreement, without holding a meeting or putting a resolution in writing, under which they reconstituted the board of directors and altered the articles of association, removing the casting vote of the chairman. After the trust was terminated, deadlock was reached in the management of the company's affairs. A. and B. contended that since C. had not been a party to the contract, she could not enforce the agreement, and they therefore sought to enforce the chairman's right to use a casting vote. C. brought an action seeking an order that P. and H., the fathers of the parties, were the only directors of the company, and declaring certain parts of the agreement void insofar as they altered the articles of association and reconstituted the board of directors.

HELD, in relation to the question of whether the agreement was effective to alter the articles of association, that despite the fact that section 10 of the Companies Act 1948 required a special resolution (three-quarters majority) to alter the articles [now section 9 of the Companies Act 1985], the agreement to alter the articles was nevertheless valid because it was the unanimous expression of the will of all the members, acting *intra vires*.

MICHAEL WHEELER, Q.C. In my judgment, section 10 of the Act is merely laying down a procedure whereby some only of the shareholders can validly alter the articles: and if, as I believe to be the case, it is a basic principle of company law that all the corporators, acting together, can do anything which is *intra vires* the company, then I see nothing in section 10 to undermine this principle. I accept that the principle requires all the corporators to "act together": but with regard to this I respectfully adopt what Ashbury J. said in *Parker and Cooper Ltd.* v. *Reading* [1926] Ch 975, 984:

"Now the view I take of both these decisions"—those were *In re Express Engineering Works Ltd.* [1920] Ch 466 and *In re George Newman & Co.* [1895] 1 Ch 674—"is that where the transaction is *intra vires* and honest, and especially if it is for the benefit of the company, it cannot be upset if the assent of all the corporators is given to it. I do not think it matters in the least whether that assent is given at different times or simultaneously."

See also Younger L.J. in *In re Express Engineering Works Ltd.* [1920] Ch 466, 471, and the passage from the judgment of Buckley J. in *In re Duomatic Ltd.* [1969] 2 Ch 365 which I have read earlier in this judgment. I should add that the evidence in the case before me is that the 1967 agreement was signed by "the two sides", if I may call them that, separately, and that they did not meet together, however informally, for the purpose of signing the document. But it is clear beyond doubt that the agreement did represent a meeting of minds, which is, after all, the essence of a meeting and the passing of a resolution.

NOTE

Statutory provision has now been made for written resolutions to be used by private companies which enables them to make decisions without having to call meetings; decisions are made in writing by all the members of the company: section 381A of the Companies Act 1985. This is, in fact, no great change in the law from the position that ruled in *In re Duomatic Ltd.* [1969] and *Cane* v. *Jones* [1981]. For an account of *In re Duomatic Ltd.* [1969], see Chapter 8 page 133 above.

In re West Canadian Collieries Ltd.

[1962] 1 Ch 370; [1962] 1 All ER 26; [1961] 3 WLR 1416
Chancery Division
The registrar of West Canadian Collieries Ltd. sent out notices convening a meeting to pass a special resolution for reduction of capital. Due to an error on his part, notice was not sent to nine members of the company. The error arose because the dividend payments to those members had been dealt with in a different way from the other members, and addressograph plates for those members were kept in a separate place from those relating to the rest of the members. Section 141(5) of the Companies Act 1948 [now section 378(6) of the Companies Act 1985] provided: '. . . notice of a meeting shall be deemed to be duly given and the meeting to be duly held when the notice is given and the meeting held in the manner provided by this act or in the articles'. The company had articles of association (article 75) which provided that the accidental omission to give notice of a meeting to, or the non-receipt of notice of a meeting

by, any person entitled to receive notice should not invalidate the proceedings at that meeting. The special resolution was passed and a petition presented to court for confirmation of the reduction of capital.

HELD that the omission to give notice was 'accidental' in terms of the articles of association and therefore did not invalidate the proceedings of the meeting. Held also that it must be implicit in article 75 that a meeting the proceedings of which were validated by article 75 must be deemed to be duly convened for the purposes of the articles, including in those purposes the manner of the meeting, since without that implication there could be no valid meeting at all.

PLOWMAN, J. In the first place, I am satisfied that the omission to give notice of the meeting to the nine members in question was "accidental" within article 75. It follows from that that the omission to give notice to the nine members did not—and I quote the article—"invalidate the proceedings at that meeting". But the question arises whether the result of this is (a) that though the proceedings of the meeting were valid, the notice of the meeting is nevertheless still not deemed to have been duly given for the purposes of section 141 or (b) that the notice of the meeting is to be deemed to have been duly given for the purposes of that section. The latter, in my judgment, is the true view. It must, I think, be implicit in article 75 that a meeting, the proceedings of which are to be taken to be valid notwithstanding the omission to give notice to members, is to be deemed to have been duly convened for the purposes of the articles, including in those purposes the manner of convening the meeting. It seems to me that, in the absence of such an implication, there would be no meeting the proceedings of which could be validated by the articles. I say that there would be no meeting, because it is well settled that as regards a general meeting failure to give notice to a single person entitled to receive notice renders the meeting a nullity.

12. Borrowing, receivership and the administration order

Summary

1. Sources of the law

In this area there are significant differences between English and Scots law. Care should be taken to work from appropriate textbooks.

(a) English & Welsh sources
The rules on debentures are generally found in case law. The rules on fixed and floating charges and their ranking one with another are also found in case law in England and Wales. The rules on registration of charges are now uniform for England and Scotland, and are found in part IV of the Companies Act 1985, as amended by sections 92ff of the Companies Act 1989 (*at the time of writing these new rules are not yet in force*). The rules on receivership are found in Part III Chapter I of the Insolvency Act 1986. The rules on the administration order are uniform for England and Wales and Scotland, and are found in Part II of the Insolvency Act 1986.

(b) Scottish sources
The rules on debentures are generally found in case law. The Scots law on securities is found partly in case law and is partly statutory. For example, the rules on the standard security over heritable property are found in the Conveyancing and Feudal Reform (Scotland) Act 1970. The rules on registration of charges are as for England. The rules on receivership in Scotland are found in Part III Chapter II of the Insolvency Act 1986. The rules on the administration order are the same as for England and Wales.

2. Company borrowing

Companies frequently issue debentures in exchange for loans to them. Debentures are acknowledgements of indebtedness by companies, and may be secured or unsecured. Secured debentures give the lender additional rights over the property charged, allowing the lender in cases of default by the company ultimately to sell the charged assets and repay the loan out of the proceeds, accounting to the company for any balance. Public companies may issue debentures or debenture stock to the public and, if so, generally trustees are appointed under a debenture trust deed, to safeguard the interests of the debenture stock holders. The issue of debentures is not subject to rules on maintenance of capital, as debenture holders are not members of the company (compare Chapter 6 above). However, it has been held that convertible debentures cannot be issued at a discount where they could be immediately converted into fully paid-up shares: see *Mosely* v. *Koffyfontein Mines Ltd.* [1904].

3. Charges

(a) England & Wales

A company can grant fixed charges over assets which are identified at the time of the creation of the charge, and floating charges over fluctuating assets. Floating charges become fixed on the happening of events which are specified in the charge documentation as causing the charge to become fixed, e.g. the appointment of a receiver.

The classic definition of a floating charge is provided by Romer, J. in *re Yorkshire Woolcombers Association Ltd.* [1903]. Some retention of title clauses can amount to a floating charge and are therefore registrable: see *In re Bond Worth Ltd.* [1980].

Section 93 of the Companies Act 1985 describes which charges must be registered. The general rule is that registrable charges must be registered within twenty-one days from the date of creation of the charge. Failure to do so can render the charge void against a liquidator or administrator, or against any person who for value acquires an interest in or right over the property subject to the charge, after the charge was created.

(b) Scotland

Scotland had fixed securities only until 1961 when floating charges were introduced by statute. The rules on the floating charge in Scotland are found in sections 462–6 of the Companies Act 1985. The floating charge in Scotland must be made in writing, specifying that the charge is a floating charge.

The same registration rules apply to registrable charges as apply in England and Wales.

4. Receivership

As can be seen in section 1 above, the rules on receivership are different between England and Wales and Scotland. The principal objective of the appointment of a receiver is to safeguard the interests of the holder of a floating charge. In England and Wales the term 'administrative receiver' is used of a receiver of the whole or substantially the whole of the company's property. The term 'receiver' in England and Wales is used of the appointee under a less extensive charge. Scots law does not make that distinction.

The receiver in both England and Wales and Scotland may be appointed in writing by the holder of the floating charge if the charge documentation so provides, or in certain circumstances by the court. In Scotland a receiver can be appointed by the holder of the floating charge, even where the document does not so specify, on the occurrence of certain events set out in section 52 of the Insolvency Act 1986.

Only qualified insolvency practitioners may act as receivers. The receiver has statutory management powers in addition to those which might be set out in the instrument creating the charge: see Schedule 1 (for England and Wales) and Schedule 2 (for Scotland) to the Insolvency Act 1986.

The receiver must ingather assets, and must pay company debts in their statutory order of priority: see section 40 (for England and Wales) and sections 59 and 60 (for Scotland). Various claims rank in priority to that of the floating charge: see *Iona Hotels Ltd.* v. *Craig* 1990.

5. The administration order

These provisions were introduced in 1985, with the object of providing similar rights for all creditors to the right which a floating charge creditor has to appoint a receiver. Administration is an alternative to a winding up for insolvent or probably insolvent companies, whereby the company can either be rehabilitated so that it can continue to trade, or the creditors' claims can be met more advantageously than would be the case if the company were to be wound up.

A petition can be made to a competent court for an administration order if the court is satisfied that the company is or is likely to become unable to pay its debts, and that the order would be likely to achieve one of the following objects:

(a) the survival of the company as a going concern;

(b) the approval of a voluntary arrangement under Part I of the Insolvency Act 1986;

(c) the sanctioning of a scheme of arrangement under section 425 of the Companies Act 1985;

(d) a more advantageous realisation of the company's assets than would be effected on a winding up.

See *Re Primlaks (UK) Ltd.* [1989]; and **Air Ecosse Ltd.* v. *Civil Aviation Authority* 1987.

The parties who can petition are: the company; the directors; a creditor or creditors; and the supervisor of a voluntary arrangement.

The legal effect of the administration order is to create a 'breathing space' by freezing civil actions against the company, execution of judgments (*diligence), and repossessions of goods from the date of the presentation of the petition, without the leave of the court. From that time also, no winding up resolution can be passed or winding-up order made. However, there is no bar to the presentation of a petition seeking a winding-up order, and no bar to a receiver being appointed. If a receiver is appointed, the court will only grant the petition for the administration order if the receiver consents (whereupon he/she leaves office), or where the appointment of the receiver is invalid. Once an administration order is granted, the moratorium continues and any petition for a winding-up order is dismissed.

The administrator has to prepare proposals for the implementation of the purposes for which he was appointed, and these must be sent to all creditors and members within three months of the order. The proposals must be approved by a simple majority at a meeting of creditors. The administrator's task is then to implement the proposals. He has management powers identical to those of the English receiver.

Mosely v. Koffyfontein Mines Ltd.

[1904] 2 Ch 108

Court of Appeal

A company proposed in a prospectus to make an issue of debentures at a discount of 20 per cent on the basis that they would be convertible in the future into fully paid shares of the company. The plaintiff, who was the largest shareholder of the company, sought an injunction to prevent the company proceeding with the allotment of the debentures until trial on the grounds that the issue of debentures was in effect an allotment of shares at a discount. Buckley, J. held that the proposed issue was not a device for issuing shares at a discount, and he refused to make the order for an injunction. The plaintiff appealed to the Court of Appeal.

HELD, reversing the decision of Buckley, J., that the proposed issue of debentures was void, on the grounds that it could be used as a means of allotting shares at a discount.

VAUGHAN WILLIAMS, L.J. If the debentures were exchanged for shares immediately after the issue of the debentures, the practical result would be that the shares, although nominally issued in exchange of the surrender of debentures, would really be issued at a discount—i.e., 100 £1 shares for a payment of £80. The answer given by the company to this is that, as a matter of business no man would surrender a £100 debenture, which would always be entitled to payment in full before the shareholders could touch a penny, in exchange for 100 £1 shares, unless and until such shares were selling at par in the market, and probably not unless and until such shares were at a premium. It is said in answer to this, that it is not impossible, especially as the circular contemplated the issue of debentures to shareholders, that such shareholders might, for the purpose of Stock Exchange operations, exchange immediately their debentures for shares. The fact, however, clearly appears that the bargain referred to in the circular has this blot, that it might result in shares being issued practically at a discount. I think that the real question is, Does this bargain give to the company that which the company as businessmen fairly regard as money's worth for the full nominal value of the shares? It is not sufficient for the company to say that the bargain was made in good faith. The company must at least establish that there is no obvious money measure on the face of this bargain shewing that the shares were issued at a discount. Is this money measure made obvious by the fact that the company bind themselves at any time after the issue of the debentures to allot shares to the full nominal value of the debentures, although those debentures were issued at a discount of 20 per cent? The case is on the border line, but I am inclined to think that Buckley J. ought to have issued the injunction asked for, on the ground that the issue of debentures on the proposed terms was open to abuse, even if the agreement was not illusory, but a real agreement honestly made.

The appeal must be allowed.

Re Yorkshire Woolcombers Association Ltd. (Illingworth v. Houldsworth and another)

[1903] 2 Ch 284

House of Lords

The Yorkshire Woolcombers Association had assigned to guarantors by deed all its present and future book and other debts to be held in trust for the benefit of the company's guarantors. The deed contained a provision that the trustee might at any time give notice, appoint a receiver and exercise the statutory power of sale, but meanwhile should not be answerable for allowing the company to receive the book debts. That deed was not registered with the Registrar of Companies. A receiver of the book and other debts was appointed in a debenture-holder's action. The trustee for the guarantors accordingly applied by motion in that action to enforce his security and allow him to collect the book debts. Farwell, J. held that the deed assigning the book and other debts was a floating charge, and that it was void for want of registration: it therefore had no validity against the receiver appointed in the debenture-holder's action. The decision of Farwell, J. was affirmed by the Court of Appeal. The trustee appealed to the House of Lords.

HELD, affirming the decision of the Court of Appeal, that on a true construction of the deed it was intended that the company should carry on its business in the ordinary way and receive the book debts for that purpose, and that the deed was a floating charge in terms of section 14 of the Companies Act 1900 (now section 396 of the Companies Act

1985), and void for want of registration in a question between the trustee and a creditor of the company.

ROMER, L.J. I certainly do not intend to attempt to give an exact definition of the term "floating charge", nor am I prepared to say that there will not be a floating charge within the meaning of the Act, which does not contain all the three characteristics that I am about to mention, but I certainly think that if a charge has the three characteristics that I am about to mention it is a floating charge: (1) if it is a charge on a class of assets of a company present and future; (2) if that class is one which, in the ordinary course of the business of the company, would be changing from time to time; and (3) if you find that by the charge it is contemplated that, until some future step is taken by or on behalf of those interested in the charge, the company may carry on its business in the ordinary way as far as concerns the particular class of assets I am dealing with.

In the present case those three characteristics do in my opinion distinguish the charge we have to consider. In the first place, the charge is one upon all the debts of the company present and future, not even limiting them (though I do not think it makes any difference) to the trade debts, present and future. In the second place, it obviously contemplates a class of asset which, in the ordinary course of the life of the company, must continually, and of necessity, change; and, thirdly, in the present case, if I look at the deed which created the charge here, to my mind it is clearly contemplated that until some step is taken by or on behalf of those who are to have the benefit of the charge, the company would be able to receive the debts due to the company in its ordinary course of business, and to deal with them for the ordinary purposes of the business.

. . . I think the decision of the Court below was quite right, and that the appeal should be dismissed.

The decision was appealed to the House of Lords.

EARL OF HALSBURY, L.C. In the first place you have that which in a sense I suppose must be an element in the definition of a floating security, that it is something which is to float, not to be put into immediate operation, but such that the company is to be allowed to carry on its business. It contemplates not only that it should carry with it the book debts which were then existing, but it contemplates also the possibility of those book debts being extinguished by payment to the company, and that other book debts should come in and take the place of those that had disappeared. That, my Lords seems to me to be an essential characteristic of what is properly called a floating security.

. . . I am not able to deduce more from the instrument itself than the Court of Appeal have done, and I entirely agree with the judgment pronounced by them, and it appears to me that this appeal ought to be dismissed.

LORD MACNAGHTEN. I should have thought there was not much difficulty in defining what a floating charge is in contrast to what is called a specific charge. A specific charge, I think, is one that without more fastens on ascertained and definite property or property capable of being ascertained and defined; a floating charge, on the other hand, is ambulatory and shifting in its nature, hovering over and so to speak floating with the property which it is intended to affect until some event occurs or some act is done which causes it to settle and fasten on the subject of the charge within its reach and grasp.

NOTE

This case was decided long before there was such a security as a floating charge in Scotland. The floating charge in Scotland is a creature of statute law (now sections 462–6 of the Companies Act 1985), and therefore this case is not binding in Scotland.

In re Bond Worth Ltd.

[1980] 1 Ch 228

Chancery Division

Supplies of the man-made fibre Acrilan were sold by Monsanto Ltd. to Bond Worth Ltd. under conditions of sale which incorporated a retention of title clause stating:

(a) . . . equitable and beneficial ownership shall remain with us [the sellers] until full payment has been received . . . or until prior resale, in which case our beneficial entitlement shall attach to the proceeds of resale or to the claim for such proceeds.

(b) Should the goods become constituents of or be converted into other products while subject to our equitable and beneficial ownership we shall have the equitable and beneficial ownership in such other products as if they were solely and simply the goods . . . .

The holding company of the buyer of the goods, and the buyer of the goods, were put into receivership by the second debenture holder. At that time the buyer owed £529,000 to the sellers in respect of goods subject to the retention of title clause. The sellers notified the receiver of their claim to ownership of the goods supplied and not paid for, whether processed or not, and the proceeds of any sales, under the retention of title clause. A few days later the business of the buyer, including all stocks of raw and processed fibre, was sold to G. Ltd. under a hiving-down agreement. Joint receivers were appointed a few days later by the first debenture holder. The joint receivers presented a summons for determination of the validity and priority of the sellers' claim.

HELD (1) that the retention of title clause created a floating equitable charge as security for the purchase price, secured over the fibre, the proceeds of its resale, and the products into which it might be converted, and the proceeds of those products; and (2) that the floating charge was void against the other creditors of the buyers for want of registration under section 95(2)(f) of the Companies Act 1948 (now section 396(1)(e) of the Companies Act 1985).

SLADE, J. There is, however, one type of charge (and I think one type only) which, by its very nature, leaves a company at liberty to deal with the assets charged in the ordinary course of its business, without regard to the charge, until stopped by a winding up or by the appointment of a receiver or the happening of some other agreed event. I refer to what is commonly known as a "floating charge".

. . . In the present case, in my judgment, the respective charges on each of the four categories of charged assets were ambulatory and shifting in their nature, and were intended to hover over them until the happening of an event which caused them to crystallise. The assets comprised in each of the four categories were of a fluctuating class, albeit in the case of the first category liable to fluctuate only by diminution. Until a crystallising event occurred, it was clearly not intended that any restriction should be placed on Bond Worth to deal with them in the ordinary course of business.

. . . In my judgment the effect of the retention of title clause was to create floating equitable charges over the four categories of charged assets, for the purpose of securing payment of the purchase prices due under the relevant orders, and to constitute Bond Worth a trustee of such assets for the purpose of such security, but for no other purpose.

. . . The judgment of Romer L.J. in *In re Yorkshire Woolcombers Association Ltd.* [1903] 2 Ch 284, 294–295, which concerned the meaning of the equivalent words "floating charge on the undertaking or property of the company" contained in section 14(1)(d) of the Companies Act 1900, shows that a charge may fall within the statutory definition, even though it does not comprise the entire undertaking and property of the company. It also shows that in considering whether a charge is a floating charge within the statutory definition, the court must deal with it as a question of substance to be answered according to the particular facts of the case. Approaching the matter in this way, I am driven to the conclusion that all the relevant charges are floating charges on property of Bond Worth within the statutory definition.

. . . Having held that the relevant charges arose by way of grant back by Bond Worth in favour of Monsanto, I think it must follow that they were "created" by Bond Worth for the purpose of section 95.

Prescribed particulars of the relevant charges in the present case were never delivered to the Registrar of Companies in accordance with section 95(1) [of the Companies Act 1948]. In my judgment, the charges must be void against any creditor of Bond Worth, but without prejudice to the contractual obligation of Bond Worth for repayment of the money thereby secured.

★ Iona Hotels Ltd. v. William Craig

1990 SCLR 614

Court of Session

On 31 December 1987 the respondent arrested £13,000 payable to the petitioners, in the hands of the Sheriff Clerk at Glasgow, on the dependence of an action by the respondent against the petitioners, and the arrestment was still on the dependence of the action at the time of the presentation of the petition. On 22 January 1988 the petitioners granted a floating charge over their whole property in favour of the Royal Bank of Scotland. On 15 November 1988 the bank appointed a receiver. The petitioners sought recall of the arrestment, claiming that the charge ranked prior to the arrestment.

HELD that an arrestment *executed* prior to the creation of a floating charge ranks before it, and the petition was refused.

LORD PRESIDENT. It is common ground that the particular issue which arises in this case is not the subject of any previous decision. In *Lord Advocate* v. *Royal Bank of Scotland* [1977 SC 155] the floating charges under which the receiver was appointed were granted before the date of the arrestment. It was held that the receiver had power to take possession of the funds which had been arrested because the arrestment had not been followed by a furthcoming prior to the date of crystallisation of the floating charge and because the arrestment itself was not a diligence effectually executed on the property of the company within the meaning of the statute. But as Lord President Emslie pointed out at p. 166, that case was not concerned with the different questions which might arise where the arrestment preceded not only the appointment of the receiver but also the creation of the floating charge under which he was appointed.

. . . The powers of the receiver comprise those, if any, given to him by the instrument creating the floating charge, together with those specified in Schedule 2 to the Act insofar as these are not inconsistent with any provisions in that instrument: section 55(1) and (2). But section 55(3)(a) provides that those subsections apply

"subject to the rights of any person who has effectually executed diligence on all or any part of the property of the company prior to the appointment of the receiver."

The phrase "effectually executed diligence on . . . any part of the property of the company" recurs in section 60(1)(b), in the context of provisions which regulate the distribution of moneys which have been ingathered by the receiver. A person who has effectually executed diligence within the meaning of that provision is accorded a priority in the order of distribution. But a person whose diligence is not of that character has no place in the order of ranking under this subsection, and he is not protected against the powers of the receiver by section 55(3)(a).

. . . In my opinion the answer to the question raised in this case is to be found by an examination of the principle of litigiosity and its effects. The principle is simply this, that an arrestment, being merely a step in diligence, renders the subject litigious as soon as it is used, with the result that the common debtor cannot defeat it by any posterior voluntary deed. . . . What it involves is a prohibition, which is addressed to the arrestee so that the thing may remain in his hands for the satisfaction of the debt. It also involves that the arrester's advantage cannot be defeated by the subsequent voluntary act of the debtor himself, by any later arrestment, or by any other diligence begun but not carried to completion. . . . To return to the analogy of the fixed security, property which is the subject of an assignation in security remains the property of the company subject to the rights of the assignee. And the litigiosity which results from the arrestment restricts the power of the common debtor to affect his own property by his subsequent voluntary act, but it does not render that act worthless for all purposes. The rights of an assignee of a subsequent assignation in security are subject to the rights of the arrester, whose advantage cannot be defeated by that security. But the extent of that advantage will depend on the outcome of the process in which the arrestment is used. If the action fails, the arrestment falls and there is no longer any restriction on the rights of the assignee, and the fixed security will be effective in regard to any balance which may remain after any successful claim by the arrester has been satisfied. In my opinion the same approach is appropriate in the case of a posterior floating charge and it is not in conflict with any of the provisions of the statute. The property to which it attaches is subject to the rights of an arrester whose arrestment was prior to the date of registration of the floating charge. The extent of those rights may be such as to render the floating charge worthless on crystallisation in regard to the property held by the arrestee, but they may not. The receiver must await the outcome of the process until the debt arrested for has been satisfied. What remains at that stage will be for him to collect because it is, as it all along has been, property of the company to which the floating charge has attached. The statute is silent on these matters, but as I see it this is because the rights of the prior arrester are provided for by the general law, just as they are in the case of a fixed security which has been tainted by the voluntary act of the debtor subsequent to the date of the arrestment.

In my opinion the receiver is not entitled in these circumstances to recall of the arrestment, and the prayer of the petition should be refused.

NOTE

For further Scots cases concerning the meaning of the phrase 'effectually executed diligence' in section 60 of the Insolvency Act 1986 see *Lord Advocate* v. *The Royal Bank of Scotland* 1977 SC 155; *Armour and Mycroft, Petitioners* 1983 SLT 453; and *Forth & Clyde Construction Co. Ltd.* v. *Trinity Timber & Plywood Co. Ltd.* 1984 SC 1.

Re Primlaks (UK) Ltd.

[1989] BCLC 734
Chancery Division

Primlaks (UK) Ltd. was part of a group of companies which traded with persons resident in Nigeria. Many of the companies in the group were indebted to banks, and Primlaks was indebted to the Bank of Credit and Commerce International (BCCI). BCCI refused to agree to a restructuring of the group's indebtedness, and obtained judgment against Primlaks and its guarantors for approximately $6,700,000. When the court refused to stay execution of the judgment, Primlaks sought the advice of an insolvency practitioner, who advised that an administration order should be sought under section 8 of the Insolvency Act 1986 to achieve one or more of the following objects: (i) the approval of a voluntary arrangement under Part I of the Insolvency Act 1986; (ii) an arrangement under section 425 of the Companies Act 1985, or (iii) a more advantageous realisation of Primlaks' assets than could be effected in a winding up.

HELD that the administration order should be granted. The words in section 8(1)(b) of the Insolvency Act 1986, 'the making of an order under this section would be likely to achieve one or more of the purposes mentioned below', did not mean 'more likely than not' but in deciding whether or not to grant an administration order the court had to be satisfied that there was a real prospect of one or more of the purposes set out in section 8(3) of the Insolvency Act 1986 being achieved. On balance the administration order was granted for the following reasons: (1) the company had been trading profitably for a number of years, and had not been trading at the expense of its creditors; (2) the company's difficulties were not caused by mismanagement, but by the collapse of the Nigerian economy; (3) a substantial majority of the company's principal banking creditors and its suppliers supported the petition for the administration order; (4) there was evidence to suggest that the company had taken steps to reduce its operating costs, that it could trade at a small profit, and the insolvency practitioner consulted took the view that trading under a clean subsidiary would enable work in progress to be realised; and (5) the insolvency practitioner, who was a man of considerable reputation, had recommended the making of the administration order.

VINELOTT, J. It is, in my judgment, plainly impossible to say that it is probable, that is more likely than not, that the making of an administration order in this case would achieve any of the objects set out in section 8(3) . . . .The question must always be, if there is a real prospect that one or more of the stated purposes would be achieved, is that a prospect sufficiently likely in the light of all the other circumstances of the case to justify the making of the order?

The judge proceeded to give his reasons for granting the order, which are as expressed in the headnote.

★ Air Ecosse Ltd. v. Civil Aviation Authority
1987 SLT 751
Court of Session Inner House, Second Division

An administration order was granted in relation to Air Ecosse Ltd. After the grant of the administration order, British Airways applied to the Civil Aviation Authority to revoke the licences of Air Ecosse Ltd. for two routes and for a grant of air transport licences to British Airways for those routes. The petitioners sought an adjournment of the respondents' hearing of the applications on the grounds that under section 11(3) of the Insolvency Act 1986 the respondents lacked jurisdiction as the administrator had not consented to the hearing, nor had the leave of the court been obtained. The motion was refused. Therefore, the petitioners presented a petition for judicial review seeking an order quashing the decision refusing the motion. The Lord Ordinary dismissed the petition on the ground that the hearing of the applications was not 'other proceedings' within the meaning of section 11(3)(d). The petitioners appealed to the Inner House of the Court of Session.

HELD that the words 'other proceedings' in section 11(3)(d) of the Insolvency Act 1986 should be interpreted narrowly, using the *ejusdem generis* rule under section 11(3)(a)–(c). Therefore, the hearing before the Civil Aviation Authority did not amount to 'other proceedings', and the reclaiming motion was refused.

LORD JAUNCEY. I consider that one must therefore look to the context in which the word is found to determine the meaning to be attached to it.

. . . The situations covered by paragraphs (a), (b) and (c) of section 11(3) appear to relate primarily, if not entirely, to steps which could be taken by creditors of a company for the purpose of enforcing their rights. The words "execution or other process" and "distress" suggest means of enforcing decrees or securities which would normally be available to creditors. If "other proceedings" covered hearings before the respondents at their instance or at the instance of someone not a creditor but a competitor this would extend the ambit of subsection (3) well beyond the other situations covered by the paragraphs thereof and would almost inevitably cover other administrative procedures such as applications by a chief constable for suspension of a public house licence under section 31 of the Licencing (Scotland) Act 1976. If the petitioners are right, a company which was subject to an administration order would be put on ice not only in relation to its creditors but in relation to administrative constraints which might otherwise apply to it.

. . . Parliament clearly intended that a company subject to an administration order should be put on ice so far as its creditors were concerned but I do not consider that it intended that this moratorium should extend to matters which directly affected not creditors but the public interest. I therefore conclude that the hearing before the respondents did not constitute "proceedings" within the meaning of section 11(3)(d) of the 1986 Act.

THE LORD JUSTICE-CLERK (ROSS). In my opinion, the whole flavour of section 11(3)(a), (b) and (c) is that it is dealing with steps which may be taken by a creditor against a company. In my opinion, this colours the interpretation which falls to be placed upon the words: "no other proceedings . . . may be commenced or continued . . . against the company" where these appear in (d). The situation might have been different if the word "other" had not appeared, since (d) would then have contained a clear prohibition against any proceedings being taken against the company. However, the word "other" does appear and effect must be given to it. The whole basis of the *ejusdem generis* rule is that the word "other" falls to be read as if it meant "similar" (*Quazi* v. *Quazi*, *per* Lord Diplock). In my opinion the word "other" in section 11(3)(d) falls to be read as if it meant "similar". That being so it is plain that what is prohibited by (d) is any proceedings which are similar to those described in (a), (b), and (c). This would confine the prohibition to proceedings which might be taken by someone such as a creditor against the company and which was in some way related to a debt due by the company. . . . In my opinion, however, the prohibition in (d) does not extend to proceedings such as those which were before the first respondents on 23 April 1987.

LORD McDONALD. The sharp issue in this reclaiming motion is an alleged conflict between the terms of two Acts of Parliament. The first Act is the Civil Aviation Act of 1982. That Act set up a controlling body called the Civil Aviation Authority (C.A.A.). No aircraft may be used for carriage for reward unless the operator holds a licence from the C.A.A. (s.64(1)). The Act specifies certain general objectives to which the activities of the C.A.A. must be directed (s.4). The C.A.A. must endeavour to satisfy all substantial categories of public demand, and that at the lowest charges consistent with safety. . . . A licence once granted may be revoked at any time by the C.A.A. under section 66 of the Act. This may be done either on the application of an interested party, or *ex proprio motu* by C.A.A. A competing airline such as the second respondents British Airways (B.A.) has a title to make such an application.

. . . It is my opinion, as already indicated, that section 11(3) of the Act of 1986 is confined to the activities of creditors of a company subject to an administration order. It does not extend beyond that to courses of action which may be open to persons who are not creditors, e.g. competitors, under a different statute. It seems to me that section 11(3) (a), (b) and (c) disclose a genus, viz. creditors of a company subject to an administration order whose rights as creditors are to be restricted, and the use of the word "other" in section 11(3)(d) is simply to bring within that genus those species of creditor who complete the genus but who have been omitted in the earlier paragraphs. In this connection I have found assistance from the clear exposition of the *ejusdem generis* rule contained in the speech of Lord Diplock in *Quazi* v. *Quazi* at pp. 807 *et seq.*

I also take the view that it is unlikely that Parliament would intend to limit the powers which it has conferred upon C.A.A. by the terms of an insolvency statute.

. . . For the foregoing reasons I would refuse the reclaiming motion.

13. Minority protection

Summary

1. Sources of the law

The law relating to minority protection is found partly in the Companies Act 1985 (throughout the statute, but note particularly sections 459–61 of the Companies Act 1985), and partly in case law.

2. Majority rule and minority protection

Companies as democracies generally reach their decisions by majority vote, except where statute or the constitution demand unanimous voting. Wherever majority voting is used, instances can occur where minorities who voted against the resolution or did not vote at all are unhappy at the decisions reached by the majority and wish to challenge them.

Generally, the principle of majority rule applies, whereby members are precluded from challenging corporate decisions which are *intra vires* the company, and which have not breached either statutory or constitutional rules. In addition, minorities may be prevented from challenging decisions which have breached constitutional rules, because the courts have long regarded actions brought to redress such a wrong as futile when the company could by ratification cure the breach of procedure by ordinary resolution. Another justification for the principle which is cited by the judges is the undesirability of allowing multiple actions to be brought by individual members for the same wrong. The principle of majority rule is associated with the case of *Foss* v. *Harbottle* (1843).

However, the principle has always had case law exceptions, and statute law also provides remedies for minority members in specified circumstances.

3. Statutory remedies

There are many statutory remedies, some specific to particular circumstances, and others of more general application. The most important is found in sections 459–61 of the Companies Act 1985 which protect minorities against unfairly prejudicial conduct: a single member or group of members can petition the court for an order on the ground that 'the company's affairs are being or have been conducted in a manner which is unfairly prejudicial to the interests of its members generally or of some part of its members (including at least himself) or that any actual or proposed act or omission of the company (including an act or omission on its behalf) is or would be so prejudicial.' The conduct must have been suffered by the member(s) as members and not in some other capacity such as employees or directors. See *Elder and others* v. *Elder & Watson Ltd.* 1952.

The court has power to grant various orders to regulate the company's affairs; it can order legal proceedings to be raised in the name of the company, and can provide for the purchase of the shares of the minorities either by the company or by other members, thereby enabling the minorities to leave the company. Much of the case law is concerned with the appropriate method of valuation of these shares, which can vary according to circumstances.

The courts have applied these provisions very flexibly since their introduction in 1980. Many of the cases have been brought by director/members of personal-relationship companies where the relationship of loyalty and trust has broken down: in such cases, the most useful remedy is often the purchase of the shares of the departing director/member by the company or by the remaining members. See *Re London School of Electronics Ltd.* [1986]; *Re Bird Precision Bellows Ltd.* [1986]; *Re Nuneaton Borough Association Football Club Ltd. (Re a Company No. 00789 of 1987)* (1989); and *Re Sam Weller & Sons Ltd. (Re a Company No. 823A of 1987)* [1989].

Another statutory remedy that can be used in cases of breakdown of the relationship between the majority and the minority is to have the company wound up by the court on the ground that it is 'just and equitable' in the circumstances so to do: section 122(1)(g) of the Insolvency Act 1986. (Cases under that section are discussed in the following chapter.)

The Companies Act 1985 contains a range of remedies covering particular circumstances. Under these provisions, often the right to challenge a decision or to bring matters to the attention of the general meeting is confined to holders of a qualifying percentage of shares or votes. For example, alterations of the objects clause of the memorandum of association can be challenged in court by holders of 15 per cent of the issued share capital or of any class of it, or in the case of a company without a share capital, 15 per cent of the membership: section 5 of the Companies Act 1985. See also sections 127, 368, and 376 of the Companies Act 1985 for further examples.

4. Common law remedies

These are of less importance since the advent of what is now sections 459–61 of the Companies Act 1985. However, the common law remedies may still be used in conjunction with or instead of the statutory remedies. The common law remedies arise as a result of a series of exceptions to the principle of majority rule laid down in *Foss* v. *Harbottle* (1843). See also *Pavlides* v. *Jensen* [1956]. The exceptions are as follows:

(1) Where the act complained of is illegal, or, until changes were made to the *ultra vires* doctrine in the Companies Act 1989, is *ultra vires* the company's objects as expressed in the memorandum of association. The reason for this exception is because the company could not ratify such an act: see *Smith* v. *Croft (No. 3)* (1987).

(2) Where the articles of association require a specific majority decision, and the decision is passed by a different majority: see *Edwards* v. *Halliwell* [1950]. This is perhaps less justifiable, since the company may ratify such breaches.

(3) Where the act is a fraud on the minority, and the wrongdoers are in absolute control of the company: see *Cook* v. *Deeks* [1916], and contrast *Prudential Assurance Co. Ltd.* v. *Newman Industries Ltd. (No. 2)* [1982].

(4) In certain cases, where a member's personal rights, e.g. his voting rights, have been infringed: see *Pender* v. *Lushington* (1877).

In England, such minority actions may be brought as representative actions, or derivative actions, depending on the circumstances. A representative action is brought by the shareholder in respect of a wrong done to himself and others. A derivative action is brought by the shareholder in respect of a wrong done to the company. Generally the defendants are the directors of the company. The company is joined in the action as a nominal defendant to enable it to be awarded damages: see *Prudential Assurance Co. Ltd.* v. *Newman Industries Ltd. (No. 2)* [1982]. In England but not in Scotland, the court can order in a minority action that the plaintiff be indemnified against costs by the company (a Wallersteiner order).

In Scotland, all such actions are brought in the form of personal actions, not representative or derivative actions, although on occasion members have been allowed by the courts to bring actions seeking damages for the company: see *Oliver's Trustees* v. *W.G. Walker & Sons (Edin.) Ltd.* 1948.

The remedies the minority might seek include: putting right a wrong, e.g. obtaining a court order compelling directors to repay or restore money or property taken from the company, or seeking damages from the directors for breach of duty; alternatively, the minority might seek to institute proceedings on behalf of the company against an outside party; in Scotland, the court could appoint a judicial factor to manage the affairs of the company on a temporary basis: see *Weir* v. *Rees* 1991.

Foss v. Harbottle

(1843) 2 Hare 461

Court of Chancery

Two shareholders brought a bill on behalf of themselves and all the other shareholders except the defendants, against the defendants, most of whom were the directors of the company, on the grounds that the defendants had defrauded the company by selling land (the Victoria Park in Manchester) to the company at an exorbitant price, and by arranging certain improper mortgages. The plaintiffs sought to have the defendants held personally liable to make good the losses caused to the company.

HELD that since the company itself could obtain redress against the defendants if it wished to do so, the plaintiffs had no interest to sue.

SIR JAMES WIGRAM, V.-C. The Victoria Park Company is an incorporated body, and the conduct with which the defendants are charged in this suit is an injury not to the plaintiffs exclusively; it is an injury to the whole corporation by individuals whom the corporation entrusted with powers to be exercised only for the good of the corporation. And from the case of *Attorney-General* v. *Wilson* (1840) Cr & Ph 1 (without going further) it may be stated as undoubted law that a bill or information by a corporation will lie to be relieved in respect of injuries which the corporation has suffered at the hands of persons standing in the situation of the directors upon this record. This bill, however, differs from that in *Attorney-General* v. *Wilson* in this—that, instead of the corporation being formally represented as plaintiffs, the bill in this case is brought by two individual corporators, professedly on behalf of themselves and all the other members of the corporation, except those who committed the injuries complained of—the Plaintiffs assuming to themselves the right and power in that manner to sue on behalf of and represent the corporation itself.

It was not, nor could it successfully be, argued that it was a matter of course for any individual members of a corporation thus to assume to themselves the rights of suing in the name of the corporation. In law the corporation and the aggregate members of the corporation are not the same thing for purposes like this; and the only question can be whether the facts alleged in this case justify a departure from the rule which *prima facie* would require that the corporation should sue in its own name and in its corporate character, or in the name of someone whom the law has appointed to be its representative. . . . Now, who are the *cestui que trusts* in this case? The corporation, in a sense, is undoubtedly the *cestui que trust*; but the majority of the proprietors at a special general meeting assembled, independently of any general rules of law upon the subject, by the very terms of the incorporation in the present case, has power to bind the whole body, and every individual corporator must be taken to have come into the corporation upon the terms of being liable to be bound. How then can this court act in a suit constituted as this is, if it is to be assumed, for the purposes of this argument, that the powers of the body of proprietors are still in existence, and may lawfully be exercised for a purpose like that I have suggested? Whilst the court may be declaring the acts complained of to be void at the suit of the present plaintiffs, who in fact may be the only proprietors who disapprove of them, the governing body of proprietors may defeat the decree by lawfully resolving upon the confirmation of the very acts which are the subject of the suit. The very fact that the governing body of proprietors assembled at the special general meeting may so bind even a reluctant minority is decisive to show that the frame of this suit cannot be sustained whilst that body retains its functions. In order that this suit may be sustained it must be shewn either that there is no such power as I have supposed remaining in the proprietors, or, at least, that all means have been resorted to and found ineffectual to set that body in motion: this latter point is nowhere suggested in the bill: there is no suggestion that an attempt has been made by any proprietor to set the body of proprietors in motion, or to procure a meeting to be convened for the purpose of revoking the acts complained of. The question then is whether this bill is so framed as of necessity to exclude the supposition that the supreme body of proprietors is not in a condition to confirm the transactions in question; or, if those transactions are to be impeached in a Court of Justice, whether the proprietors have not power to set the corporation in motion for the purpose of vindicating its own rights.

. . . The foundation upon which I consider the plaintiffs can alone have a right to sue in the form of this bill must wholly fail, if there has been a governing body of directors *de facto*. There is no longer the impediment to convening a meeting of proprietors, who by their vote might direct proceedings like the present to be taken in the name of the corporation or of a treasurer of the corporation (if that were necessary); or who, by rejecting such a proposal, would, in effect, decide that the corporation was not aggrieved by the transactions in question.

. . . I am of opinion that this question—the question of confirmation or avoidance—cannot properly be litigated upon this record, regard being had to the existing state and powers of the corporation, and that therefore that part of the bill which seeks to visit the directors personally with the consequences of the impeached mortgages and charges, the benefit of which the company enjoys, is in the same predicament as that which relates to the other subjects of complaint.

★ Elder and others v. Elder & Watson Ltd.

1952 SC 49; 1952 SLT 112
Court of Session

A petition was presented by certain shareholders of the company under section 210 of the Companies Act 1948 (which has now been replaced by a different remedy in sections 459–61 of the Companies Act 1985) seeking purchase of their shares by the company on the ground that the affairs of the company 'were being conducted in a manner oppressive to some parts of the members (including himself)' . It was averred that two of the petitioners who were shareholders in the company had been removed from office as directors and deprived of their employment as factory manager and company secretary. This followed a breakdown of relations between the parties which culminated in an assault by Walter Elder, one of the directors, upon one of the petitioners, his brother George Elder. It was also averred that Walter Elder had instigated these acts in order to win control of the company for himself. There was no averment of mismanagement of the business. Before presenting the petition, the petitioners had unsuccessfully sought to dispose of their shares to the company at a price fixed by arbitration.

HELD that the petition failed because the petitioners had not been affected in their capacity as *members*, but in their capacity as directors and employees. The section was only concerned to grant a remedy in relation to oppression suffered by members; and that there was no evidence that would justify a winding up on the 'just and equitable' ground. The petition was accordingly dismissed as irrelevant.

LORD PRESIDENT (COOPER). I search the petition in vain for any relevant averment that the petitioners have suffered in their character as members of the company. *Qua* members, their position does not seem to me to differ significantly from that of any other shareholder. The true grievance is that two of them, George Elder and James Glass, have lost the positions which they formerly held as directors and officers of the company. I do not consider that section 210 was intended to meet any such case, the ''oppression'' required by the section being oppression of members in their character as such. I do not think that a ''just and equitable'' winding-up has ever yet been ordered merely because of changes effected in the board of directors or the dismissal of officers, and very strong grounds would be needed to justify such a step.

LORD KEITH. An employee who has been treated oppressively has no remedy under this section and a member who is an employee can, in my opinion, have no recourse to this section merely because of treatment he has suffered as an employee. The same holds, in my opinion, of a member who is a director or who holds other office in the company and whose only complaint is of deprivation of such office by whatever manner achieved. I do not suggest that such conduct towards a director, officer or employee may not have some relevance in an application under section 210 if it is part and parcel of conduct designed to react on the rights of members as such or to further a scheme whereby the rights of a section of members may be prejudiced. It may seem unnecessary to stress this aspect of the matter, but there was more than a suggestion in the argument to which we listened that oppressive conduct towards a member in his capacity as director might *per se* justify an application under section 210. I can find no warrant for this view in the statute.

I should also dispose of another argument that was presented to us. It was maintained on the authority of such cases as *Yenidje Tobacco Co.* [1916] 2 Ch 426 that this company should be treated as a partnership and that, if there were shown such a loss of confidence between the principal shareholders as would in the case of partners justify a winding-up of a partnership, the petitioners were entitled to the remedy sought. I would say in the first place that this case is far removed from the *Yenidje Tobacco Co.* case, where there were only two shareholders, with equal voting powers, and where the conduct of business between them had become quite impossible. But, apart from this, the question of absence of mutual confidence *per se* between partners, or between two sets of shareholders, however relevant to a winding up, seems to me to have no direct relevance to the remedy granted by section 210. It is oppression of some part of the shareholders by the manner in which the affairs of the company are being conducted that must be averred and proved. Mere loss of confidence or pure deadlock does not, I think, come within section 210. . . . In the present case I am satisfied that there are no circumstances averred in the petition relevant to infer oppression within the meaning of the section. The petition discloses differences of opinion between the first-named petitioner and his brother as directors of the company, some violence used to him in the course of a quarrel, removal or exclusion from office of the first and second-named petitioners as directors, forced retiral or dismissal from employment of the first and second-named petitioners as secretary and factory manager respectively and declinature of an offer of the same petitioners to sell their shareholdings to the then board of directors. I can find, however, no suggestion that anything that was done was designed to injure the petitioners in their rights as shareholders or did in fact do so. At the most, the averments seem to me to disclose no more than differences of opinion as to the management of the company, giving rise perhaps to animosities and to exclusion of the first and second-named petitioners from office and employment in the company. There is nothing to suggest that the company is not being conducted efficiently by the existing board in the interests of the members as a whole.

NOTE

Although the law has changed since this case was decided, the case is still of relevance for the clear assertion that for a member to have a remedy under what was then section 210 of the Companies Act 1948, and what is now section 459–61 of the Companies Act 1985, the member must have been affected by some act of the company *in his capacity as member* and not in some other capacity, such as employee or director.

The modern statutory remedy does not require proof of oppression, but only of unfairly prejudicial conduct, and so is easier to establish.

Re London School of Electronics Ltd.

[1986] 1 Ch 211
Chancery Division
The petitioner was a director of and held 25 per cent of the issued share capital in London School of Electronics Ltd. The remaining 75

per cent was held by another company, CTC, of which Athanasiou (A.), and George (G.), held most of the shares and acted as the directors. The petitioner had been a teacher employed by CTC. The company operated as a personal relationship company. The relationship between the parties broke down, and a resolution was passed to remove the petitioner as a director of the London School of Electronics Ltd. A. and G. had also made an agreement with an American university to grant recognition for a BSc degree course to CTC, from the benefit of which the London School of Electronics was excluded. A. and G. put up a notice at the centre where CTC operated stating that the petitioner had been dismissed from the company. The petitioner then set up his own college in the same centre where CTC traded, and took with him twelve students who had previously been students of the London School of Electronics. The petitioner presented his petition which claimed that A. and G. had behaved in a manner that was unfairly prejudicial to his interests by diverting the electronics students of the London School of Electronics to CTC, by his dismissal as a director, and displaying in public his notice of dismissal. He sought an order under section 75 of the Companies Act 1980 (now sections 459–61 of the Companies Act 1985) to compel CTC to purchase his shares or obtain purchasers for his shares.

HELD that section 75 of the Companies Act 1980 empowered the court to grant a remedy as it thought fit, provided unfairly prejudicial conduct had been established; there was no need to establish that it was just and equitable to grant the remedy, and therefore it was not essential that the petitioner should come to court with clean hands, although his conduct in relation to the whole circumstances was nevertheless relevant; that the overriding cause of the breakdown in relations was the appropriation by CTC of the students enrolling on the BSc course in electronics, which was unfairly prejudicial to the interests of the petitioner, notwithstanding the fact that the petitioner had himself removed twelve students to his new college; that in all the circumstances the petitioner's shares should be valued as at the date of presentation of the petition, on the basis that the students removed by the petitioner had remained with the company, and that the valuation should view the petitioner's shares according to the value of the company's shares as a whole, and not as a minority holding.

NOURSE, J. In my judgment it was CTC's decision to appropriate the BSc students to itself which was the effective cause of the breakdown in the relationship of mutual confidence and trust between the quasi-partners. Furthermore, that was clearly conduct on the part of CTC which was both unfair and prejudicial to the interests of the petitioner as a member of the company. It is possible, although I do not so decide, that CTC would have been entitled to relieve the petitioner of his teaching duties before June 1983. It is even possible, although it is much less likely, that CTC had it gone through the appropriate formalities, could have properly removed the petitioner as a director of the company. But none of that is to say that CTC was entitled to take the extreme step of determining to deprive the petitioner of his 25 per cent interest in the profits attributable to the BSc students. Furthermore, I do not think that the petitioner's removal of a dozen or so students to LCEE in August and September can have any effect on the question of unfair prejudice. It was Mr Athanasiou and Mr George who had unfairly brought about the petitioner's departure from the company and his remaining a director was little more than a technicality. His removal of the students is certainly something which will have consequences later in the case. It did not in my view have the effect of rendering the prejudicial conduct no longer unfair.

. . . In the present case I have held that the conduct which was unfairly prejudical to the interest of the petitioner as a member of the company was CTC's decision to appropriate the BSc students to itself. Had that conduct not taken place the petitioner would effectively have become entitled to 25 per cent of the profits attributable to the BSc students. Since those profits would not have been earned until the academic year 1983–84, it would not in my view be fair to value the petitioner's shares as at June 1983. He is at the least entitled to have them valued at some date during the academic year 1983–84, and, since no other date has been suggested, the date of the presentation of the petition—10 February 1984—is as good as any other.

. . . I am also in no doubt that the valuation ought to be made on the footing that the students which the petitioner removed to LCEE remained with the company. Mr Oliver's primary submission here was that the petitioner's continuing status as a director rendered him accountable to the company in a fiduciary capacity for any profits earned by LCEE in respect of those students. I do not dissent from that submission, but it seems to me that it would in any event be fair to treat those students as having remained with the company, since the whole object of the exercise is that the petitioner should be bought out on the footing that the unfair prejudice had never occurred, in which event both he and the students would have remained with the company.

Finally, it is clear that the price must be fixed *pro rata* according to the value of the shares as a whole and not discounted: see *Re Bird Precision Bellows Ltd.* [1984] Ch. 419.

Re Bird Precision Bellows Ltd.

[1986] Ch 658; [1985] 3 All ER 523; [1986] 2 WLR 158
Court of Appeal

Bird Precision Bellows Ltd. was a personal relationship or quasi-partnership company. B. had expertise in the manufacture of precision bellows, and was appointed managing director; A. was appointed chairman and director; and N. was appointed finance director. B. was the only one of the three who received a salary. The petitioners, A., N. and N.'s family held 26 per cent of the issued share capital. Restrictions were placed by the articles of association on the transfer of shares. The relationship of trust between the parties broke down, culminating in the removal of A. and N. from their directorships at an extraordinary general meeting. A. and N. presented a petition to court under section 75 of the Companies Act 1980 (now section 459–61 Companies Act 1985) for an order that their shares be bought by the majority shareholders at their fair value. The court had ordered that the shares of the removed directors be bought by the majority shareholders 'at such price as the court shall hereafter determine'. A hearing took place in the High Court to determine the purchase price, when it was held by Nourse, J. that the company was a quasi-partnership company in which A. and N. had suffered unfairly prejudicial conduct in being unfairly excluded from management and that, therefore, the fair basis for valuation of the shares was to fix a price according to the value of the shares of the company as a whole without any discount for the fact that the shares were a minority holding. Interest was held not to be due for the period before the price had been determined. An appeal was made to the Court of Appeal.

HELD, dismissing the appeal, that section 75 provided discretion to the court to do what was fair and equitable so as to put right the prejudice to the petitioner, and therefore the proper price for the sale of the shares was the price which the court determined; the judge had been right to treat the company as a quasi-partnership and to value its shares as a whole, of which the petitioners had paid a proportionate part.

OLIVER, L.J. It seems to me that the whole framework of the section, and of such of the authorities as we have seen, which seem to me to support this, is to confer on the court a very wide discretion to do what is considered fair and equitable in all the circumstances of the case, in order to put right and cure for the future the unfair prejudice which the petitioner has suffered at the hands of the other shareholders of the company.

. . . Speaking for myself, I am quite satisfied, as a matter of construction of the terms of the order, that the judge was entitled to exercise in full his discretion under section 75(3) and (4). Those subsections give him a very wide discretion, and I am quite satisfied that no ground has been shown for interference by this court with the actual manner in which the judge in fact exercised the discretion which was vested in him by the section, and by which he concluded that this was a quasi-partnership case, and that being so it would be appropriate that the shares of the company should be valued as a whole and that the petitioners should then simply be paid their proportionate part of that value which was represented by their shareholding, without there being made a discount for the fact that this was a minority shareholding.

NOTE

In *Re Castleburn Ltd.* [1991] BCLC 89, it was held in the High Court that, as there was a provision for ascertaining the method of valuation set out in the articles of association in this company, in the circumstances of the case it was *not* unfairly prejudicial conduct within section 459 of the Companies Act 1985 for a discount to be applied to a sale of shares which took place according to provisions in the articles, rather than following a court order, reflecting the fact that the shares being sold were a minority interest. Conduct of the directors which was in terms of the articles of association could not be unfairly prejudicial conduct. The sale of shares followed a breakdown in relations between shareholder/directors of a personal relationship company.

Accordingly, where a procedure for valuing shares has been set out in advance in the articles, that procedure should be followed, rather than requesting the court to perform a valuation. See also *Re a Company* [1987] 1 WLR 102 and *Re a Company* (1988) 4 BCC 80.

Re Nuneaton Borough Association Football Club Ltd. (Re a Company No. 00789 of 1987)

(1989) 5 BCC 792; [1989] BCLC 454

Chancery Division

A petition was presented to the Companies Court under section 459 Companies Act 1985, alleging unfairly prejudicial conduct. No annual general meeting had been held in 1981 or 1983, and the annual general meetings in 1982 and 1984 were of doubtful effect, because 'double meetings' covering two years were held on these occasions. Because of this the board of directors was not properly constituted, as the directors had vacated office under retirement by rotation provisions in the articles of association, and had not been re-elected. Two extraordinary general meetings were held on two days' notice, to increase the nominal share capital, and these meetings were later established to be invalid, resulting in the invalidity of the share issue. Some of these shares had been issued to the petitioner, Shooter, who was also co-opted on to the board. He also purchased further shares which belonged to the invalid batch, and two of the original, valid, shares of the company. The chairman convened an extraordinary general meeting to remove the petitioner as director, whereupon the petitioner obtained an injunction restraining the holding of the meeting, and presented his petition under section 459 Companies Act 1985. His allegations were: failure to hold annual general meetings; depriving the company of a proper board of directors and of properly appointed auditors; failure to lay accounts before the members; failure to file accounts; failure to file annual returns; and holding invalid extraordinary general meetings. He also alleged that the shares he bought were worthless.

HELD, the failure to hold annual general meetings and lay accounts before members, but not the absence of filing of returns (although it was conduct prejudicial to the interests of members), affected all members equally, and therefore was not conduct affecting part only of the membership, within the meaning of section 459(1); that the holding of invalid extraordinary general meetings was unfairly prejudicial to the petitioner because he had paid large sums for shares which were invalid; that there was power to make such an order as would enable the company to be properly run for the future: the chairman should be ordered to sell his shares to the petitioner on terms fair to the chairman, and the valuation of the shares should reflect the prestige element of a football club: valuation according to expected dividend stream was inappropriate because a dividend is rarely paid by football clubs, as was valuation according to the value of assets because the constitutions of football clubs generally forbade the return of assets to members above the par value of the shares.

HARMAN, J. The result is that there are, plainly, serious irregularities which, in my judgment, do amount to conduct unfairly prejudicial to the interests of the members. One difficulty is that the conduct, unfortunately, affects all members equally, since they are all deprived of any remedy, and my own decision in *Re a Company No. 00370 of 1987* (1988) 4 BCC 506 holds that conduct which affects all members equally is not conduct prejudicial to the interest of some part of the members because one cannot, I thought, read the phrase in the statute "some part of the members" as being "some part, including all of the members". It is not good English and I do not believe at the time that Parliament so intended.

That decision, however, has not been relied upon because Mr Potts goes on to point to other matters. He points, in particular, to Mr Shooter's position resulting from the abortive extraordinary general meetings. The conduct of the extraordinary general meetings is, plainly, the conduct of the company's affairs. To hold an extraordinary general meeting to enable the company to raise money, but, by reason of the deliberate (I am afraid), although not malicious, holding of the meeting on short notice resulting in the meeting being totally ineffective, must be prejudicial to the interests of members, and when it comes to Mr Shooter, unfairly particularly to his interests because he paid the company money—a substantial sum—for shares which did not exist. Further, he was led to pay money to others on the faith of the company's representation made by the issue of share certificates to them for shares which did not exist. Thus, as it seems to me, Mr Shooter has, plainly, been prejudiced by the conduct of the affairs of the company.

NOTE

Since the time when *Re Nuneaton Borough Association Football Club Ltd.* was decided, the wording of section 459 of the Companies Act 1985 has been changed in the Companies Act 1989 to include cases of conduct affecting *all* members as well as conduct affecting *some* members of the company and, therefore, in relation to the failure to hold annual general meetings or to file accounts, a different judgment might be expected today.

Re Sam Weller & Sons Ltd. (Re a Company No. 823A of 1987)

[1989] 3 WLR 923; (1989) 5 BCC 810

Chancery Division

A petition was presented to the Companies Court under section 459 Companies Act 1985 by a brother and sister who were shareholders in a family company. They alleged that their interests as members were unfairly prejudiced by (1) payment by the company of 'the same derisory dividend for many years past'; (2) by the purchase by the company of a holiday flat in Wales for two other members of the family who were employed by the company; (3) the proposed capital expenditure of the company of £130,000 without evidence that it would prove profitable; and (4) by the refusal of the sole director, Mr Sam Weller, to register transfers of shares to the petitioners, and to disclose the emoluments of himself or of the two family employees of the company. A dividend of 14p per share had been paid for the past thirty-seven years, and the company appeared able to support a higher dividend. The petitioners sought an order for the purchase by Mr Weller of their shares at a value representing the appropriate proportion of the value of the whole issued share capital.

The company, and other family members applied to the court to strike out the petition on the ground that all members were affected equally by the size of the dividend and, therefore, the petition was not appropriate because it was not conduct prejudicial to *some* part of the membership including the petitioners.

HELD the word 'interests' was wider than the term 'rights', and that members might have the same rights, but different interests in relation to payment of a dividend; that the petitioners might have a claim even where those responsible for the unfairly prejudicial conduct suffered the same or greater prejudice; that section 459 imported an objective test; that the court could not be satisfied that the allegations in the petition regarding the payment of dividends were incapable of amounting to unfair prejudice. Therefore the striking-out petition was dismissed.

PETER GIBSON, J. To my mind, the wording of the section imports an objective test. One simply looks to see whether the manner in which the affairs of the company have been conducted can be described as "unfairly prejudicial to the interests of some part of the members''. That, as Mr Instone submitted, requires an objective assessment of the quality of the conduct. Thus, conduct which is ''unfairly prejudicial'' to the petitioner's interests, even if not intended to be so, may nevertheless come within the section.

. . . To return to the facts alleged in the present case, here it is asserted by the petitioners that the sole director is conducting the affairs of the company for the exclusive benefit of himself and his family, and that while he and his sons are taking an income from the company, he is causing the company to pay inadequate dividends to the shareholders. The facts are striking because of the absence of any increase in the dividend for so many years and because of the amount of accumulated profits and the amount of cash in hand. I ask myself why the payment of low dividends in such circumstances is incapable of amounting to conduct unfairly prejudicial to the interests of those members, like the petitioners, who do not receive directors' fees or remuneration from the company. I am unable to see any sufficient reason. It may be in the interests of Mr Sam Weller and his sons that larger dividends should not be paid out in order to enhance the capital value of their holdings. Their interests are not necessarily identical with those of the other shareholders. It may well be in the interests of the other shareholders, including the petitioners, that a more immediate benefit should accrue to them in the form of larger dividends. As their only income from the company is by way of dividend, their interests may be not only prejudiced by the policy of low dividend payments, but unfairly prejudiced.

I do not intend to suggest that a shareholder who does not receive an income from the company except by way of dividend is always entitled to complain whenever the company is controlled by persons who do derive an income from the company and when profits are not fully distributed by way of dividend. I have no doubt that the court will view with great caution allegations of unfair prejudice on this ground. Nevertheless, concerned as I am with an application to strike out, I must be satisfied, if I am to accede to the application, that the allegations in the petition relating to the payment of dividends are incapable of amounting to unfair prejudice to the interests of some part of the members, including the petitioners. For the reasons that I have given, I cannot be so satisfied.

I confess that I am the happier to reach this conclusion when the only alternative is to petition on the same facts for the winding up of the company. It would seem to me deplorable if the only relief which the court could give, were the alleged facts proved and were such relief sought on the petition, was the drastic remedy of a winding-up order. That would mean that the shareholders have been left in a worse position under the current legislation than they were when sec. 210 [of the Companies Act 1948] was in force. In the *Scottish Co-operative* case [*Scottish Co-operative Wholesale Society Ltd.* v. *Meyer and another* [1959] AC (HL) 324] the House of Lords ordered the purchase of the petitioner's shares, notwithstanding that it could have wound up the company on the just and equitable ground.

NOTE

Again, this case was decided before the change in the law in the Companies Act 1989 to allow petitions where the act complained of affected all members and not merely some of them.

There are a great many cases based on section 459 of the Companies Act 1985, such as:

Re a Company (No. 00314 of 1989), ex parte Estate Acquisition and Development Ltd. and others [1991] BCLC 154;

Re Castleburn Ltd. [1991] (see page 247);

Re a Company (No. 006834 of 1988), ex parte Kremer [1989] BCLC 365;

Re D.R. Chemicals Ltd. (1989) 5 BCC 39;

Re Ringtower Holdings plc (1989) 5 BCC 82;

Re a Company [1988] 1 WLR 1068;

Re Blue Arrow plc [1987] BCLC 585;

Re a Company [1986] BCLC 376;

Re a Company [1986] BCLC 391;

*Weir v. *Rees* 1991 SLT (OH) 345.

Pavlides v. Jensen and others

[1956] 1 Ch. 565; [1956] 2 All ER 518; [1956] 3 WLR 224
Chancery Division

A minority shareholder brought an action in his own name and that of all the other shareholders except three, who were also directors of the company, against these directors and the company for damages for negligence. He contended that the defendants had been grossly negligent in allowing an asbestos mine in Cyprus to be sold for much less than its true value. He did not claim that the sale was fraudulent or *ultra vires*. The company was itself controlled by another company in which the same defendant directors held the majority voting power. The defendants applied to court for a preliminary determination as to whether on the facts alleged by the plaintiff the action was maintainable.

HELD that as the sale was *intra vires*, and in the absence of proof of fraud, the action did not come within one of the exceptions to *Foss* v. *Harbottle*, and was not therefore maintainable.

DANCKWERTS, J. It is contended on behalf of the defendants that the matters in respect of which the plaintiff complains, and in particular the question whether proceedings should be taken against the directors, is a matter of internal management of the company, with which, on the principle stated in *Foss* v. *Harbottle* (1843) 2 Hare 461, the court normally will not interfere. It is contended further on behalf of the defendants that the present case—based on negligence of directors—is not within the few recognised exceptions to the above-mentioned rule, namely, cases of ultra vires, illegality, or fraud (including fraudulent oppression of a minority by the majority of the shareholders). Further, it is said, the case is not a case where the control of the voting power is in the hands of the directors of the company whose actions are impugned; for they are not the share-holders; the shares are held by another company of which the defendant directors merely happen also to be among the directors.

For the plaintiff, it is contended that the above-mentioned exceptions are not exhaustive, and the court will grant relief whenever justice requires on any ground, and particularly where an otherwise helpless minority shareholder is in need of assistance by the court. As regards control, it is contended that, except for an immaterial period, the defendant directors, being a majority of the directors of Portland

Tunnel Cement Co. Ltd. (the holders of the vast bulk of the shares of the company) were in a position to stifle any attempt to institute proceedings in the name of the company against them.

. . . Lord Davey [in *Burland* v. *Earle* [1902] AC 83, 93] refers to an action by shareholders (instead of the company) being allowed ''in order to give a remedy for a wrong done which would otherwise escape redress''. But he points out that this is purely a matter of procedure, and he expressly confines the cases in which such proceedings can be brought to those in which the acts complained of are of a fraudulent character (in which he includes appropriation by a majority in fraud of the minority of the shareholders) or beyond the powers of the company. Where the act complained of is within the powers of the company and the intention of the majority of the shareholders, in other cases than these exceptions the action is not maintainable. Lord Davey adds that, ''Unless otherwise provided by the regulations of the company, a shareholder is not debarred from voting or using his voting power to carry a resolution by the circumstance of his having a particular interest in the subject-matter of the vote.''

On the facts of the present case, the sale of the company's mine was not beyond the powers of the company, and it is not alleged to be *ultra vires*. There is no allegation of fraud on the part of the directors or appropriation of assets of the company by the majority shareholders in fraud of the minority. It was open to the company, on the resolution of the majority of the shareholders, to sell the mine at a price decided by the company in that manner, and it was open to the company by a vote of the majority to decide that, if the directors by their negligence or error of judgment had sold the company's mine at an undervalue, proceedings should not be taken by the company against the directors. Applying, therefore, the principles as stated by Lord Davey, it is impossible to see how the present action can be maintained.

Smith and others v. Croft and others (No. 3)

(1987) BCC 218; [1987] BCLC 355

Chancery Division

This was a motion to strike out a minority shareholders' derivative action on the grounds that it was frivolous, vexatious or an abuse of process. The action was brought by three shareholders claiming that various payments in the name of the company were improperly paid and should be repaid to the company. They alleged that excessive remuneration had been paid to the executive directors, and that payments to associated companies for services rendered and expenses payments to the directors constituted *ultra vires* gifts; they also alleged that the directors were in breach of their fiduciary duty and had committed a fraud on the minority, and that the company had given unlawful financial assistance for the purchase of its own shares by associated companies in breach of rules which are now found in sections 151–8 of the Companies Act 1985. All the payments were, however, made out of distributable profits, and there was no suggestion that there had been a fraud on creditors. The case was brought under the exceptions to *Foss* v. *Harbottle*. The three plaintiffs together held 11.86 per cent of the voting rights. The defendants were the chairman, the executive directors and companies associated with them who together held a large majority of the voting rights. The plaintiffs had a further 3 per cent support from other shareholders, while an additional 20 per cent opposed the action.

HELD that the plaintiff's statement of claim should be struck out: the court held that the payments of remuneration to directors might be an abuse of power, but could not be *ultra vires*, where power of remuneration was vested by the articles of association in the board of directors; the same was true of the payments to the associated companies, and the expenses payments; there was a prima facie case for holding that there had been a breach of the statutory rules relating to the provision by the company of financial assistance for the purchase of shares; a minority cannot have a larger right of relief than the company would have were it the plaintiff, and if there were a valid reason why the company should not sue, that would also affect the plaintiff; in relation to whether the minority action would be allowed, the court held that the important question was whether the plaintiff was being improperly prevented from bringing proceedings on behalf of the company; if it was an expression of the will of the company by an appropriate independent organ that was preventing the plaintiff bringing an action, then the plaintiff was correctly prevented; therefore it was appropriate to consider the views of a simple majority of the independent shareholders.

KNOX, J. In my judgment the arguments addressed to me on this aspect of the case raise two questions of law and one of mixed law and fact, before an answer that the action does not fall within the proper boundaries of the exception to the rule in *Foss* v. *Harbottle* could be given. The questions of law can be formulated as follows:

(1) Is a minority shareholder always entitled as of right to bring and prosecute an action for the company to recover money paid away in the course of a transaction which was *ultra vires* the company, or is the prosecution of such an action susceptible of coming within the rule in *Foss* v. *Harbottle* so that there can be circumstances in which the court will not allow it to continue?

(2) If the latter view is the correct one in relation to those categories of claims based on *ultra vires* transactions, and also in all cases of minority shareholders' actions to recover money for the company in respect of acts which constitute a fraud on the minority, will the court pay regard to the views of the majority of shareholders who are independent of the defendants to the action on the question whether the action should proceed?

. . . The third question which arises is whether in this case Wren Trust should be treated as independent, if the views of an independent majority are relevant.

. . . Ultimately the question which has to be answered in order to determine whether the rule in *Foss* v. *Harbottle* applies to prevent a minority shareholder seeking relief as plaintiff for the benefit of the company is: "Is the plaintiff being improperly prevented from bringing these proceedings in behalf of the company?" If it is an expression of the corporate will of the company by an appropriate independent organ that is preventing the plaintiff from prosecuting the action he is not improperly but properly prevented and so the answer to the question is, "No". The appropriate independent organ will vary according to the constitution of the company concerned and the identity of the defendants who will in most cases be disqualified from participating by voting in expressing the corporate will.

Finally on this aspect of the matter I remain unconvinced that a just result is achieved by a single minority shareholder having the right to involve a company in an action for recovery of compensation for the company if all the other minority shareholders are for disinterested reasons satisfied that the proceedings will be productive of more harm than good.

NOTE

Knox, J. also provides a useful classification of the case law exceptions to the principle laid down in *Foss* v. *Harbottle*. See (1987) BCC 218, 246–50.

Edwards and another v. Halliwell and others

[1950] 2 All ER 1064

Court of Appeal

Although the rules of the defendant trade union provided that alteration to members' contributions could only be made after a two-thirds majority had been obtained in a ballot of the membership, a delegate meeting passed a resolution to increase the contributions without holding a ballot. Two members of the union sought a declaration that the resolution was invalid. Vaisey J. granted the declaration and the defendants appealed.

HELD that as the matter was not a mere irregularity of internal management, but a matter of substance and tainted with oppression, the court would grant the plaintiffs relief as an exception to the rule in *Foss* v. *Harbottle*, which did not apply to invasions of the private rights of members.

ASQUITH, L.J. The other point relied on by the defendants was that, even if they were wrong on the point of construction, the court either could not, or should not, grant the plaintiffs the relief which they claim. Under this head counsel for the defendants relied on the alleged principle that, when an action is brought by an individual in respect of a mere irregularity in a matter that is *intra vires* a trade union and concerns its internal management, the court will not as a rule intervene. For this purpose he conceded that a "mere irregularity" meant something not involving fraud, oppression or unfairness. I confess I should have thought the action complained of here was strongly tinctured, not, indeed, with fraud, but with "oppression" and "unfairness". Here were men who had a right not to have their contributions increased except after a ballot resulting in a two-thirds majority. This right was clearly violated. An unauthorised increase was sought to be extorted, and when they refused to pay, as they were entitled to do, severe penalties were imposed or threatened. To call this a mere informality or irregularity without any element of oppression or unfairness would be an abuse of language. When in circumstances such as I have described a remedy is sought by an individual, complaining of a particular act in breach of his rights and inflicting particular damage on him, it seems to me the principle of *Foss* v. *Harbottle* (1843) 2 Hare 461, which has been so strongly relied on by the defendants, does not apply either by way of barring the remedy or supporting the objection that the action is wrongly constituted because the union is not a plaintiff. Nor, lastly, can I accept the submission that, if the action is maintainable at law, it should nevertheless be dismissed because the vast majority of the members approved the action taken by the defendants. . . . I think the appeal should be dismissed.

JENKINS, J. As to the contention that, even though the purported alteration of the tables of contributions was invalid, the court should not interfere because the omission to hold a ballot and obtain a two-thirds majority as required by r. 19 was a mere irregularity in point of form, in my judgment, that argument can be shortly dismissed by saying that this was not a matter of form. It was a matter of substance. The relevant part of r. 19, I conceive, was designed to protect members against increases in the rates of contributions unless those increases were agreed to by a particular majority of members on a vote obtained in a particular way—that is to say, a two-thirds majority on a ballot vote. It seems to me that the executive committee's disregard of that express provision in the rules was a wrong done to each individual member on a point of substance.

. . . The rule in *Foss* v. *Harbottle*, as I understand it, comes to no more than this. First, the proper plaintiff in an action in respect of a wrong alleged to be done to a company or association of persons is *prima facie* the company or the association of persons itself. Secondly, where the alleged wrong is a transaction which might be made binding on the company or association and on all its members by a simple majority of the members, no individual member of the company is allowed to maintain an action in respect of that matter for the simple reason that, if a mere majority of the company or association is in favour of what has been done, then *cadit quaestio*. No wrong had been done to the company or association and there is nothing in respect of which anyone can sue. If, on the other hand, a simple majority of members of the company or association is against what has been done, then there is no valid reason why the company or association itself should not sue. In my judgment, it is implicit in the rule that the matter relied on as constituting the cause of action should be a cause of action properly belonging to the general body of corporators or members of the company or association as opposed to a cause of action which some individual member can assert in his own right.

The cases falling within the general ambit of the rule are subject to certain exceptions. It has been noted in the course of argument that in cases where the act complained of is wholly *ultra vires* the company or association the rule has no application because there is no question of the transaction being confirmed by any majority. It has been further pointed out that where what has been done amounts to what is generally called in these cases a fraud on the minority and the wrongdoers are themselves in control of the company, the rule is relaxed in favour of the aggrieved minority who are allowed to bring what is known as a minority shareholders' action on behalf of themselves and all others. The reason for this is that, if they were denied that right, their grievance could never reach the court because the wrongdoers themselves, being in control, would not allow the company to sue. Those exceptions are not directly in point in this case, but they show, especially the last one, that the rule is not an inflexible rule and it will be relaxed where necessary in the interests of justice.

There is a further exception which seems to me to touch this case directly. That is the exception made by ROMER J. in *Cotter* v. *National Union of Seamen* [1929] 2 Ch 58. He pointed out that the rule did not prevent an individual member from suing if the matter in respect of which he was suing was one which could validly be done or sanctioned, not by a simple majority of the members of the company or association, but only by some special majority, as, for instance, in the case of a limited company under the Companies Act, a special resolution duly passed as such. As ROMER J. pointed out, the reason for that exception is clear, because otherwise, if the rule were applied in its full rigour, a company, which, by its directors, had broken its own regulations by doing something without a special resolution which could only validly be done by a special resolution could assert that it alone was the proper plaintiff in any consequent action and the effect would be to allow a company acting in breach of its articles to do *de facto* by ordinary resolution that which according to its own regulations could only be done by special resolution. That exception exactly fits the present case inasmuch as here the act complained of is something which could only have been validly done, not by a simple majority, but by a two-thirds majority obtained on a ballot vote. In my judgment, therefore, the reliance on the rule in *Foss* v. *Harbottle* in the present case may be regarded as misconceived on that ground alone.

I would go further. In my judgment, this is a case of a kind which is not even within the general ambit of the rule. It is not a case where what is complained of is a wrong done to the union, a matter in respect of which the cause of action would primarily and properly belong to the union. It is a case in which certain members of a trade union complain that the union, acting through the delegate meeting and the executive council in breach of the rules by which the union and every member are bound, has invaded the individual rights of the complainant menbers, who are entitled to maintain themselves in full membership with all the rights and privileges appertaining to the status so long as they pay contributions in accordance with the tables of contributions as they stood before the purported alterations of 1943, unless and until the scale of contributions is validly altered by the prescribed majority obtained on a ballot vote. Those rights, these members claim, have been invaded. The gist of the case is that the personal and individual rights of membership of each of them have been invaded by a purported, but invalid, alteration of the tables of contributions. In those circumstances, it seems to me the rule in *Foss* v. *Harbottle* has no application at all, for the individual members who are suing sue, not in the right of the union, but in their own right to protect from invasion their own individual rights as members.

Prudential Assurance Co. Ltd. v. Newman Industries Ltd. and others (No. 2)

[1982] 1 Ch 204; [1982] 1 All ER 354; [1982] 2 WLR 31
Court of Appeal

The facts of this case were very complex: Prudential Assurance Co. Ltd. (P. Ltd.), (the plaintiffs), were 3 per cent shareholders in Newman Industries Ltd. (N. Ltd.). On their own behalf and that of N. Ltd. and its shareholders, they brought a derivative action and a representative action against Mr Bartlett and Mr Laughton, respectively the chairman and vice-chairman of N. Ltd. and another company, TPG, and also against N. Ltd. and TPG. They claimed damages on the grounds, firstly, that N. Ltd. had agreed to buy TPG's holdings in two companies to relieve TPG's financial difficulties, an agreement that was not disclosed to the whole board of directors. Secondly, that Mr Bartlett, the chairman of N. Ltd., had contracted on behalf of the company to purchase almost all the assets and take over the liabilities of TPG, a contract which had to be approved by the shareholders of both companies. Although the extraordinary general meeting of N. Ltd. to approve the contract had been postponed under pressure from dissenting parties to allow time for a report to be prepared by a merchant bank on the proposed purchase, the meeting had been held before the report was ready, and a resolution was passed to proceed with the purchase of TPG's assets. The plaintiffs alleged fraud on the part of the chairman and vice-chairman. The chairman and vice-chairman did not have a majority of the shares in N Ltd. The defendants then sought a court ruling as to whether the plaintiffs, as minority shareholders, were entitled to institute proceedings, because of the rule in *Foss* v. *Harbottle*. In the High Court Vinelott, J. held that the interests of justice demanded that the plaintiffs be allowed to raise the action. The defendants appealed to the Court of Appeal.

HELD in relation to the propriety of the bringing of the action by the plaintiffs, that where fraud had been committed against a company, the company itself was the proper plaintiff, and that a derivative action was appropriate only where the board of directors was under the control of the fraudsters: the question of whether the company was so controlled should have been determined before the action was brought by the plaintiffs. In relation to the personal action, since the plaintiffs' rights as shareholders were rights to participate in the company on the terms laid down in the articles of association, they had not suffered damage to those rights, and hence the action was misconceived. Therefore, instances where the wrongdoers have *de facto* as opposed to absolute control over corporate decision making, do not come within the exceptions to the rule in *Foss* v. *Harbottle*.

CUMMING-BRUCE, TEMPLEMAN, and BRIGHTMAN, L.J.J. (joint judgment). . . . In our view, whatever may be the properly defined boundaries of the exception to the rule [in *Foss* v. *Harbottle*] the plaintiff ought at least to be required before proceeding with his action to establish a *prima facie* case (i) that the company is entitled to the relief claimed, and (ii) that the action falls within the proper boundaries of the exception to the rule in *Foss* v. *Harbottle*. On the latter issue it may well be right for the judge trying the preliminary issue to grant a sufficient adjournment to enable a meeting of shareholders to be convened by the board, so that he can reach a conclusion in the light of the conduct of, and proceedings at, that meeting.

We turn to the personal action. . . . In our judgment the personal claim is misconceived. It is of course correct, as the judge found and Mr Bartlett did not dispute, that he and Mr Laughton, in advising the shareholders to support the resolution approving the agreement, owed the shareholders a duty to give such advice in good faith and not fraudulently. It is also correct that if directors convene a meeting on the basis of a fraudulent circular, a shareholder will have a right of action to recover any loss which he has been personally caused in consequence of the fraudulent circular; this might include the expense of attending the meeting. But what he cannot do is recover damages merely because the company in which he is interested has suffered damage. He cannot recover a sum equal to the diminution in the market value of his shares, or equal to the likely diminution in dividend, because such a ''loss'' is merely a reflection of the loss suffered by the company. The shareholder does not suffer any personal loss. His only ''loss'' is through the company, in the diminution of the value of the net assets of the company, in which he has (say) a 3 per cent shareholding. The plaintiff's shares are merely a right of participation in the company on the terms of the articles of association. The shares themselves, his right of participation, are not directly affected by the wrongdoing. The plaintiff still holds all the shares as his own absolutely unencumbered property. The deceit practised upon the plaintiff does not affect the shares; it merely enables the defendant to rob the company.

. . . The plaintiffs in this action were never concerned to recover in the personal action. The plaintiffs were only interested in the personal action as a means of circumventing the rule in *Foss* v. *Harbottle*. The plaintiffs succeeded. A personal action would subvert the rule in *Foss* v. *Harbottle* and that rule is not merely a tiresome procedural obstacle placed in the path of a shareholder by a legalistic judiciary. The rule is the consequence of the fact that a corporation is a separate legal entity. Other consequences are limited liability and limited rights. The company is liable for its contracts and torts; the shareholder has no such liability. The company acquires causes of action for breaches of contract and for torts which damage the company. No cause of action vests in the shareholder. When the shareholder acquires a share he accepts the fact that the value of his investment follows the fortunes of the company and that he can only exercise his influence over the fortunes of the company by the exercise of his voting rights in general meeting. The law confers on him the right to ensure that the company observes the limitations of its memorandum of association and the right to ensure that other shareholders observe the rule, imposed on them by the articles of association.

Pender v. Lushington

(1877) 6 ChD 70

Chancery Division

The Direct United States Cable Co. Ltd. had articles of association which stated that every member was entitled to one vote for every ten shares held, but that no member should be entitled to more than 100 votes in all, and that no member could vote at a general meeting unless he had been possessed of his shares for three months previously. The articles also provided that the company should not be affected with notice of trust.

The action was brought by a shareholder on behalf of himself and certain other shareholders, against the company and the directors, to restrain the defendants from ruling out 649 votes which had been cast against an amendment to a resolution proposed by the plaintiff, Pender. The reason given by the chairman for ruling out the votes was that the shares had been transferred by large shareholders to nominees to evade the rule restricting shareholders to 100 votes in all, and that the nominees had no beneficial interest in the company. The transfers had, however, taken place more than three months previously as required by the articles.

HELD that the members of the company were the people whose names appeared on the register of members, and that only those people who were entered on that register, and under the articles of association, had been so entered for three months, could vote at general meetings: the purpose for which they came to acquire the shares was irrelevant; that the plaintiffs were entitled to an injunction, and that until a general meeting could be called to decide whether or not the company's name should be used as plaintiff, the company's name could continue to be used in the proceedings; and that a shareholder had rights of property in his shares, and was therefore entitled to use legal proceedings if those rights were not respected.

JESSEL, M.R. In all cases of this kind, where men exercise their rights of property, they exercise their rights from some motive adequate or inadequate, and I have always considered the law to be that those who have the rights of property are entitled to exercise them, whatever their motives may be for such an exercise—that is as regards a Court of Law as distinguished from a court of morality or conscience, if such a court exists.

. . . It is admitted that the votes tendered were votes of persons on the register of shareholders, and it is admitted that they had been possessed of those shares for at least three months previously to the time of holding the general meeting, which is what is required by the 59th article. That being so, their votes were rejected on this ground: It was said that the persons who gave the votes were trustees for other persons, and that these other persons, the *cestuis que trust* of those trustees, were also either holders in their own name or as *cestuis que trust* of other shares, amounting in the whole to more than 1000 shares, so that if all the shares to which the persons were entitled had been registered in one name, that person could not have been given more than 100 votes, the 56th section of the articles saying, that every member holding at least ten shares shall have one vote for every complete number of ten shares, with this limit, that no shareholder shall be entitled to more than 100 votes in all.

Now the argument is, that the words "every member" mean, not a man registered on the list of shareholders, but any person beneficially entitled to shares, because if not carried to that extent I do not understand the argument at all.

. . . It comes, therefore, to this, that the register of shareholders, on which there can be no notice of trust, furnishes the only means of ascertaining whether you have a lawful meeting or a lawful demand for a poll, or of enabling the scrutineers to strike out votes.

The result appears to me to be manifest, that the company has no rights whatever to enter into the question of the beneficial ownership of shares. Any such suggestion is quite inadmissible, and therefore it is clear that the chairman had no right to inquire who was the beneficial owner of the shares, and the votes in question ought to have been admitted as good votes independently of any inquiry as to whether the parties tendering them were or were not, and to what extent, trustees for other persons beneficially entitled to the shares.

. . . But there is another ground on which the action may be maintained. This is an action by Mr *Pender* for himself. He is a member of the company, and whether he votes with the majority or the minority he is entitled to have his vote recorded—an individual right in respect of which he has a right to sue. That has nothing to do with the question like that raised in *Foss* v. *Harbottle* (1843) 2 Hare, 461 and that line of cases. He has a right to say "Whether I vote in the majority or minority, you shall record my vote, as that is a right of property belonging to my interest in this company, and if you refuse to record my vote I will institute legal proceedings against you to compel you". What is the answer to such an action? It seems to me that it can be maintained as a matter of substance, and that there is no technical difficulty in maintaining it.

★ Oliver's Trustees and another v. W.G. Walker & Sons (Edin.) Ltd.

1948 SLT (OH) 140
Court of Session

A minority action was brought against a company and its directors in which the pursuers sought to reduce directors' minutes which sought to increase the directors' salaries and bonuses; they also sought declarator that the directors were liable to repay what they had received from the company; and the pursuers alleged *mala fides* on the part of the directors. The Lord Ordinary had allowed a proof restricted to the pursuers' averments: (1) that remuneration was excessive and grossly unfair; and (2) that the directors acted in *mala fide* at the general meetings on 1 August 1945 and 23 October 1946.

HELD by Lord Mackintosh that as fixing directors' remuneration was *intra vires*, though *ultra vires* the directors, the court had no jurisdiction to entertain the action brought by a minority except so far as based on fraud by the directors.

LORD MACKINTOSH. The wider question in this case is whether this is a matter upon which a minority of shareholders can competently ask for and get relief from the court, or whether it is not such a matter as can only be dealt with by the company in general meeting. In the Privy Council case of *Burland* v. *Earle* [1902] AC 83, the law on this question was laid down by Lord Davey in a well-known passage. . . ."The cases in which the minority can maintain such an action are therefore confined to those in which the acts complained of are of a fraudulent character or beyond the powers of the company."
    . . . I think therefore that the pursuers have relevantly averred that the remuneration voted by the directors to themselves was excessive to the amount of something like £900 per annum and that they must be given an opportunity of proving this if they can . . . While I have thought it right to allow enquiry here in view of the pursuers' pleadings, and particularly their averment that the remuneration in

question was excessive and grossly unfair, I think I have said enough to indicate that in my view the onus which the pursuers have to discharge is a heavy one. Before they can establish that the actings of the directors on 25 August 1944 were of a fraudulent character they would have to prove not only that the remuneration then voted was on the high side, but that it was out of all proportion to the services rendered, or in other words, that a substantial portion of it was in effect just a gift made by the directors to themselves out of the company's funds.

★ Weir v. Rees

1991 SLT (OH) 345
Court of Session

A power struggle had taken place within Bremner plc, as a result of which the company was left without any directors, after the removal of the entire board of directors. Until a further election of directors could be held, control of the company was in the hands of two of the deposed directors, one functioning as the company secretary, and the other by virtue of his appointment as manager. Some of the shareholders petitioned the court for the sequestration of the property and undertaking of the company, and for the appointment of an interim judicial factor, on the grounds that the secretary and the manager could not be relied on to act impartially.

HELD that an interim judicial factor should be appointed, to safeguard the interests of the members until a fresh board of directors could be appointed.

LORD CAPLAN. I concluded that it was reasonable in all the circumstances to appoint a judicial factor *ad interim*. For the moment there are no proper arrangements for the control and management of the company. As manager and secretary respectively Mr Rowland-Jones and Mr Rees, in the absence of directors to whom they can refer, do not have proper authority to deal with a whole range of matters which could arise and require urgent attention. Nor are they suitable persons to have unsupervised control of the company in the circumstances which have now arisen. They are in serious conflict with what appears to be a majority of the shareholders on a number of issues and by removing them summarily fron their office as directors such shareholders have shown that they have no confidence in them as persons to look after the company. I must say that I am not in a position to have any views at all as to the character or capacities of either of the respondents. My opinion as to their suitability to continue to be in control is governed by the obvious difficulty that each would have in acting impartially were a situation to arise which was in conflict with their personal interests and also the more general consideration that pending a resolution of the company's affairs it is important to have an independent person in charge who will protect the interests of all concerned parties until new and properly appointed directors resume control of the company.

. . . In the whole circumstances I therefore thought that it was appropriate to grant the motion.

14. Winding up

Summary

1. Sources of the law

The law on winding up is found in sections 73–251 of the Insolvency Act 1986, and in case law. The case law detailed in this Chapter consists largely of cases on the discretion of the court to wind up companies on the 'just and equitable' ground (section 122(1)(g) of the Insolvency Act 1986) and cases on personal liability for fraudulent and wrongful trading (sections 213–14 of the Insolvency Act 1986). The procedure for winding up is contained in the Insolvency Rules 1986 and Insolvency (Scotland) Rules 1986.

2. The winding-up process

The process of winding up involves the appointment of a liquidator whose task it is to ingather the assets of the company, pay the creditors in a statutorily approved order, and to pay any remaining funds to the shareholders. The company is then dissolved and removed from the Register of Companies kept by Companies House.

Most companies are insolvent when they are wound up, but it is possible for a company which is solvent to be wound up, for example because the need for the company no longer exists, or because of serious mismanagement by the directors.

Companies can be wound up by the court or voluntarily. The grounds on which a company can be wound up by the court are set out in section 122 of the Insolvency Act 1986. These grounds include the fact that the company is unable to pay its debts (the commonest cause), and the fact that the court is of the opinion that it is just and equitable that the company be wound up. Winding up on the 'just and equitable' ground provides discretion to the court to wind up the company if it considers that winding up is appropriate in the circumstances. Winding up orders have been granted on this ground where there is deadlock in administration (*Re Yenidje Tobacco Co. Ltd.* [1916]), where one party has been excluded from management in a quasi-partnership company, or personal relationship company (*Ebrahimi* v. *Westbourne Galleries Ltd.* [1973]; **Gammack, Petitioner* 1983), and in cases of general maladministration by directors, for example, where there is misapplication of assets and a lack of provision of information to members (**Hyndman* v. *R.C. Hyndman & Co. Ltd.* 1989). It would also be appropriate in cases where the purpose for which the company had been formed had been completed, although a just and equitable winding up was refused for this purpose in *Re Abbey Leisure Ltd.* [1989].

The grounds on which a company can be wound up voluntarily are set out in section 84 of the Insolvency Act 1986. These are: that the period for the duration of the company has expired, that a special resolution has been passed by the company authorising its winding up, and that the company has passed as an extraordinary resolution that it cannot by reason of its liabilities carry on in business and that it is advisable to wind up. Most liquidations proceed as voluntary liquidations because the process is both quicker and cheaper.

A voluntary winding up can be a creditors' voluntary winding up or a members' voluntary winding up. A members' voluntary winding up is one in which a declaration of solvency is passed by the directors stating that the company will be able to pay its debts in full within a year from the commencement of the winding up (section 89 of the Insolvency Act 1986). The creditors have less involvement in a members' voluntary winding up because they will be paid in full.

3. Personal liability of directors and others for company debts

Directors and other persons can be made personally liable in the liquidation of the company under a number of statutory provisions. The first of these is section 212 of the Insolvency Act 1986, which allows the Official Receiver, liquidator, a creditor or a contributory to apply to court for an order compelling the repayment of money or the restoration of goods to the company, or the payment of compensation to the company, to the extent that the court considers just, in respect of misapplication of company money or property, or misfeasance or breach of fiduciary or other duty. The persons who can be found liable are officers of the company, liquidators, administrators and administrative receivers, or any person who has taken part in the management of the company.

Fraudulent trading is provided for in section 213 of the Insolvency Act 1986. This section had been part of the law since the Companies Act 1929. A liquidator can apply to a court for an order holding a person liable if there is proof that that person is responsible for the company's carrying on business with intent to defraud creditors or for any fraudulent purpose. The court can hold the person liable to contribute to the assets of the company to the extent the court thinks proper. Personal liability under this section has been difficult to establish because of the requirement of proving fraud (see *In re Sarflax Ltd.* [1979]). However, in *Re Gerald Cooper Chemicals Ltd. (in Liquidation)* [1978] a creditor was held liable. See also *Re a Company (No. 001418 of 1988)* [1991]. There are also criminal penalities for fraudulent trading which are contained in section 458 of the Companies Act 1985. These apply whether or not the company is in liquidation: see *R. v. Kemp* (1988).

Wrongful trading is provided for in section 214 of the insolvency Act 1986, and was first introduced into the law in 1985. This applies only where the company is in insolvent liquidation, and only affects directors and shadow directors. For the section to apply, it has to be established that the company is in insolvent liquidation, that the director prior to the commencement of the winding up knew or ought reasonably to have concluded that there was no reasonable prospect of the company's avoiding going into insolvent liquidation, and that the director was a director at that time. The director's behaviour is measured against both the general knowledge, skill and experience that may reasonably be expected of a person carrying out the same functions as are carried out by that director in relation to the company, and also the general knowledge, skill and experience that that director has. It is a defence to establish that the director took every step with a view to minimising the potential loss to the company's creditors as (assuming him to have known that there was no reasonable prospect that the company would avoid going into insolvent liquidation) he ought to have taken: see *Re Produce Marketing Consortium Ltd.* [1989]; and *Re Purpoint Ltd.* [1991].

There are no statutory criminal penalties attached to wrongful trading. Wrongful trading ought to be easier to prove than fraudulent trading because it does not involve proof of deliberate intention to deceive and allows the director's conduct to be measured not only against the subjective standard of his own state of knowledge, but also against the objective standard of the average company director.

Under section 216 of the Insolvency Act 1986, the name of a company which has gone into insolvent liquidation cannot be re-used by the directors without the leave of the court for five years following the liquidation: see *Re Bonus Breaks Ltd.* (1991).

4. Dissolution and restoration of the company to the register

Once a company has been dissolved following liquidation, or without liquidation under section 651 of the Companies Act 1985, the court may declare the dissolution void to enable the company to be liquidated. Other than in cases of damages for personal injuries, or under the Fatal Accidents Act 1976 or the Damages (Scotland) Act 1976, which can be brought at any time, unless another enactment sets a time limit, such an application must be brought within two years from the date of dissolution. Generally, this provision will be used by employees and others who wish to bring industrial injuries compensation claims. See *In re Workvale Ltd.* [1991].

Re Yenidje Tobacco Co. Ltd.

[1916] Ch 426

Court of Appeal

Weinberg and Rothman were each sole traders operating as tobacconists. They agreed to amalgamate and formed a private limited company in which they were the only directors and shareholders. According to the articles they had equal voting power, and the quorum of the directors was one. If agreement could not be reached, there was provision in the articles for reference to arbitration. After a costly reference to arbitration, Rothman refused to implement the award. He sued Weinberg for fraudulent misrepresentation in relation to the agreement for the sale of his business, whereupon the parties refused to speak to each other and communicated when necessary through the company secretary. The company continued to be profitable. Weinberg presented a petition for winding up on the 'just and equitable ground' under legislation which is now found in section 122(1)(g) of the Insolvency Act 1986, claiming that deadlock had arisen, and that the substratum of the company had gone. At first instance the court granted a winding-up order which was appealed.

HELD that if this had been a partnership it would have been dissolved; the same principle should apply to a limited company which was in essence a partnership in all but name, and the decision of the trial judge was affirmed.

LORD COZENS-HARDY, M.R. When one of the two partners has commenced, and has not discontinued, an action charging his co-partner with fraud in the inception of the partnership, is it likely, is it reasonable, is it common sense, to suppose that these two partners can work together in the manner in which they ought to work in the conduct of the partnership business? Can they do so when things have reached such a pass, as they have here, that after an arbitration lasting eighteen days, an arbitration on the only point which was referred, which terminated in favour of Mr Weinberg, and to which Mr Rothman declines to give effect, in this sense, that although the award decided that Litiger had not been dismissed and ought to continue as a servant of the firm until removed, Mr Rothman will not allow him to come and do his business, so that he, Litiger, is in the happy position now of receiving his wages of £5 per week without being allowed to do any work for the company in respect of which he is a servant?

The matter does not stop there. It is proved that these two directors are not on speaking terms, that the so-called meetings of the board of directors have been almost a farce or comedy, the directors will not speak to each other on the board, and some third person has to convey communications between them which ought to go directly from one to the other. . . . . Certainly, having regard to the fact that the only two directors will not speak to each other, and no business which deserves the name of business in the affairs of the company can be carried on, I think the company should not be allowed to continue. I have treated it as a partnership, and under the Partnership Act of course the application for a dissolution would take the form of an action; but this is not a partnership strictly, it is not a case in which it can be dissolved by action. But ought not the same principles to apply to a case like this where in substance it is a partnership in the form or guise of a private company? . . . I think that in a case like this we are bound to say that circumstances which would justify the winding up of a partnership between these two by action are circumstances which should induce the Court to exercise its jurisdiction under the just and equitable clause and to wind up the company.

. . . In my opinion the appeal fails and ought to be dismissed with costs.

Ebrahimi v. Westbourne Galleries Ltd. and others

[1973] AC 360; [1972] 2 All ER 492; [1972] 2 WLR 1289
House of Lords

The appellant and Nazar (N.) had been in partnership as dealers in oriental carpets, and transferred their business to a private limited company in which they were the sole directors and shareholders. No dividends were paid, the profits being paid to the directors as remuneration. Some time later G., the son of N., was made a director and acquired sufficient shares to give N. and G. a majority at a general meeting. A disagreement arose between the appellant and N. and G., as a result of which the appellant was removed as a director by an ordinary resolution. The appellant petitioned for an order under s. 210 of the Companies Act 1948 (the forerunner to ss. 459–61 of the Companies Act 1985, which required evidence of 'oppressive conduct' and not, as now, 'unfairly prejudicial conduct'), to compel the other two shareholder-directors to purchase his shares, or sell their shares to him on such terms as the court should think fit, or alternatively for a winding-up order under section 222(f) of the Companies Act 1948 (the forerunner of section 122(1)(g) of the Insolvency Act 1986) on the ground that it was just and equitable that the company should be wound up.

At first instance Plowman, J. refused to make an order under section 210, but granted a winding-up order. An appeal was made to the Court of Appeal by the respondents, which allowed the appeal and held that in a quasi-partnership company the removal of a director under the articles was not a ground for a winding-up order unless there was evidence that the power of removal had not been exercised *bona fide* in the interests of the company as a whole, or that no man could have thought the removal in the interests of the company, and that there was insufficient evidence that the removal was not justified. The appellant then appealed to the House of Lords.

HELD that the company should be wound up on the just and equitable ground: a limited company was more than a mere legal entity, and the court could take account of equitable considerations of a personal nature between individuals, and in this case the agreement between the parties had been that the appellant should have a continuing right to take part in management. Since the appellant had been deprived of his management rights and was unable to dispose of his shares without the consent of the other two shareholder-directors, the court should wind up the company.

Per curiam: elements which give rise to the application of equitable considerations include one, or probably more, of the following: (1) an association formed or continued on the basis of a personal relationship involving mutual confidence; (2) an agreement that some or all of the shareholders shall participate in management; and (3) a restriction on the members' right to transfer shares. The fact that the company is a small one, or a private company is not enough.

LORD WILBERFORCE. The foundation of it all lies in the words ''just and equitable'' and, if there is any respect in which some of the cases may be open to criticism, it is that the courts may sometimes have been too timorous in giving them full force. The words are a recognition of the fact that a limited company is more than a mere legal entity, with a personality in law of its own: that there is room in company law for recognition of the fact that behind it, or amongst it, there are individuals, with rights, expectations and obligations *inter se* which are not necessarily submerged in the company structure. That structure is defined by the Companies Act and by the articles of association by which shareholders agree to be bound. In most companies and in most contexts, this definition is sufficient and exhaustive, equally so whether the company is large or small. The "just and equitable" provision does not, as the respondents suggest, entitle one party to disregard the obligation he assumes by entering a company, nor the court to dispense him from it. It does, as equity always does, enable the court to subject the exercise of legal rights to equitable considerations; considerations, that is, of a personal character arising between one individual and another, which may make it unjust or inequitable, to insist on legal rights, or to exercise them in a particular way.

It would be impossible, and wholly undesirable, to define the circumstances in which these considerations may arise. Certainly the fact that a company is a small one, or a small private company, is not enough. There are very many of these where the association is a purely commercial one, of which it can safely be said that the basis of the association is adequately and exhaustively laid down in the articles. The superimposition of equitable considerations requires something more, of the following elements: (i) an association formed or continued on the basis of a personal relationship, involving mutual confidence—this element will often be found where a pre-existing partnership has been converted into a limited company; (ii) an agreement, or understanding, that all, or some (for there may be "sleeping" members), of the shareholders shall participate in the conduct of the business; (iii) restriction upon the transfer of the members' interest in the company—so that if confidence is lost, or one member is removed from management, he cannot take out his stake and go elsewhere.

LORD CROSS OF CHELSEA. What the minority shareholder in cases of this sort really wants is not to have the company wound up—which may prove an unsatisfactory remedy—but to be paid a proper price for his shareholding. With this in mind Parliament provided by section 210 of the Companies Act 1948 that if a member of a company could show that the company's affairs were being conducted in a manner oppressive to some of the members including himself, that the facts proved would justify the making of a winding-up order under the "just and equitable" clause but that to wind up the company would unfairly prejudice the "oppressed" members the court could (*inter alia*) make an order for the purchase of the shares of those members by other members or by the company. To give the court jurisdiction under this section the petitioner must show both that the conduct of the majority is ''oppressive'' and also that it affects him in his capacity as a shareholder. Mr Ebrahimi was unable to establish either of these preconditions. But the jurisdiction to wind up under section 222(f) continues to exist as an independent remedy and I have no doubt that the Court of Appeal was right in rejecting the submission of the respondents to the effect that a petitioner cannot obtain an order under that subsection any more than under section 210 unless he can show that his position as a shareholder has been worsened by the action of which he complains.

 . . . It was not suggested that Mr Ebrahimi had been guilty of any misconduct such as would justify one partner in expelling another under an expulsion clause contained in partnership articles. All that happened was that without one being more to blame than the other the two could no longer work together in harmony. Had no company been formed Mr Ebrahimi could have had the partnership wound up and though Mr Nazar and his son were entitled in law to oust him from his directorship and deprive him of his income they could only do so subject to Mr Ebrahimi's right to obtain equitable relief in the form of a winding up order under section 222(f). I would, therefore, allow the appeal.

NOTE

The modern remedies under section 459–61 of the Companies Act 1985 are a great deal easier to prove than was 'oppressive' conduct under section 210 of the Companies Act 1948. Acordingly, if *Ebrahimi* v. *Westbourne Galleries Ltd.* [1973] were to come before the court today, the court would most probably grant one of the remedies under those sections, and there would be no need for the company to be wound up.

★ **Gammack, Petitioner**

1983 SLT (OH) 246
Court of Session

Three individuals carried on business as a private company until the death of one of them, whereupon the two survivors carried on as the directors until the death of one of the others. Thereafter four new directors were co-opted on to the board, who were connected with the two deceased directors. The two directors who were connected with one of the deceased directors were voted off the board, and replaced by persons connected with the other deceased director. One of the deposed directors, who was also a shareholder, presented a petition on his own behalf and that of his family under section 222(f) of the Companies Act 1948 (now section 122(1)(g) of the Insolvency Act 1986), claiming that it was just and equitable that the company be wound up. The current directors held a controlling interest in the company. The petitioner claimed that the company had been set up on the basis that both families should participate in management, and that the shareholders with the controlling interest had shown an intention to take money from the company in the form of directors' fees, salaries and benefits to the prejudice of the petitioners as shareholders. He also alleged that the inexperience of the board had caused the company to make a loss, and that the respondents refused to allow the petitioner and his family to take their share capital out of the company by selling their shares at a fair price. The respondents alleged that they were making efforts to restore profitability to the company, and that any benefits received were justified in terms of work done for the company.

HELD, refusing the winding-up order, (i) that the company was not a personal relationship company and that there was not proved to be an agreement whereby members of both families were to take part in management; (ii) that the petitioners had not averred that the respondents' motives were purely selfish and that the remuneration and benefits were not so out of proportion as to justify the inference that the respondents were acting solely in their own interests; and (iii) that the refusal to accept an offer if made to buy the shares at a stated price, the reasonableness of which was a matter of dispute, did not justify the averment of a refusal to allow the petitioners to take their capital out of the company by selling their shares at a fair price, and that there were no grounds in the averments for supposing that the respondents were not willing to negotiate a sale of the shares.

Observed that the availability of an alternative remedy under section 75 of the Companies Act 1980 (now section 459–61 of the Companies Act 1985) and the reasonableness of the parties in seeking a winding-up order would be factors in assessing whether the order should be granted.

LORD KINCRAIG. The first ground is: "The company is a private company and was set up and has been conducted until the events previously described on the footing that both the families concerned should participate in the management of its affairs'' from which the Munro family have now been excluded. In my judgment the averments do not justify this assertion. It would appear that only the founders of the company took part in its management prior to their respective deaths, none of the members of their respective families having been concerned at all in management until after their deaths. . . . I can find nothing in the averments to suggest that there is some special underlying obligation on the members of this company that so long as the business continues any one member is entitled to management participation. I have in mind in dealing with these matters the considerations relevant to the making of a winding-up order on the just and equitable ground formulated by Lord Wilberforce in the case of *Re Westbourne Galleries Ltd.*

The second ground of winding up is stated as follows: ''Further by their actings the respondents have shown an intention to take money from the company in the form of fees, salaries, and benefits to the prejudice of the petitioners as shareholders.'' . . . The remuneration and benefits given to certain members of the Mitchell family, having regard to the previous history of the company are not so out of proportion as to justify the inference that they are acting solely in their own interests and without regard to the interests of the company.

. . . The third ground is stated as follows: ''In addition the respondents have declined to permit the petitioners to take their capital out of the company by selling their shares at a fair price.'' It is not easy on the averments to discover on what this ground is based. The refusal to accept an offer, if made, to buy shares at a stated price, the reasonableness of which is a matter of opinion and is in dispute, does not seem to me to justify the averment of a refusal to allow the petitioners to take their capital out of the company by selling their shares at a fair price. No attempt is averred to have been made to negotiate on the price for the purchase of the shares, or to operate the elaborate provisions of article 6 of the articles of association of the company which provides the procedure where a member wishes to sell his shares. I can see no grounds in the averments for supposing that the respondents are not willing to negotiate a sale of the shares or to concur in the operation of article 6. This ground also therefore is unsupported by averments.

For these reasons I am of opinion that a winding up order of this company is not justified.

⋆ Hyndman v. R.C. Hyndman Ltd.

1989 SCLR 294

Sheriff Court

A petition was presented for the winding up of a family company on the 'just and equitable' ground under section 122(1)(g) of the Insolvency Act 1986. The petitioner had received her shares from a family trust. Originally her father and his brother had run a business in partnership as the County Inn, Cambuslang. The business had later been converted into a company. After her father's death the petitioner had been excluded from the business and had received no dividend. The accounts for 1987 for the group of companies of which R.C. Hyndman Ltd. had become part contained a qualified auditor's report to the effect that the auditors had not been able to satisfy themselves of the completeness and accuracy of the accounting records. The whole assets of the business had been sold, including the County Inn, and the company was to be put into voluntary liquidation. The basis for the winding-up order was (1) that the substratum of the company had gone, and that mutual trust had been lost; and (2) there was a suspicion of lack of honesty in the conduct of the directors. The respondents argued that allegations of fraud should be specifically averred in the petition, and that the petition was unnecessary since the company was to be put into voluntary liquidation.

HELD, granting the petition, that there was no need to aver fraud for a petition to be made on the 'just and equitable' ground and that, in the circumstances, the petitioner was not acting unreasonably within the meaning of section 125(2) of the Insolvency Act 1986 in seeking to have the company wound up rather than adopting some other remedy.

SHERIFF G.J. EVANS. The first matter for consideration is whether or not, irrespective of the necessity or reasonableness of seeking a winding up order, it appears *prima facie* just and equitable to do so. I realise that the necessity and reasonableness of the order are factors that have a bearing on the ultimate view I take of the matter, but I consider it permissible to form a personal view on the general equities of the factual situation before putting those very factors into the balance.

That being my approach, I have come to the view that the general equities are clearly in favour of the petitioner. The principal factors appear to me to be as follows:

1. The family background to the formation of the company from an equal ownership of two brothers whose share in the company profits reflected their former share in the partnership.

2. The total exclusion of the petitioner from the respondents' premises and affairs for a period of sixteen years since her father's death without the receipt of any dividend or benefit whatsoever, such as her father intended her to have received, and the way in which her reasonable requests for information and enlightenment about the respondents' affairs have been consistently ignored.

3. The dissipation of assets of other close relatives of the respondent directors and the apparent build-up of personal assets that cannot be accounted for from directors' salaries alone.

4. The unsatisfactory state of the group accounts as detailed and commented on by Mr Grant [solicitor for the pursuer] and the suspicion that the directors intend to secure large sums for themselves.

5. The substratum of the company has now gone.

. . . I cannot conceive further of any kind of rule under Part XVII of the Companies Act 1985 that would deal effectively with the present state of affairs. It could be said that the petitioner should have invoked her right to bring such a petition at a much earlier stage, once it became clear that the trustees were going to be of no use to her. The remedy itself, however, only came into existence by virtue of section 75 of the Companies Act 1980. Moreover, the petitioner was only eighteen at the time of her father's death and would have to rely largely on what advice her trustees then gave her. Even after she had gone on to seek independent legal advice in 1984, some eight years later, it proved to be initially ineffective. Throughout this time and since, however, she has been met, until only recently, with a blank wall of indifference.

. . . I shall, accordingly, grant the craves of the initial writ and appoint Mr Redman to be an interim liquidator.

Re Abbey Leisure Ltd.

[1989] BCLC 619; (1989) 5 BCC 183

Chancery Division

A petition was presented to court for the winding up of the company on the 'just and equitable' ground under section 122(1)(g) of the Insolvency Act 1986, or for an order under sections 459–61 of the Companies Act 1985 that the respondents should purchase the petitioner's shares. The respondents were the company and two other shareholders who were also directors. The petitioner also sought an injunction to prevent the respondents from dealing with the company's assets pending the hearing of the motion. The company presented a cross-motion to strike out the petition as an abuse of process. The petitioner held 40 per cent of the issued share capital, the remainder being held by the two individual respondents. The petition stated that the company had been formed to acquire and manage a night-club which was sold in 1988. The petitioner had proposed to the directors that he should transfer his shares to them if they would pay him 40 per cent of the proceeds of the sale of the night-club. The directors then offered to purchase his shares in terms of the articles of association, at a price to be agreed between seller and buyers or at a price certified as fair by an independent accountant. This was refused by the petitioner. The petition alleged that the petitioner had been excluded from management, and that the directors were intending to acquire a new business for the company in which the petitioner did not wish to participate, as he alleged that there was an understanding at the outset that the company would only be concerned to operate a night-club. The memorandum of association did permit the company to engage in all kinds of businesses. The respondents denied any such agreement, and relied on section 125(2) of the Insolvency Act 1986 which rules out a winding-up order on the 'just and equitable' ground if there is another appropriate remedy and the petitioner is acting unreasonably in not pursuing that remedy. They also claimed that the remedy under ss. 459–61 of the Companies Act 1985 was inappropriate when a fair offer had been made for the shares.

HELD that the petition should be struck out: despite any agreement between the parties, it was an open question how the parties should proceed once the need for the company came to an end. The parties could proceed by winding-up order or by a sale of the petitioner's shares to the respondents, as was provided for in the articles. It was unreasonable for the petitioner to refuse the offer for the matter to be submitted to the accountant for a valuation. Any dispute that arose on the valuation could be resolved in accordance with the terms of breach of the contract created by the articles rather than either by winding up or by the court fixing a method of valuation of the petitioner's shares.

HOFFMANN, J. Mr Virdi [the petitioner] in his evidence has put forward a number of reasons why he says that it would be unfair to expect him to sell his shares in accordance with the articles. In particular he says that he cannot be assured that the accountant valuing the shares will not apply some discount from the proportionate value of the company's assets to reflect the fact that he is a minority shareholder. The position therefore is that while the procedure under the articles balancing one thing with another may give Mr Virdi the same or more than he would obtain upon a winding up it may well give him less. Does that make it reasonable for him to insist upon the company being wound up? In my judgment, it does not. On the hypothesis which I have accepted, that the agreement between the parties, notwithstanding the terms of the memorandum, was that they were only venturing their capital in a particular night-club in Worcester, it would still be an open question as to how the matter was to be resolved when that particular venture came to an end. There is no suggestion in Mr Virdi's evidence that it was expressly agreed that upon that venture coming to an end there would be a winding up. That might be one way of dealing with the matter but not necessarily the only way. The other obvious way would be for Mr Virdi to sell his shares to the others and this is a matter for which the articles make express provision. Taking into account the potential damage which a winding-up order could do to the company and to the interests of those shareholders who wish it to carry on in business and taking into account the fact that Mr Virdi not only submitted to but actually drafted the terms of the articles in question, I do not see why it is unreasonable to expect him to use their provisions notwithstanding the fact that they may produce a somewhat rough and ready method of valuation. That is something which could have cut both ways at the time when the parties entered into this bargain and I think something which they were willing to accept.

NOTE

For further cases on winding up on the 'just and equitable' ground see:

Loch v. *John Blackwood* [1924] AC 783;

Re K/9 Meat Supplies (Guildford) Ltd. [1966] 3 All ER 320;

*Symington and Symington v. *Symington's Quarries Ltd.* 1905 SC (Series VIII) 121;

*Thomson v. *Drysdale* 1925 SC 311.

In re Sarflax Ltd.

[1979] Ch 592; [1979] 1 All ER 529; [1979] 2 WLR 202
Chancery Division

Sarflax Ltd. had supplied a press to an Italian company (SAFE). The product was defective, and the Italian company sought damages, eventually obtaining judgment against Sarflax Ltd. in the Italian courts. Sarflax Ltd. ceased trading and transferred its fixed assets, stock-in-trade and work in progress at book value to F. Ltd., its parent company, to which it had become indebted. There was no suggestion that the indebtedness was not genuine. Other debts of Sarflax Ltd. were settled out of the remaining assets, but without settling the debt of the Italian company. A liquidator was appointed to Sarflax Ltd., who admitted the claim of the Italian company. The liquidator issued proceedings under section 332 of the Companies Act 1948 (now section 213 of the Insolvency Act 1986) seeking a declaration that business had been carried on with intent to defraud creditors and in particular the Italian company. The respondents were two directors of both the parent company and of Sarflax Ltd. The respondents applied to have the summons struck out on the ground that it disclosed no reasonable cause of action and was an abuse of process.

HELD that the expression 'carrying on any business' used in the statute was not synonymous with carrying on a trade and could include ingathering and distributing assets in settlement of debts; and that short of bankruptcy a person could dispose of assets as he pleased, and that simply preferring one creditor over another when the company was not in or approaching liquidation did not of itself constitute fraud. Accordingly the liquidator's summons was struck out.

OLIVER, J. I feel quite unable to say that the expression ''carrying on any business'' in the section is necessarily synonymous with actively carrying on trade or that the collection of assets acquired in the course of business and the distribution of the proceeds of those assets in the discharge of business liabilities cannot constitute the carrying on of "any business" for the purposes of the section. . . . Mr. Price's (counsel for the respondents) next submission is, however, a much more formidable one. Granted, he says, that the collection of assets and payment of debts can constitute the carrying on of a business, nevertheless what the court is concerned with here is a composite expression "*has carried on business with intent to defraud creditors*". . . . All that is alleged is (a) the collection and realisation of assets, which cannot possibly, without more, constitute fraud and (b) the application of the proceeds of collection and realisation in paying creditors, as to the validity of whose debts no contest is raised, in preference to the claims of SAFE.

. . . What is alleged here—and it is all the liquidator relies upon—is the bare fact of preference and in the light of the authorities to which I have referred the proposition that that, *per se*, constitutes fraud within the meaning of the section is not one which is, in my judgment, arguable with any prospect of success.

In re Gerald Cooper Chemicals Ltd. (In Liquidation)

[1978] 1 Ch 262; [1978] 2 All ER 49; [1978] 2 WLR 866
Chancery Division

C. Ltd. borrowed from another company, J. Ltd., to finance a plant for the production of indigo. Thereafter, C. Ltd. became insolvent and never began production. However, C. Ltd. accepted part payment in advance from a customer for a supply of indigo. The money received from the customer was paid to J. Ltd. in part discharge of the loan. The customer sought a declaration under section 332 of the Companies Act 1948 (now section 213 of the Insolvency Act 1986) against J. Ltd. and its two directors on the grounds that they were knowingly parties to the carrying on of business by the company with intent to defraud creditors and for other fraudulent purposes and were, therefore, personally liable without limitation for the outstanding balance due to the customer. J. Ltd. applied to have the summons struck out as disclosing no ground of action.

HELD, dismissing the summons, that the facts showed that C. Ltd. had been carrying on business fraudulently in accepting a payment when it had no prospect of being able to fulfil the contract, and that the part repayment of the loan was a fraud on the customer: if it was proved that J. Ltd. knew that the part repayment had been made with moneys obtained by fraud, the customer would be entitled to a declaration under section 332.

TEMPLEMAN, J. In the present case, the Cooper companies were carrying on the business of selling indigo. In my judgment, they carried on that business with intent to defraud creditors if they accepted deposits knowing that they could not supply the indigo and were insolvent. They were carrying on business with intent to defraud creditors as soon as they accepted one deposit knowing that they could not supply the indigo and would not repay the deposit. It does not matter for the purposes of section 332 that only one creditor was defrauded, and by one transaction, provided that the transaction can properly be described as a fraud on a creditor perpetrated in the course of carrying on a business.

. . . I agree that a lender who presses for payment is not a party to a fraud merely because he knows that no money will be available to pay him if the debtor remains honest. The honest debtor is free to be made bankrupt. But in my judgment a creditor is party to the carrying on of a business with intent to defraud creditors if he accepts money which he knows full well has in fact been procured by carrying on the business with intent to defraud creditors for the very purpose of making the payment. Mr Evans Lombe said truly that section 332 creates a criminal offence and should be strictly construed. But a man who warms himself with the fire of fraud cannot complain if he is singed.

Re a Company (No. 001418 of 1988)

[1991] BCLC 197

Chancery Division

A company went into creditors' voluntary liquidation with outstanding debts to unsecured creditors, including Crown debts. The liquidator sought to make the chairman and managing director personally liable in respect of fraudulent trading under section 630 of the Companies Act 1985 (now section 213 of the Insolvency Act 1986).

HELD (1) that a person is knowingly party to the business of a company having been carried on with intent to defraud creditors if (a) at the time when debts were incurred by the company he had no good reason for thinking that funds would be available to pay those debts when they became due or thereafter, and (b) there was dishonesty involving real moral blame according to current notions of fair trading. A person intended to defraud a trade supplier if he deceived the supplier into believing that he would be paid at the time stipulated or shortly thereafter. A person intended to deceive an involuntary creditor such as the Inland Revenue, if he continued to incur liabilities to that creditor when he did not honestly believe that the liability would be discharged when it became due or shortly thereafter and, on the facts, the defendant had knowingly been a party to fraudulent trading from 31 July 1984 until the voluntary liquidation; (2) a declaration under section 630 of the Companies Act 1985 could include a punitive element as well as a compensatory element; a declaration would be granted that the defendant was personally liable to the extent of £156,420 for the company's debts and liabilities and that that sum should form part of the general assets in the liquidation.

JUDGE BROMLEY QC. The first defendant told me that he did not intend to defraud creditors and he did not know about fraudulent trading. I am satisfied that he was in full control of the company and had full knowledge of its affairs. He is an experienced businessman. . . . In my judgment, within the principles I have referred to, from the end of July 1984 at least the first defendant had no reason for thinking that the company could pay its debts as they fell due or shortly thereafter. There was in my judgment real moral blame according to current notions of fair trading in his procuring the company to continue to trade i.e. within the meaning of the section, dishonestly. I accordingly determine that there was fraudulent trading and, as a convenient date for its start, that it began on 31 July 1984.

As to 1985 onwards little, in my judgment, needs to be said. The position continued to deteriorate. The accounts sent to the bank for January 1985 showed a net assets deficiency of £185,451. There was a significant scale of dishonoured cheques from February 1985 onwards and on 26 March 1985 the bank wrote to the company suggesting that it find other bankers and repay the indebtedness. It was at about that time that the company arranged to sell its premises, and that sale was completed—it seems after some delays—in July 1985 and the bank was paid off. Also in that month Brayford Plastics Ltd. sued the company and, as I have said, eventually the company progressed into a creditors' voluntary liquidation on 6 June 1986 showing a very substantial deficiency as to unsecured creditors.

The question now arises as to the form of the relief. . . . The following principles are in my view relevant on this application by a liquidator.

(1) The declaration should specify responsibility for a definite sum and not be in general terms as, for example, to creditors whose debts were incurred after commencement of the fraudulent trading (see *Re William C. Leitch Bros. Ltd.* [1932] 2 Ch 71 at 77–79 [1932] All ER Rep 892 at 895–6 per Maugham J.).

(2) The provision being applied is in the nature of a punitive provision (see *Re William C. Leitch Bros. Ltd.* [1932] Ch 71 at 80 [1932] All ER Rep 892 at 896). It follows that the declared sum may be or contain a punitive element as well as a compensatory element (see *Cyona Distributors Ltd.* [1967] 1 All ER 281 at 284 [1967] Ch 889 at 902 *per* Lord Denning MR).

(3) The usual order on an application by a liquidator is that the sum for which the person concerned is declared to be personally liable ought to be dealt with as part of the general assets in the liquidation (see *Re William C. Leitch Bros. Ltd. (No. 2)* [1933] Ch 261; [1932] All ER 897, *per* Eve J. approved by Lord Denning M.R. in *Re Cyona Distributors Ltd.* [1967] 1 All ER 281 at 284, [1967] Ch 889 at 902).

(4) So far as the sum for which the person in question is declared to be responsible is compensatory, then in my judgment it is more appropriate under this particular statutory provision to adopt the approach of Maugham J. in the first *Leitch* case, [1932] 2 Ch 71 at 80 [1932] All ER Rep 892 at 896, i.e. to limit the sum to the amount of the debts of the creditors proved to have been defrauded by the fraudulent trading. . . . Where the context is fraudulent trading with intent to defraud creditors, there is a clear logic in asking what the creditors have lost as a result of the fraudulent trading.

R. v. Kemp

(1988) 4 BCC 203

Court of Appeal

Kemp was convicted of the criminal offence of fraudulent trading under what is now section 458 of the Companies Act 1985. He had carried out, through the medium of two companies, a fraud in which employees of several businesses were induced to believe that their businesses had ordered large amounts of carbon paper which in fact had not been ordered. The civil remedies for fraudulent trading (now section 213 of the Insolvency Act 1986) had not been used because the companies had no assets. Kemp appealed against conviction on the ground that the persons defrauded were not 'creditors' as specified in the statute, since they had not obtained judgment against Kemp's companies.

HELD that the words 'or for any fraudulent purpose' in what is now section 458 of the Companies Act 1985 clearly were wide enough to include a fraud against customers.

Re Produce Marketing Consortium Ltd.

[1989] 3 All ER 1; [1989] 1 WLR 745; [1989] BCLC 513

Chancery Division

The liquidator of Produce Marketing Consortium Ltd. sought an order from the court under section 214 of the Insolvency Act 1985 (wrongful trading) declaring that the two directors, Mr David and Mr Murphy (D. and M.) were personally liable to contribute to the assets of the company. The company were importers of fruit. Gradually the company had drifted towards insolvency (which was demonstrated in the accounts since 1981) and eventually went into creditors' voluntary liquidation in 1987. While the company was still trading, the auditors had warned the directors of the possibility of their being liable for fraudulent trading. A decrease in the level of the company's overdraft was achieved, which was funded by increasing the company's liability to its largest shipper. The directors attempted to justify continuing to trade after the time when they realised liquidation was inevitable, on the ground that they had perishable fruit in cold store, which they argued constituted a defence under section 214(4).

HELD that both directors were liable to contribute to the assets of the insolvent company. They were held jointly and severally liable to contribute £75,000, but between the parties D. was to indemnify M. up to £50,000, beyond which they were to be jointly liable; that the directors had continued trading longer than was necessary to realise the fruit in the cold store from the time when they ought to have concluded that there was no reasonable prospect of the company's avoiding going into insolvent liquidation; and that the amount of liability of a director under section 214 of the Insolvency Act 1986 was the amount by which the company's assets had been depleted by his conduct.

KNOX, J. The knowledge to be imputed in testing whether or not directors knew or ought to have concluded that there was no reasonable prospect of the company avoiding insolvent liquidation is not limited to the documentary material actually available at the given time. This appears from section 214(4) which includes a reference to facts which a director of a company ought not only to know but those which he ought to ascertain, a word which does not appear in section 214(2)(b). In my judgment this indicates that there is to be included by way of factual information not only what was actually there, but what, given reasonable diligence and an appropriate level of general knowledge, skill and experience, was ascertainable. This leads me to the conclusion in this case that I should assume, for the purposes of applying the test in section 214(2), that the financial results for the year ending September 1985 were known at the end of July 1986 at least to the extent of the size of the deficiency of assets over liabilities.

. . . That deals with their actual knowledge, but, in addition, I have to have regard to what they have to be treated as having known or ascertained, and that includes the actual deficit of assets over liabilities of £132,870. . . . Nor, in my judgment, do the facts that the bank was throughout willing to continue its facilities and that Mr Tough [the auditor], although expressing the grave warnings that he did when the accounts for the years ending 30 September 1985 and 1986 were available to him, was willing to accompany Mr David and Mr Murphy to the bank in February 1987 to see if further facilities would be granted, detract from the conclusion I have reached that Mr David and Mr Murphy ought to have concluded at the end of July 1986 that there was no reasonable prospect the PMC would avoid going into insolvent liquidation.

. . . The next question which arises is whether there is a case under section 214(3) for saying that after the end of July 1986 the respondents took every step with a view to minimising the potential loss to the creditors of PMC as, assuming them to have known that there was no reasonable prospect of PMC avoiding insolvent liquidation, they ought to have taken. This clearly has to be answered "No", since they went on trading for another year.

. . . In my judgment the jurisdiction under section 214 is primarily compensatory rather than penal. *Prima facie* the appropriate amount that a director is declared to be liable to contribute is the amount by which the company's assets can be discerned to have been depleted by the director's conduct which caused the discretion under section 214(1) to arise. But Parliament has indeed chosen very wide words of discretion and it would be undesirable to seek to spell out limits on that discretion, more especially so since this is, so far as counsel were aware, the first case to come to judgment under this section. The fact that there was no fraudulent intent is not of itself a reason for fixing the amount at a nominal or low figure, for that would amount to frustrating what I discern as Parliament's intention in adding section 214 to section 213 in the Insolvency Act 1986, but I am not persuaded that it is right to ignore that fact totally.

I take into account the following factors in addition to those set out above, which give rise to the existence of the court's discretion under section 214(1):

(1) This was a case of failure to appreciate what should have been clear, rather than a deliberate course of wrongdoing.

(2) There were occasions when positive untruths were stated which cannot just be treated as unwarranted optimism . . . .

(3) The most solemn warning given by the auditor in early February 1987 was effectively ignored . . .

(4) Mr David has given a guarantee to the bank with a limit of £50,000. The bank will have a charge over anything which Mr David or Mr Murphy contributes pursuant to my order. *Pro tanto* that will relieve Mr David from his guarantee liability.

(5) The affairs of PMC were conducted during the last seven months of trading in a way which reduced the indebtedness to the bank, to which Mr David had given a guarantee, at the expense of trade creditors and in particular Ramona.

(6) The evidence regarding the disappearance of debtors from the statement of affairs is not entirely clear and there remains in my mind an element of speculation on the extent to which it is right to fix on £22,000 as the amount to be treated as having been overstated in September 1986.

Taking all these circumstances into account I propose to declare that Mr David and Mr Murphy are liable to make a contribution to the assets of PMC of £75,000.

As between the two of them it seems to me right that Mr David should indemnify Mr Murphy as to £50,000 and that above that figure they should be jointly liable.

Re Purpoint Ltd.

[1991] BCLC 491; [1991] BCC 121

Chancery Division

Purpoint Ltd. had been in existence since 1986 when it took over the business of another company which had not been profitable. Purpoint Ltd. had maintained no proper books of account and was erratic in the payment of debts. Mr Meredith (M.), a director of the company, sought to leave the company in 1987 to go into business with others. He informed the auditors who advised him that the company was insolvent, and informed him about the potential liability of directors under sections 212 and 214 of the Insolvency Act 1986 if they allow the company to continue to trade after they are aware of its insolvency. The company was wound up insolvent in May 1988, owing debts to the Crown and to trade creditors. The liquidator sought an order to make M. personally liable under sections 212 and 214 of the Insolvency Act 1986.

HELD that under section 212 of the Insolvency Act 1986, M. was liable to repay £12,666.79 to the company in respect of a Nissan Prairie car which he had had the use of, drawings which had not been accounted for, and for the loss made by the company on a contract with the firm with which M. had sought to go into partnership; further, that M. was also personally liable under section 214 of the Insolvency Act 1986, but because of the lack of adequate accounting records the court should aggregate all the debts which were incurred after

1 January 1987 and that M. should be made personally liable for them (the date from which the court held that M. should have realised that the company could not avoid going into insolvent liquidation). It would, however, be imposing too high a standard of care for the court to hold that M. should have realised that the company was doomed from the start.

Per curiam: The purpose of an order under section 214 of the Insolvency Act 1986 is to recoup the loss to the company so as to benefit all the company's creditors, and the court has no jurisdiction to direct payment to a particular class of creditors.

VINELOTT, J. I have felt some doubt whether a reasonably prudent director would have allowed the company to commence trading at all. It had no capital base. Its only assets were purchased by bank borrowing or acquired by hire purchase. And its working capital was contributed by a loan from Mr Froome. The business it inherited from Winnersh Printing Services Ltd. had proved unprofitable and with the winding up of that company the creditors, other than the Royal Bank of Scotland, were left with an empty shell. The new company assumed the additional burden of paying a salary to Mr Meridith. However, I do not think it would be right to conclude that Mr Meridith ought to have known that the company was doomed from the moment it started to trade. That would, I think, impose too high a test. Mr Meridith believed that his connections in the advertising and publicity field would enable him to introduce new business and that the failure of the old company had been due not to any want of skill or organising ability on Mr Froome's part, but on his inability to attract custom. I cannot say that that was a belief which could not have been entertained by a reasonable and prudent director conscious of his duty to persons to whom the company would incur liabilities in the ordinary course of carrying on a business.

On the other hand, in my judgment, it should have been plain to Mr Meridith by the end of 1986 that the company could not avoid going into insolvent liquidation. The company could not meet its trade debts as they fell due. In addition it owed very large Crown debts and it had no prospect whatever that it could turn its trading into profit sufficiently quickly to pay them off. The difficulty is that it is impossible, because of Mr Meridith's total failure to ensure that proper records were kept and that proper cash flow calculations and net worth calculations were made, to ascertain the precise extent to which the company's net liabilities at the end of 1986 or the extent to which the net liabilities were increased by the continuance of the company's trading after the end of 1986.

I think the only solution to this difficulty is to quantify the loss caused by the continuation of trading after the end of 1986 by aggregating the debts owed to creditors incurred after 1 January 1987 and unpaid when the company ceased trading and the amount of the Crown debts incurred after 1 January 1987.

. . . The court, in making an order under section 214 [of the Insolvency Act 1986], is concerned to ensure that any depletion of the assets of the company attributable to the period after the moment when the directors knew or ought reasonably to have concluded that there was no reasonable prospect of the company's avoiding an insolvent winding up—in effect, while the company's business was being carried on at the risk of creditors—is made good: see *Re Produce Marketing Consortium Ltd. (No. 2)* [1989] BCLC 520 at 553 *per* Knox J. The purpose is to recoup the loss to the company so as to benefit the creditors as a whole. The court has no jurisdiction to direct payment to creditors or to direct that moneys paid to the company should be applied in payment of one class of creditors in preference to another. Moreover, creditors whose debts are incurred after the critical date in fact have no stronger claim than those whose debts were incurred before that date. The former class also suffers to the extent that the assets of the company are depleted by wrongful trading.

Re Bonus Breaks Ltd.

(1991) BCC 546

Chancery Division

An application was made to court by a director in the liquidation of Bonus Breaks Ltd. for leave to re-use the name of the liquidated company under section 216 of the Insolvency Act 1986. The director intended to act as a director of a new company to be called Bonus Breaks Promotions Ltd. The applicant and a colleague had acquired the original company by means of a management buy-out. The company's insolvency had been considerable at the time of its liquidation, but there was no evidence that the failure was due to dishonesty. The old company had been insolvent for nearly two years before its eventual liquidation. The liquidator reported that the company should have ceased trading at the time of the onset of insolvency, but that the applicant had continued to trade on the advice of the auditor and the bank manager; he reported also that proper books of account were kept, and that the applicant had lost substantial sums of her own money. The new company was to have a paid-up share capital of £50,000 divided into 1,000 ordinary shares and 49,000 redeemable shares. The applicant was to be one of two directors, the other being responsible for the management and financial side of the business. The creditors of the old company knew of the application and two of them supported it.

HELD, giving leave to re-use the name, that the court would require an undertaking to ensure that the new company's capital base was maintained, that the company would not redeem any redeemable shares or purchase shares out of distributable profits for a period of two years, unless that was approved by a third director unconnected with either of the other two.

MORRITT, J. The application is supported by two major creditors of the old company, no doubt hoping that the prosperity of the new company will assist them in the recovery of their debts from the royalty due to the old company. It is also worthy of note that in the liquidator's notice and report to the creditors, the fact of this application was notified to the creditors, complying to that extent with the requirements of the first excepted case to which I have referred. It seems, therefore, that the creditors of the old company know what is proposed. Those that have responded do not object to what is proposed and, subject to one point, the arrangements made for the conduct of the business of the new company, seem to me to be entirely satisfactory in so far as anybody can forecast what the commercial climate which the new company will face is likely to be.

The one point that concerned me was the fact that the share capital of £50,000 is plainly crucial to the attainment of the figures given in the cash-flow forecast because without the paid-up share capital, there would have to be bank borrowing which would be expensive. On further enquiry, it appeared that the shares were redeemable only at the option of the company within one and three years after its incorporation. Even then, it seems to me to be undesirable that the capital base should be capable of being removed at the option of the applicant and Mr Leader alone. Accordingly, I enquired and was informed that an undertaking would be given, that the company would not redeem any redeemable shares nor purchase its own shares out of distributable profits for a period of two years from today, unless, effectively, that was approved by a third director who was not himself connected with either of the other two. That seems to me to be satisfactory. . . . It seems to me that this, in the circumstances, is therefore an application which I can approve on the giving of that undertaking.

In re Workvale Ltd. (In Dissolution)

[1991] WLR 294; (1991) BCC 109

Chancery Division

An employee was injured while erecting partitions in a building on behalf of the company. Although a claim for compensation had been intimated to the company, the company was liquidated and dissolved without any settlement being made. A writ was issued by the employee against the company for damages for the industrial injuries. The writ was issued about twenty-four days before the end of the primary limitation period for actions for personal injuries under the Limitation Act 1980. While the case was proceeding, the petitioner died. The claim was allowed to become time barred under the Limitation Act 1980. However, there was a change in the law by virtue of section 141 of the Companies Act 1989 (amending section 651 of the Companies Act 1985), which removed the time bar in such cases, except where another enactment set a time limit. Section 33 of the Limitation Act 1980 allowed a court a discretion to dispense with the time limit if it appeared just and equitable to do so. An application was made to court to restore the company to the register under section 651 of the Companies Act 1985.

HELD that the application to restore the company to the register should be granted, since it was not plain that an order under section 33 of the Limitation Act 1980, overriding the time limitation in section 11, would not be granted. The widow of the injured employee could therefore 'test her luck' in the courts, in the words of Harman, J., and sue for damages, which if she was successful, would be met by the company's insurers.

NOTE

The Limitation Act 1980 does not apply in Scotland. The equivalent legislation for Scotland is the Prescription and Limitation (Scotland) Act 1973 (as amended).